OXFORD STUDIES IN ISLAMIC ART

VI

Frontispiece. The head of Walīd's statue.

for Merlin & Anny Channon
with best wishes & thanks
from Robert Hamilton

WALID AND HIS FRIENDS
An Umayyad Tragedy

Robert Hamilton

Published by Oxford University Press
for
the Board of the Faculty of Oriental Studies,
University of Oxford

Oxford University Press, Walton Street, Oxford OX2 6DP
London Glasgow New York Toronto
Delhi Bombay Calcutta Madras Karachi
Kuala Lumpur Singapore Hong Kong Tokyo
Nairobi Dar es Salaam Cape Town
Melbourne Auckland
and associate companies in
Beirut Berlin Ibadan Mexico City

British Library Cataloguing in Publication Data
Walid and his friends.
—(Oxford studies in Islamic art; 6)
1. Arabian Peninsula—History
I. University of Oxford. *Faculty of Oriental Studies*
953'.02'0922 DS236

ISBN 0-19-728011-0
ISBN 0-19-728012-9 Pbk

Designed by Richard Foenander
Typeset on a Monotype Lasercomp at Oxford University Computing Service.
Printed in Great Britain by The Alden Press, Oxford

CORRIGENDA

p.7, l.3 for تَحَامُونَ read تُحَامُونَ

" " l.5 for أَيُّهَا read أَيُّهَا

p.18 fig.3 delete "Mosque" where printed; insert correctly in building N. of Palace

p.21, note 7. Insert "Appendix III, no.3"

p.35 l.14 for "He had" read "Abu Harun had"

p.47, notes for 36 read 37; for 37 read 36

p.58, figs. 25A and 25B Interchange captions

p.88 l.6 from end before "Yes" insert "I said"

p.92 n.111 Text omitted from Appendix III

قَدْ جَعَلْنَا طَوَافَنَا بِالدِّنَانِ حِينَ طَافَ الْوَرَى بِرُكْنِ الْيَمَانِي
سَجَدَ السَّاجِدُونَ لِلَّهِ حَقًّا وَجَعَلْنَا سُجُودَنَا لِلْقِنَانِي

p.113, l.17 delete "from"

p.123 l.28 for "Thrilling" read "trilling"

p.149 n.219 for 83 read 84

p.157 ll.9,24 for Sulaymah read Sulaymā

" " n.233 Text omitted from Appendix III

دَعُوا لِي سُلَيْمَى وَالطِّلَاءَ وَقَيْنَةً وَكَأْسًا أَلَا حَسْبِي بِذَلِكَ مَالَا
إِذَا مَا صَفَا عَيْشٌ بِرَمْلَةِ عَالِجٍ وَعَانَقْتُ سَلْمَى لَا أُرِيدُ بَدَالَا
خُذُوا مُلْكَكُمْ لَا ثَبَّتَ اللَّهُ مُلْكَكُمْ ثَبَاتًا يُسَاوِي مَا حَيِيتُ عِقَالَا
وَخَلُّوا عِنَانِي قَبْلَ عَيْرٍ وَمَا جَرَى وَلَا تَحْسُدُونِي أَنْ أَمُوتَ هُزَالَا
أَبِالْمُلْكِ أَرْجُو أَنْ أُخَلَّدَ فِيكُمُ أَلَا رُبَّ مُلْكٍ قَدْ أُزِيلَ نِزَالَا
أَلَا رُبَّ دَارٍ قَدْ تَحَمَّلَ أَهْلُهَا فَأَضْحَتْ قِفَارًا وَالدِّيَارُ خِلَالَا

p.178, no.17 l.1 for مَشْغُولَةً read مَعْسُولَةً

p.179, no.20 l.3 for الطَّلَبُ read طَلَبَ

p.180 no.29 l.5 for ثَمَّ read ثُمَّ

p.181, n.34 l.2 for عَزَحًا read عِزَحًا

p.182 n.36 l.5 for تَلَافِيَتُهُ read تَلَافِيَتُهُ

" " n.37 l.5 for عَنْهَا read عَنَّا

" .38 l.5 for الْجَذْبِ read الْجَذْبِ

p.183 no.40 l.2 for فَارْبَعْ read فَأَرْجِعْ

" " .41 l.4 for الْيَمَنِ read الْيَمَنِ

" .42 l.2 for غَزَوْتُ read عَزَوْتُ

p.185 no.50 l.8 for قَبْلُ read قَبْلَ

" " " l.9 for فَوْقَهَا read نَوْقَهَا

p.185 l.12 for p.165 read p.111

p.186 no.59 l.1 for عَزِيمَاةً read عَزِيمَةً

p.187 no.60 l.3 for بِكَفِّيْ read بِكَفِّيْ

p.188 no.64 l.7 for الْحَنَّةَ read الْجَنَّةَ

" " .65 l.1 for وَجْهُهَا read وَجْهُهَا

" 191 no.82 l.1 for مُوْضِعْ read مَوْضِعْ

" 193 no.90 l.1 for تَعَانِقُنِي read تُعَانِقُنِي

" 194 no.96 l.1 for وَاسْتَرْنَارَا read وَاسْتَنَارَا

" 195 no.101 l.3 for انْدَرِجْ read انْدَرِجْ

Contents

لَيْتَ شِعْرِى مَا حَالُ أَهْلِكَ يَا قَصْـ　　رُ وَأَيْنَ ٱلَّذِينَ عَالَوا بِنَاكَا
مَا لِأَرْبَابِكَ ٱلْجَبَابِرَةِ ٱلأَمْـ　　لَاكِ شَادُوكَ ثُمَّ حَلُّوا سِوَاكَا
أَلِزُهْدٍ يَا قَصْرُ فِيكَ تَحَامُو　　كَ أَلَا تُبْتَنَى وَلَسْتَ هُنَاكَا
لَيْتَ شِعْرِى وَلَيْتَنِى كُنْتُ أَدْرِى　　مَا دَهَاهُمْ يَا قَصْرُ ثُمَّ دَهَاكَا

أَيُّهَا ٱلسَّائِلُ ٱلْمُفَكِّرُ فِيهِمْ　　مَا إِلَى ذَا ٱلسُّؤَالِ قُلْ لِى دَعَاكَا
أَوَ مَا تَعْرِفُ ٱلْمَنُونَ إِذَا حَلَّـ　　تْ دِيَارًا فَلَنْ تُرَاعِى هَلَاكَا
إِنَّ فِى نَفْسِكَ ٱلضَّعِيفَةِ شُغْلاً　　فَٱعْتَبِرْ وَٱمْضِ فَٱلْمَنُونُ وَرَاكَا

Would that I knew, thou palace, what had become of thy people!
And where are they that raised high thy walls?
What hath befallen thy proud masters, the kings
Who made thee strong, then passed away from thee?
Was it for abstinence that they deserted thee?
Yet wast thou not built? Wast thou not there? Would that I knew
And had knowledge what had overtaken them, and then,
Thou palace, overtaken thee!

O thou that askest, who thinkest on them, tell me:
What made thee ask? Dost thou not know that Death,
When she alighteth on homes, recks not of desolation?
Within thine own weak soul is business enough!
Take warning, then. Pass on! Death followeth thee behind!

Read on a palace of the Umayyads in Damascus, ʿUmarī (1924), i, 250.

Editor's Note

The book that follows begins with a tragedy—the great earthquake of A.D.746. This earthquake levelled, among other places, an elaborate palace complex just outside Jericho. It is one of Hamilton's great achievements that he published such a meticulous record and analysis of the site that it has become the best known of all Umayyad palaces. Hamilton realized, however, that idiosyncrasies in the architecture and decoration must reflect the whims and desires of its patron, whom he subsequently identified as al-Walid ibn Yazid. In this book Hamilton has undertaken another form of archaeology; by combing early Arab literary and poetical accounts, including Walid's own poetry, he has sought to recreate a picture of Walid's life. Hamilton enables us to picture Khirbat al-Mafjar peopled by its patron and his entourage.

There will, though, be those who will be offended by this picture, for it is dominated by Walid's fleshly appetites. This is a tale not only of physical and emotional excess, but of gross religious irreverence. Let those who are offended read this as a moral tale. It begins with a tragedy—an earthquake which ruins Walid's palace—and ends with a tragedy—Walid's own assassination. Let these tragedies be viewed as the twin vengeance of God and man.

Julian Raby
Series Editor

Foreword

It is the persons of an ancient society even more than its works and arts that can enlighten and reward the curiosity of an archaeologist. He is best of all served when both written records and material remains, reflecting each other, survive to evoke the personality of a known individual. For that reason, having some years ago examined and described in detail the architectural remains of a palace of Walīd ibn Yazīd, the Umayyad Caliph, exposed by excavation in the ruins known as Khirbat al-Mafjar, in the Jordan Valley (*Ghawr*) of Palestine, and having found those remains evocative of a lively and eccentric character, I conceived that it might be rewarding to seek out and bring together in a continuous narrative such memories of the man as were recorded in early books and might give further substance and a historical setting to the impression of an entertaining personality conveyed by the ruins.

It was, in fact, entertainment as much as factual history that I expected to derive in this case from a confrontation of literary records with architectural novelties. Both the nature of the buildings and the content of the relevant texts led to this expectation. At least four contiguous buildings were exposed by the excavations: a palatial mansion, a mosque, a bath and a garden pavilion. Of all these the first to be built and brought into use during the lifetime of the owner was the bath, which from the opulence and variety of its structures and ornament appeared to have served as the social and artistic centre for assemblies and private interviews dedicated to luxurious and pleasurable relaxation. The novelty of its design seemed also to denote the presence of a patron or architect of no common talent.

The texts, largely anecdotal in character, described just such a society centred on just such a person. Their confrontation with peculiar features in the ruins not only helped to identify the owner of the buildings as certainly Walīd, successor designate to the Umayyad Caliph Hishām, and thereafter the second Caliph Walīd in that dynasty, but also illuminated with lively and sometimes hilarious episodes the imprint of exuberant aestheticism perceptible in the ruins.

The picture emerging was of a society which, in its way of life and predilections, flouted the standards of behaviour preferred by conventionally orthodox Muslims. Its leader was rebuked in his own time, and castigated by future historians, not only for giving too much of his time and talents to pleasure (*ladhdhah*) and relaxation (*lahw*)—the pleasures of wine and field, music, song and women—but, more generally, for mixing too freely with professionals in the arts he enjoyed, drinking with them as good fellows and lowering the dignity of the ruling family. What could not have appealed to his contemporaries, but which we today can give credit for, was the enrichment of Mediterranean architecture, which this black sheep of history would, if politically wiser, have been initiating.

My story, against this background, is of "Walīd and his Friends"; or so it should have been. But that story could not be told without the intrusion of enemies; and these in the end prevailed, turning what might have been a light-hearted tale into a tragedy. A biography of Walīd has not been my aim—only a leisured re-enactment of the pastimes and friendships that could be imagined as animating the precincts of the establishment in the valley; and a fresh look at some aspects of individual buildings which appear to show affinity with the character of their owner and illustrate new ventures in architecture inspired by his whims.

Walīd's father, Yazīd II ibn 'Abd al-Malik, by whose example he was inevitably influenced as a boy, must come into the story; even more so his uncle Hishām, who exercised over his early and later adult years an influence and authority which lasted through a longer period even than his father's. Walīd's friends, too, had histories, some of which deserve at least a cursory account. Their stories come mostly from "The Book of Songs" (*Kitāb al-Aghānī*), of Abū'l-Faraj al-Iṣfahānī. The same book has much entertaining as well as serious matter on Walīd himself, and on his father and Hishām. On these persons the principal historical narrator is Abū Ja'far Muḥammad al-Ṭabarī (*Ta'rīkh al-Rusul wa'l-Mulūk*). He and Iṣfahānī repeat much of their subject matter in nearly identical words, doubtless copied from the same sources. These people lived from about one hundred to one hundred and fifty years after the death of Walīd (126/744); they are joined by Balādhurī, Mas'ūdī and many others. I have felt free to browse eclectically, but not exhaustively, amongst these authorities. And I have not thought it necessary to record all repetitious sources for a given incident.

In reading many of the stories it is hard to distinguish between fact and fiction. It would be naîve to accept the whole record as history, but pedantic to dissect it too critically. Except for dates of birth and death and the durations of life between them, compilers were not much interested in chronology. In Abū'l-Faraj's narrative Walīd is usually addressed as Amīr al-Mu'minīn, "Commander of the Faithful", although sometimes the conversation must have taken place before he became Caliph. Likewise, it sometimes happens that the time sequence of events implied in one chapter of "The Book of Songs" is reversed when the same persons or events come into a later chapter. The compiler accepted such anomalies, or did not notice them; the picture is impressionistic but not necessarily false.

In describing incidents narrated by the ancient compilers, or quoting the speeches of their characters, I have kept fairly close to their own words. Exceptionally, I have more or less drastically pruned the too tedious verbosity of certain sermonizing discourses of which the general tenor was nevertheless valuable. The pastimes of Walīd and his friends could not be described in prose narrative alone: the poems they sang or recited were part of their conversation and cannot be omitted. Therein lies a formidable obstacle for the translator. A gulf separates not only the idiom of English and Arabic, but often also the kind of thought that an Arab or an Englishman might feel to be poetical. Sometimes, therefore, a translation of Arabic verses in natural-sounding English must be somewhat further removed from the original than would be thought proper in an English version of Latin or Greek.

For the sake of readers who might wish to refer to the original passages where such poems or narrated incidents occur, I have given references in footnotes; and the poems themselves may be read in Arabic at the end of the book. A few references are to numbered items in the collection of Walīd's poems edited by Francesco Gabrieli in his article "al-Walīd ibn Yazīd. Il califfo e il poeta", *Rivista degli Studi Orientali*, 15, fasc. i (1934), 1-64. For the architecture and ornament of the buildings readers may refer to my book: *Khirbat al Mafjar, an Arabian Mansion in the Jordan Valley*; or, on questions of identification and interpretation, to my articles: "Who built Khirbat al Mafjar?", *Levant*, 1, (1969), 61-67; and "Khirbat al-Mafjar: The Bath Hall reconsidered", *Levant*, 10, (1978), 126-38.

Acknowledgement

I wish particularly to thank Professor A.F.L. Beeston, Laudian Professor Emeritus of Arabic at Oxford University, for his great help in elucidating the Arabic of several poems that were obscure to me. At the same time I must acknowledge that all translations in what follows, with all their imperfections, are my own.

Walīd and his Friends: An Umayyad Tragedy

The Earthquake

In the sixth year of the Emperor Constantine V, inelegantly surnamed Copronymus, a year which is computed as corresponding to A.D.746, there occurred in Palestine and Syria a calamity which cannot better be described than in the words of one or another of those Byzantine chronographers in whose compendious histories many facts and many figments of their times are recorded. I choose, for its picturesque fantasy, the account of events given by Georgius Cedrenus, who closely follows in his *Compendium* the eighth- to ninth-century *Chronography* of Theophanes. This is how Cedrenus describes what happened:

"In that same time there befell in Syria an earthquake with a great and terrible collapse, wherein some cities were utterly and others in part overwhelmed. Some cities with their walls and houses were transported safe and entire from mountainous sites to the underlying plains, as much as six miles distant. In Mesopotamia for a length of two miles the earth was cleft and from the depth of it was belched forth a dead-white sandy earth; whence there emerged, unblemished, a mule-like beast which uttering human speech foretold a raid on the Arabs by a people from the wilderness. Which indeed came to pass."[1]

The same event was more soberly described by Severus ibn al-Muqaffa', a bishop in Egypt in the tenth century. "In that same night (of the Virgin's Dormition) the mighty wrath of God in a great earthquake smote the land. In all the cities many houses fell, not one escaped nor a single soul. At sea that night ships foundered in every coast from Gaza to the farthest confines of Persia. I reckon the tale of towns and villages destroyed that night at six hundred. The souls that perished were beyond counting."[2]

These convulsions of the earth were portents of a different tragedy in human affairs. For eighty-five years the empire of the Muslims had been governed and extended by the talents and ambitions of the Umayyad family. In the same time, throughout the wide lands of Syria, both in the towns and remoter areas—desert or sown—the arts of architecture, of sculpture, painting and mosaic, had enjoyed a spectacular rejuvenation. Impelled in

1. Migne (1857 *et seq.*), 885-86.
2. Muqaffa' (1910), 139-40.

Figure 1. (A) ‘Ayn al-Nuway‘imah; (B) Aqueduct crossing Wādī al-Nuway‘imah.

part by reasons of state, religious zeal or the appearance of it, in part by personal taste and addiction to a certain manner of life and luxury, the Umayyads had poured immense public or personal fortunes into the construction and embellishment of trading cities, mosques and princely palaces, of luxurious baths and desert hunting lodges. Wide tracts of inhospitable landscape had been watered from remote springs, and transformed into parks and fertile groves, wherein mills turned and streams flowed; and wherein Umayyad princes and their retainers might indulge and refine their traditional pastimes—talk and poetry, the exercise of fast horses, the pursuit of game and, in the years of their decline, the company of musicians, poets and accomplished slave-girls. The aesthetic vitality and boundless extravagance with which certain of the Umayyads pursued their policies and pleasures did wonders for the arts and architecture of Syria. The demand for new kinds of buildings, backed by well-stocked treasuries and easy-going finance, called forth inexhaustible resources of invention from local builders and craftsmen. The remains of their masterpieces in Damascus and Jerusalem, and of lesser works in many desert or country retreats, throw a spectacular light on the accomplishment and sophistication of contemporary masters in building, and on the drive and artistic awareness of the dynasty that employed them.

But in worldly and domestic affairs some of these same mercurial rulers, endowed with fabulous wealth and almost unlimited power, were capable of every folly and excess. Their fortunes, on the night of the great earthquake, had in recent years been moving toward a calamitous end. Apart from flaws of character and impassioned hatred between cousins, the seed of their downfall had been implanted in their origins. The eponymous ancestor, Umayyah ibn 'Abd Shams, from whom the dynasty was descended by two branches, was not the Prophet's grandfather but only the grandfather's cousin. This circumstance, which set the direct descendants of Muḥammad and the Hashimite line in opposition to the ruling family, was fated to arouse in the hot blood of an Arabian aristocracy perilous and ultimately destructive resentments. Within less than a century of their rise to power, feud, instability and vice, which the virtuous among them had not the power or resolution to curb, had engulfed and destroyed the fortunes, the rule, and with few exceptions the lives of the descendants of Umayyah.

So the havoc on that night of the Eve of the Virgin's Dormition, manifesting to Christian bishops the wrath of God, could have been seen, by the rulers of the Muslim world, as an ominous warning. Only three years before, the most respected of them, 'Abbās ibn al-Walīd ibn 'Abd al-Malik, had said with foresight that God seemed to him to have given his consent to their destruction. He put his feelings into verse:

> Pray God forfend your family strifes, that rear their peaks
> And start an avalanche.
> Creation wearies of your politics; refrain,
> And grasp the pillar of your faith.
> Feed not your own flesh to the wolfish pack; the wolves
> Once tasting flesh will take their fill.
> Spare your own bowels from your ravening hands; or grief
> And bitter tears too late will weep in vain.[3]

His prayer was not granted, and the doom portended on that night in 746 was soon fulfilled.

3. Ṭabarī (1966), ii, 1788; Iṣfahānī (1905), vi, 132-33. Ṭabarī calls 'Abbās "*sayyid banī Marwān*", Ṭabarī (1966), ii, 1784. For the original text, see Appendix III, no.2.

Robert Hamilton

A Pleasance in the Valley with Intimations of an Owner

Amid the general devastation there fell at a quiet spot in the Ghawr of Palestine, the valley of the river Jordan, a cluster of elegant and luxurious buildings which stood within a rambling estate of some hundred and fifty acres, to which a three-mile aqueduct brought sweet water from springs at the foot of the western hills (**Fig.1**). The property was enclosed in a sinuous wall. It lay on gently sloping ground that fell eastwards to the river Jordan, four miles distant. The river there twisted a serpentine way through a deeper depression to the Dead Sea. The broader valley was threaded by gullies, which carried occasional falls of rain to game-infested thickets clothing the deep and muddy channel of the river. Beyond, to the east, the high lands of 'Ajlūn formed a semi-mountainous wooded horizon.

Of the buildings themselves the most conspicuous, though not the largest, was a high-domed and spacious hall or, in practice, music room; to one side of which the rounded roofs of a bath, and the lower dome of a smaller building, could be seen annexed (**Fig.2**). A few yards away, and separated by a walled courtyard containing a small mosque, there rose a palatial dwelling or castle disposed about an inner quadrangle overlooked by arcaded porticoes in two storeys. Facing to the east the palace had a projecting gate tower between external arcaded porticoes, also two-storeyed, and round towers on its outer walls. Before all these buildings there extended a long garden or forecourt at the centre of which a fountain played into a pool beneath a domed octagonal pavilion (**Fig.3**).

Although on that eve of the Virgin's Dormition these buildings were all violently overthrown, parts of walls remained standing high enough to give some shelter in later years to transitory squatters; but the greater part in the ensuing centuries displayed to passers-by only broken stumps, with piles of twisted stonework or crumbling brick, over which the annual weeds and grasses of the region threw an alternate covering of green or brown, perhaps in patches fertilized by a trickle of water oozing its way from distant springs through the surviving channel of the aqueduct.

So things remained, with silence and oblivion reigning in the valley, for twelve centuries until the curiosity of a later generation was tempted to explore the ruins. Then there were exposed successively the remnants of a palace, mosque, fountain and pavilion, music room and bath; while from the dust enough was gradually recovered of their fallen columns, arches, vaults and domes to create an image of their ancient form and multifarious ornament.

From these relics there emerged the spectre of a personality—their owner and creator—extravagant, imaginative, witty and eccentric. The time of his

Figure 2. The bath, restored isometric view.

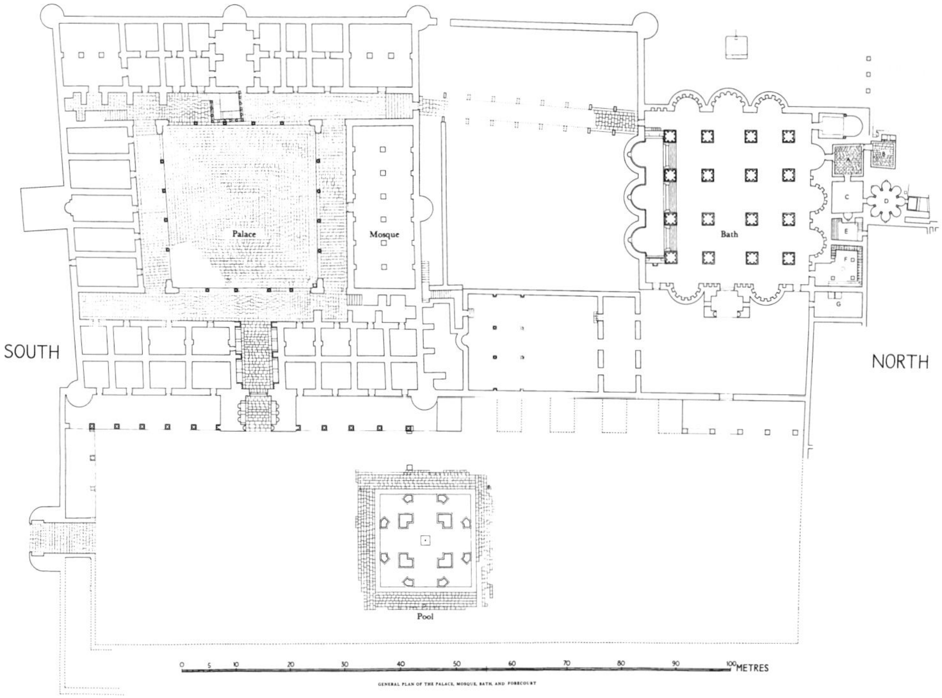

Figure 3. General plan of Khirbat al-Mafjar.

activity was revealed by graffiti in Arabic script, which named among other worthies of the time the reigning Caliph Hishām ibn ʻAbd al-Malik ibn Marwān, who ruled the Muslim world for twenty years in the first quarter of the second century of Islam (105-25/724-43).

On the owner himself these documents were silent; but what revealed at once his identity and his humour was his name enigmatically enciphered in a pictorial emblem incorporated at a focal point in the mosaic floor of the music room. The cipher comprised three elements: a knife, a palpably female and parturient vegetable form, and a leafy shoot emerging from the nethermost extremity of that (**Fig.4**). All this filled a square panel at the centre of a finely-drawn and richly-coloured semicircular design conspicuously located in an apse on the main axis of the room. Incomprehensible as a literal image, as a rebus the cipher is not too obscure: it depicts a child being born from the stylized image of a mother flanked by the condensed and abstract hieroglyph of a male consort. Expressed in words the "newborn child" of the rebus becomes in Arabic speech *al-walīd*—the name, as it proves, of the Caliph's nephew and successor, Walīd ibn Yazīd ibn ʻAbd al-Malik ibn Marwān.

Figure 4. Walīd's cipher in mosaic.

Picture of a Prince

This, then, was the master and creator of those domes and towers: Walīd ibn Yazīd.[4] It was to be the fortune of this man, years after the building of his first residence in the Ghawr, to occupy for a brief fourteen months the office of Caliph in the Islamic state, and there, by his personal eccentricities and contempt for social and religious conventions, both to invite assassination for himself, and to contribute fatally to the ultimate dissolution of the Umayyad dynasty.

Walīd was an eccentric and non-conformist but also the possessor of widely-admired talents and abilities. The historians who reprobate his moral vagaries would admit him to be one of thc bcst pocts of his time, and a respectable performer on various musical instruments. He enjoyed the skills and commanded the company of the most famous singers, from whom he himself acquired the style and standards of performance fashionable amongst professional artists of the Ḥijāz. He was also an outstanding athlete and huntsman, known for spectacular tricks performed on the back of a horse or in mounting upon it. Ṭabarī even thought his strength and the length of his toes to be worth mentioning.[5]

Walīd was notoriously addicted to the pleasures of the chase, as well as of wine and love, which latter he prized as the crown of privilege and fortune. He put it thus:

> I would that all wine were a *dīnār* a glass
>   And all cunts on a lion's brow.
> Then only the liberal would drink
>   And only the brave make love.[6]

Walīd's drinking was abhorrent to members of his family. Hearing of their objections he merely retorted: "If they liked it they would do it themselves." Then he composed these lines:

> White hairs! What of them? Enemies! Who cares?
>   I've had my joys.
> Ripe girls like statues, slaves, and mounts to hunt,
>   And dizzy wine.
> No humble youths my friends, but lordly proud
>   In their nobility;

4. For further evidence of this identification see Hamilton (1969), 61-67; Hamilton (1978), 126-38.

5. Ṭabarī (1966), ii, 1811.

6. Iṣfahānī (1905), vi, 126. He did not versify these reflections.

Seeking revenge they get it, but sought from them
They yield it not.[7]

We do not, in fact, hear so much of the "lordly proud" friends as of the singers and musicians with whom historians preferred to link his name; and it was assuredly the company and entertainment of these less aristocratic companions, as much as of the "lordly proud", that inspired Walīd to plan his establishment in the Ghawr, and which determined the nature of the buildings it comprised. For, as I have already suggested, there is an unmistakable resonance between the defiant and often humorous eccentricity of Walīd and peculiar features discernible in the buildings.

This raises a general question very pertinent to an understanding of Walīd's buildings in the Ghawr: to what extent in antiquity did the patrons of art and architecture intervene personally in the work of artists they employed? We can be sure, I think, that in their use of local materials and stock ornamental motifs, craftsmen would, as a rule, operate within the traditions of their trade uninfluenced by their employers. But in the planning and equipment of buildings they must have been subject to direction, and the question is how often, if ever, would the patron of a major work, independently of official supervisors, entertain original ideas of his own and cause them to be given practical expression. Study of Walīd's establishment in the Ghawr leads to the impression that he, at least, was closely involved in the planning of his buildings, and might almost be called the inventor of some of them.

From the literary record Walīd emerges as a person who enjoyed teasing, disconcerting or sometimes shocking his company, whether friends or critics.[8] In his establishment in the Ghawr there are puzzling, unexpected and even amusing features where the hand of just such a person can be recognized. The most conspicuous of these, which most certainly proclaims the personal initiative of Walīd himself, is the rebus of his name paradoxically asserting, and at the same time disguising, his authorship of what I have called the "music room". In the 1940s this curious mosaic picture was a puzzle to the excavators and others; it may equally have puzzled those of Walīd's contemporaries who were unaware that in innumerable Christian churches the threshold of an apse, paved in mosaic, was the place where a founder or benefactor would commonly inscribe his name and dedication. This picture, therefore, inevitably stood for the creator of the building, and when deciphered identified him as Walīd. However his friends may have interpreted Walīd's turning of his name into a riddle, or whatever we in our time may

7. Iṣfahānī (1905), vi, 103.

8. For an example of this see Iṣfahānī (1905), vi, 131, and my comments on that (quoting from a different edition) in Hamilton (1978), 132-33.

make of it, it is inconceivable that the idea emanated from anyone but himself. Undoubtedly it was his own, and I have suggested elsewhere the source from which he may have got it.[9]

Anatomy of a Music Room

The solution of Walīd's riddle turned on its situation at a focal point in the grandest of his buildings. This building, too, like its hieroglyphic dedication, conformed to no earlier pattern and appears as an original creation. I have called it a "music room" prompted partly by a conspicuous feature of its plan suggesting a design for acoustic resonance, and partly by literary references to Walīd's possession of just such a room. It was, I believe, a product of his own imagination inspired to create a spectacular and spacious setting for the social activity he enjoyed above all others—listening to music. A member of Walīd's circle, one Khālid Ṣāma, a skilled singer to the lute, relates how he was once summoned to join an assembly of renowned performers gathered to sing for Walīd. After listing their names Khālid continues: "...the company sang; and we were in a *majlis*—and what a *majlis*!"[10]

Such musical sessions of Walīd's were commonly enlivened by liberal potations, which sometimes ended in not too dignified horseplay. We may see in the music room of the Ghawr a setting convenient for such proceedings. Its sportive character was prefigured in the decoration of a projecting porch through which it was entered (**Fig.5**). This was adorned within and without, above a certain level, with a varied configuration of carved stucco panels and sculptured effigies. Within the porch, looking up, one could descry at the summit a hemispherical dome encrusted with vine and floral scrolls. Below that, from fourteen decorative niches in a cylindrical wall, an array of human figures modelled in plaster and painted in red, black and yellow looked out from their elevated stance, holding baskets of flowers and other symbols of sport or relaxation in their arms. They included young men in loincloths and buxom girls with breasts and fleshy navels bare, elaborately dressed hair and patterned fold-over skirts. Below these figures there knelt on a frieze of acanthus foliage a continuous ring of gazelles and fat-tailed sheep. These surmounted four pendentives on which four dancing male figures in loin cloths modelled in the round, with arms and one foot raised, appeared precariously to sustain the frieze (**Fig.6**).

At the far side of this porch an inner door admitted to the music room. It stood between moulded jambs, and its lintel was carved with a design of grouped palmettes beneath rosettes. A semi-circular light above the lintel was

9. Hamilton (1978), 136, citing 'Umarī (1924), 358.

10. Iṣfahānī (1905), vi, 127.

Figure 5. Bath porch façade.

Figure 6. Two pendentives from the bath porch.
Far Right—partly reassembled.

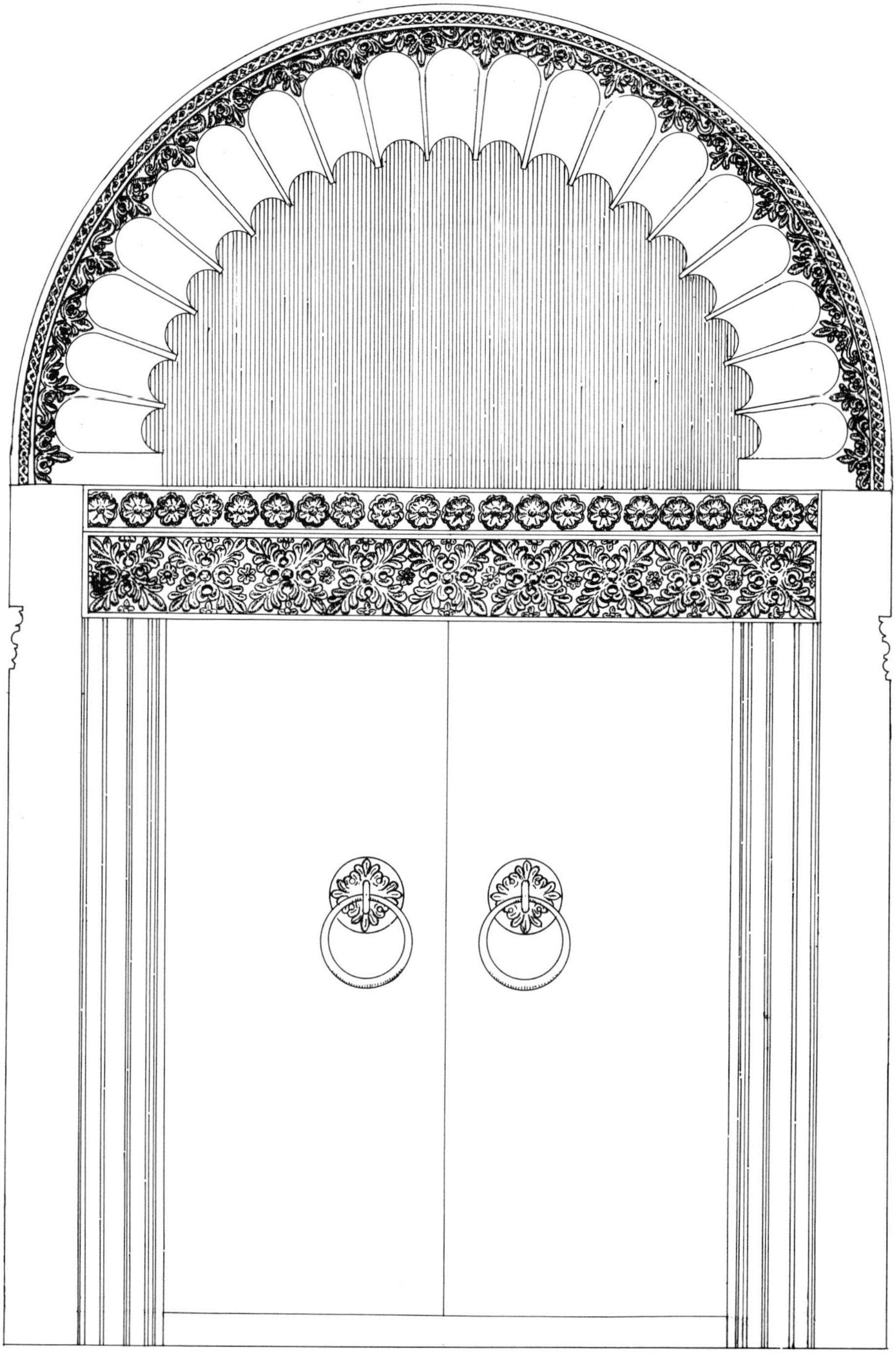

Figure 7. Main doorway to music room.

Figure 8. The music room, looking toward the entrance.

spanned by an elegant cusped arch decorated in front with a fan of small radiating niches (**Fig.7**).[11]

The music room within was a vast hall, thirty yards square, paved with what could at first glance appear as an expanse of brightly coloured carpets but was in fact a giant orderly patchwork of stone mosaic floors (**Fig.8**). From this there rose sixteen massive piers carrying arches, above which intersecting

11. This was a motif used again by Walīd's architect, but on a larger scale, for the main entrance of the palace and there given an ingenious development, as described below. The lintel was a monolith found nearly complete; Hamilton (1959), pl.xviii. The door knockers were not recovered, but have had to be invented here to fit the story of the entry of one of Walīd's singers into his assembly.

Figure 9. The performer's circle.

fenestrated walls sustained a vaulted roof (**Fig.3**). On each axis the spacing of the piers defined a broad central nave between successively narrowing pairs of aisles. The crossing of the naves formed a great square which enclosed a majestic circular mosaic carpet at the centre of the plan. The spacing and intersections of the walls above dictated a cruciform system of vaulting, which rose at the centre to a dome raised above the surrounding vaults by a cylindrical drum wall (**Fig.2**). The circle of the dome was reflected by the great circular carpet on the ground beneath it (**Fig.9**). In counterpoint to the cruciform accent of the two broad naves, the aisles surrounding their crossing could be seen as two concentric ambulatories, each of four straight walks. They were lit by clerestory windows, and the central square by eight additional high windows set in the drum wall.

The special role of this room as an auditorium for music was achieved by a series of eleven semicircular apses, capped by semidomes, which broke the lines of the four enclosing walls, two flanking the entrance, and three on each of the other sides. The reflecting concavities of these structures, with the dome above the central square, were calculated to flatter the voice of a singer shrewd enough to place himself on the central carpet, the position designed for him. Before him, and fifteen yards away, was the central apse of the wall opposite to the entrance, an apse distinguished above all the others by a ring of ornamental niches and greater elaboration of structure beneath a carved and painted front arch. This might be called the "Royal Box". Here Walīd presided over the assembly, seated above a sumptuous mosaic floor filling the semicircle of the apse (**Fig.10**). This was closed along the front by a border, at the centre of which was the cryptic rendering of his name.

High above his seat, depending from the keystone of the superincumbent semidome, was another whimsy of Walīd's humour—a seven-linked stone chain ending in a cigar-shaped pendant (**Fig.11**). The joke here was that the curious contraption, six feet in length including the keystone, could be seen to have been carved, with consummate skill and patience, out of a single block of stone. It hung directly above Walīd's seat, and in its coarse material—a local limestone of poor quality—may have suggested, to the more knowing, a humorous burlesque of the fabulous gold chain and jewelled crown recalled by legend as having hung above the throne of Khusrau Anūshīrwān.[12]

Appended to the music room, on the north or right side, was a range of four bathing rooms, two of them heated; a capacious latrine planned round an ornamental fountain; and a richly appointed domed reception room. To supplement the baths Walīd caused a generous area in the music room, against the left wall, to be given over to a swimming pool. This was formed by a barrier built between the four piers nearest to that wall and joining the first and fourth to it, thus enclosing all three apses and an area seventy feet long and up to twelve feet wide. This could be filled with water to a depth of over four feet. Broad flights of steps along the length of the pool invited the company to enter the water, and another on the inside made it easy to get out.

12. For a view that this was taken seriously, see Ettinghausen (1972), 28-34. I see it rather as a *jeu d'esprit* deriding an overrated wonder of the past and celebrating the ingenuity of Walīd's masons. If it was not from the first an idea of Walīd himself, the cynical humour of it must have won his approval. For my comments, see Hamilton (1978), 132.

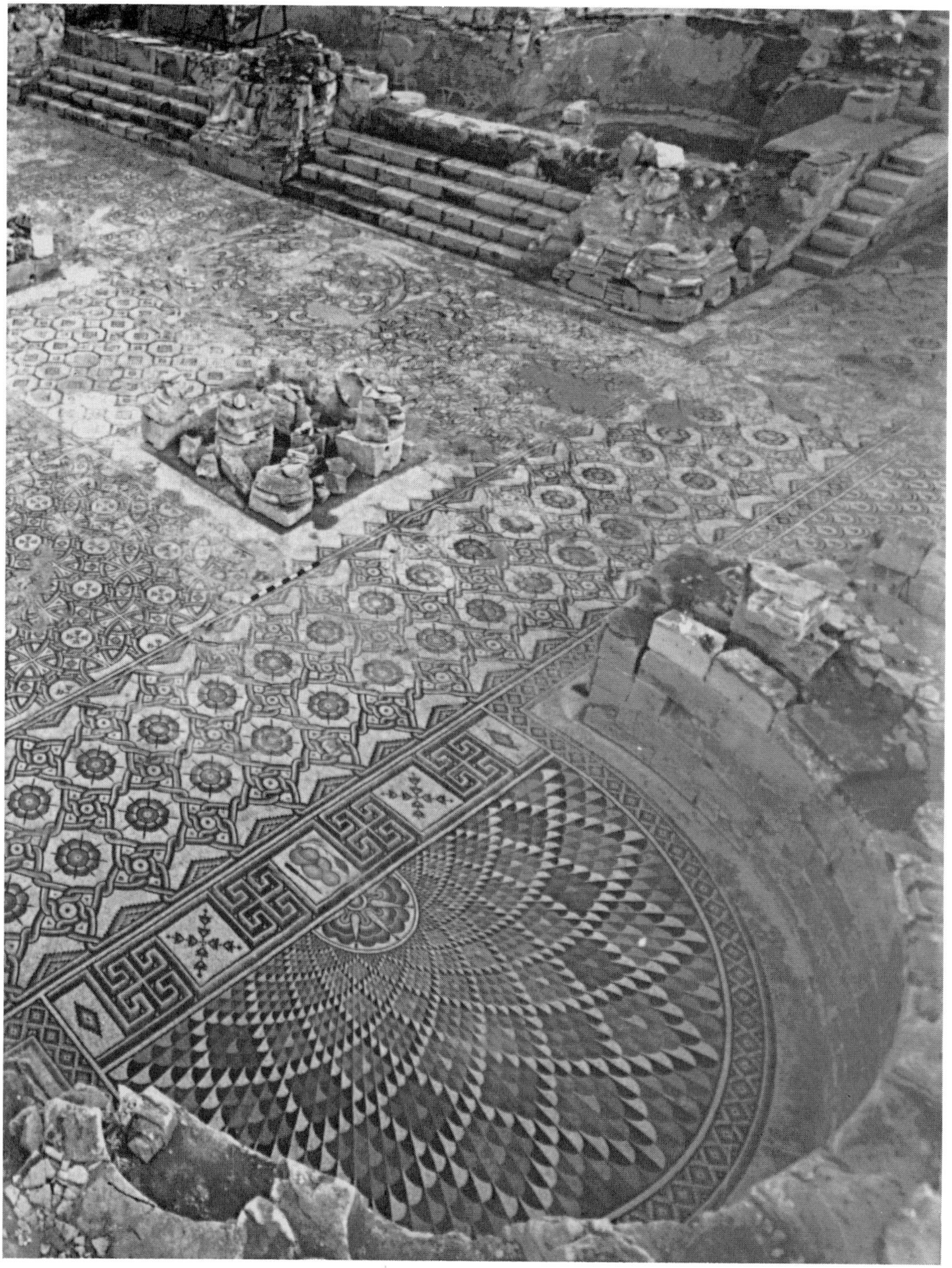

Figure 10. Walīd's places in the central apse and beside the pool.

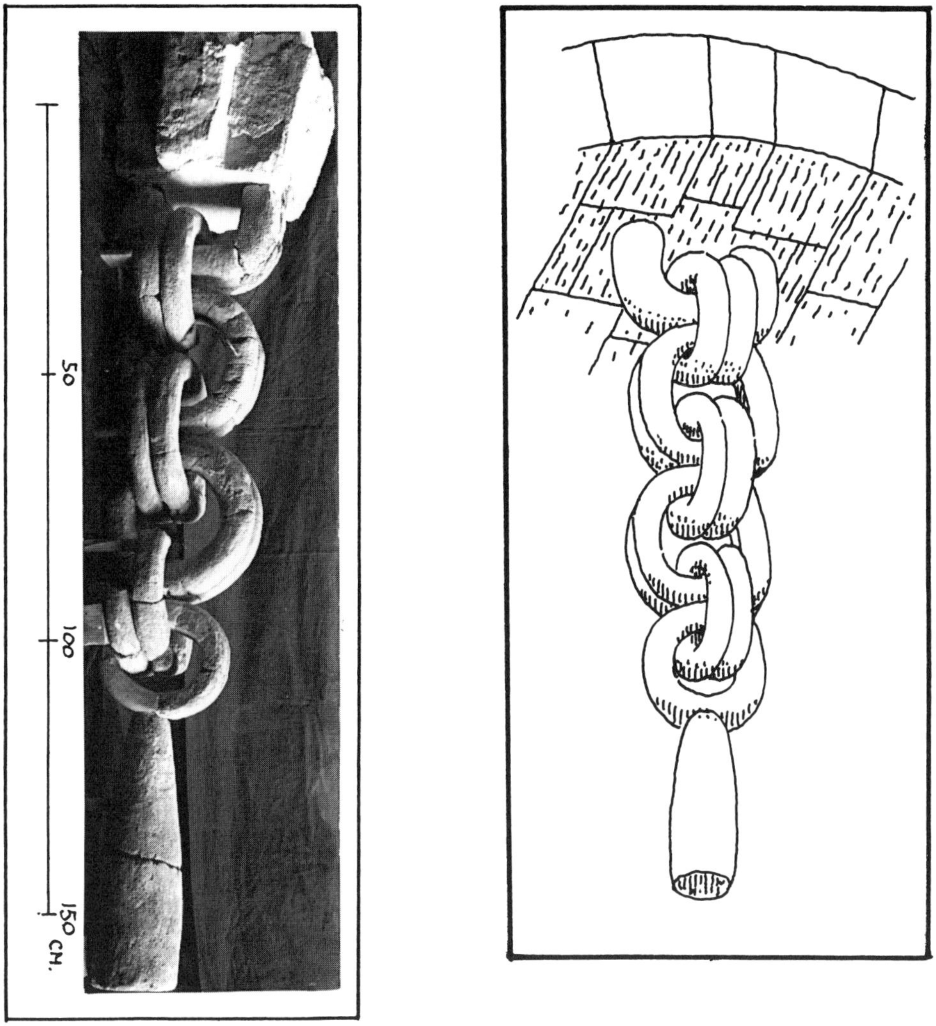

Figure 11. Stone pendant over the principal apse.

The prominence of this pool and propinquity of the hot baths and, further, the existence of convenient cupboards round the free walls for bathers' clothes have caused the music room to be designated as a *frigidarium* or even *apodyterium*, borrowing terms proper to a Roman bath. Walīd would have called it nothing of the sort. For him it was a *majlis*, an assembly room such as that admired by Khālid Ṣāma, perhaps the very same. Even the swimming pool, as we shall see, could serve as a *majlis* in special circumstances.

Abū'l-Faraj al-Iṣfahānī has described, in lively detail, a gathering of musicians that took place perhaps in this room, at which Walīd formed an important friendship. Iṣfahānī calls the scene of his story a *majlis al-lahw*—a "*lahw* assembly room". The significant word *lahw* is that which historians commonly used conjoined with *ladhdhah*, "pleasure", and *sharb*, "drink", when they wrote of Walīd's addiction to sport and frivolities.[13] It has the general sense of what banishes care and relieves anxiety. But it comprehends in particular the virtues of listening to music. Since in the context of Iṣfahānī's story the occasion was specifically a musical one, I choose here, and elsewhere, to render his expression as "music room" and apply it to Walīd's bath hall, with the allied notions of "sport" and "play" also in mind.

The Beginning of a Friendship: Mālik ibn Abī Samḥ

The story of Walīd's new friendship begins at a time when he had in attendance two famous singers, Ma'bad ibn Wahb and Ibn 'Ā'ishah. One day, in a fit of humorous banter or petulance Walīd had exclaimed, "You two, Ma'bad wailing like a woman and Ibn 'Ā'ishah squalling like a baby, both of you pain my ears. Now for God's sake find me a man who sings in a style between the two of you."[14] They both replied, "Mālik ibn Abī Samḥ!" So Walīd sent for Mālik. He arrived in due course with other singers from the Ḥijāz, and was received by Walīd's younger brother, Ghamr ibn Yazīd. Introduced the next day into the assembly Mālik sang his piece; but strangely, since he was an established singer, and in earlier days had been Ibn 'Ā'ishah's teacher, he somehow failed; and the kindly Ghamr had later to tell him that the Prince had by no means liked his performance.

Mālik did not lose heart. He pleaded nervousness and persuaded Ghamr to get him one more hearing. Next day Walīd took his seat in his music room for the next assembly. Mālik, meanwhile, determined not to fail, contrived with three successive gold *dīnār*s to elicit from a servant three glasses of strong wine. His courage fortified, he advanced on the door of the *majlis*, seized and rattled the handle, and tottering in without formality of any kind burst into song with the words:

> Life is not life without Mālik son of Abū Samḥ,
> Abuse or blame me not!

Walīd was delighted. He flung up his arms in a vulgar gesture displaying his armpits and, crying out to Mālik to approach, stood up and embraced him. The song continued:

> White as full moon or lightning's gleam in darkest night. . .[15]

13. Ṭabarī (1966), ii, 1775; Mas'ūdī (1830), ii, 185.

14. Iṣfahānī (1905), iv, 171.

15. For the original text, see Appendix III, no.4.

Walīd joined in, and the song was on their lips for the next few days, Walīd inventing a rude parody of the second line:

> Cross-eyed as ape or watchful thief in darkest night.[16]

So began a friendship between Walīd and one of his favourite singers, which was to last until the day of Walīd's death. It invites a digression here.

Digression on the Education of a Singer

Mālik was of noble descent but impoverished parentage.[17] His grandfather was an Arab of Ṭayyi' and had married a girl of the Banū Makhzūm. They had been driven by drought to migrate south to the city of Madīnah, where they were befriended by 'Abd Allāh ibn Ja'far, a grandson of Abū Ṭālib the Prophet's uncle. The grandfather died in Madīnah leaving Abū Samḥ, his orphan son, under the protection of 'Abd Allāh, who adopted and cared for him, getting him admitted into the Hashimite family. There Mālik was born, and could thus claim to be a Hashimite. But when Abū Samḥ died, Mālik and his brothers, still children, were left with their mother all penniless. To help the family live Mālik would be sent into the streets of Madīnah to beg.

One day, it is related, he was doing this at the door of one of the aristocratic grandees of the city, Ḥamzah, son of the dissident Caliph 'Abd Allāh ibn al-Zubayr, when he heard a voice singing within the house, which filled him with a kind of rapture. He could not tear himself away, but forgetting everything else remained at Ḥamzah's door until nightfall. He returned to his mother having gained not a single penny, and got a beating. But from then on he resorted day by day to Ḥamzah's door. He began to memorize the tunes he heard. Humming them over again and again, without the words, he would practise all the variations of tone and pitch and ornament. As time passed, Ḥamzah coming and going from his house, began to notice the boy always hanging around his door. One day he told his servant: "Bring in that Arab boy from outside." When Mālik appeared, Ḥamzah asked him who he was. "I am a boy of Ṭayyi' from Jabalayn;" said Mālik, "we had bad years there and were driven to come here to Madīnah. I have my mother and brothers with me. I was sitting by your door and heard a voice singing which pleased me, and I have been staying there on account of it." Ḥamzah said: "Do you know anything about that singing?" Mālik replied: "I know all his tunes but not the words."

Now, the owner of that voice was none other than Ma'bad ibn Wahb, a

16. For the original text, see Appendix III, no.5.

17. Iṣfahānī (1905), iv, 166-68.

renowned singer of Madīnah, who was patronized by Ḥamzah and sang every day in his house. "If what you say is true," said Ḥamzah, "you must be very clever." Then he sent for Ma'bad, and told him to sing something. "Can you sing that?" said Ḥamzah to Mālik. "Yes," said Mālik, and opening his mouth proceeded to sing the tune (but without the words) exactly copying Ma'bad's every nuance and subtlety of technique. "You must take this lad and train him," said Ḥamzah to Ma'bad, "for he will certainly make a name." "Why should I do that?" said Ma'bad. "Because," said Ḥamzah, "his excellence will bring you credit; otherwise," said he, "you must send me someone else who will get that credit." "You are right," said Ma'bad, "I will do as you command." Ḥamzah then turned to Mālik and asked him: "How do you now find your having haunted our door?" Mālik ventured to reply that, if the Prince preferred candour to flattery, his door had not filled his belly nor given him the wherewithal to help his family. Accordingly Ḥamzah arranged housing and sustenance for the mother and brothers, and gave them a servant to look after them and a slave to fetch their water.

Mālik under Ma'bad's tuition soon became proficient. One day, happening to hear a mourning woman utter an elegy for the victim of a recent battle, he stayed to listen; then extemporized two tunes to the woman's words, one in imitation of her wailing, with modulation from soft to loud, the other in the style and manner of Ma'bad. He then went in to Ḥamzah and asked permission to sing a composition of his own on a poem he had heard and liked. Ḥamzah told him to sing. Mālik gave his version in imitation of Ma'bad, and was congratulated on having exactly hit off the master's style and manner. "But just wait," said Mālik, "and hear something of my own, which has nothing to do with Ma'bad," and he sang the second version in the manner of the woman. Ḥamzah was delighted and instantly gave the lad the fine robe he was wearing, with two hundred *dīnār*s according to the narrator. Ma'bad at that point came in and was disapproving when he saw the lad so richly attired. Ḥamzah explained the reason and made Mālik again sing the two tunes. When Ma'bad heard the first he was furious: "This young fellow," he said, "has learnt my way of singing and now claims it for himself." "Just wait," said Ḥamzah, "and hear his own version." Mālik then sang the second tune. Ma'bad went silent, but was appeased when Ḥamzah rewarded him, too, with a robe and a gift of money. Mālik at the same time rose and kissed Ma'bad's head, and solemnly swore that he would never claim for himself the credit for any song that he sang, but would always acknowledge Ma'bad as his teacher and inspiration. And to that promise, according to the narrator, he kept substantially faithful for as long as Ma'bad lived.

Such was the early life of Mālik ibn Abī Samḥ, recommended in later years to Walīd by his old master, and introduced at a gathering in the *majlis al-lahw*. He will remain in this story until its end.

Wine and Water with Song

Music was not the only pleasure with which Walīd sought in his *majlis* to banish care. For it was his delight to associate song both with wine and with water. Beside the pool in his music room, he arranged to find in a much smaller adjoining room not only water but also wine, and wine not only to drink but also to soak in. This was a private marble-paved chamber reached through one of the unheated rooms that served as ante-chamber to the hot baths. It had in one wall two small tanks, or tubs, some four foot square and deep, interconnected and fed by two pipes of unequal diameter about one inch and four inches respectively. The tubs were lined with a smooth grey stone, the colour of lead; and beside them, and round the room, ran a marble-revetted bench (**Fig.12**).[18]

In this room, or some other very like it, there took place a memorable encounter between Walīd and a singer of Madīnah named Abū Harūn 'Uṭarrad.[19] He had a fine voice and a handsome face; he was a composer as well as a singer, a man of upright character and good intelligence. He was a learned reader of the Qur'ān and respected in Madīnah for his integrity. With all these qualities his estimate of Walīd should be of interest; in fact he has described an uncommonly demonstrative listener to music.

Walīd had lately succeeded to the Caliphate, and wrote to his agent in Madīnah to summon 'Uṭarrad, who tells this story: "The agent read me the letter, gave me journey money and sent me to him. I was admitted and found him in his palace sitting on the edge of a *birka* [tank] lined with lead and filled with wine. It was not a large one, but a man could turn round in it immersed. I could hardly greet him before he said: 'Are you 'Uṭarrad?' I said: 'Yes, Commander of the Faithful.' 'Abū Harūn,' said he, 'I have longed to hear you; sing me "Ḥayya'l-ḥumul"...' So I sang:

Up now! The litters—they keep them who arm not; [20]
    Their fashion and mine are not in accord!
God prosper the vengeance you ride in pursuit of;
    Good faith is the surest provision to take.
Rope tied to rope I come as your comrade;
    My arrows I feather with feathers of yours.
The place of my heart and its metal you know them;
    And your dogs when I come to you late do not bark.

18. Today nothing above the rim of the tubs has survived, Hamilton (1959), 54, fig.20. In **Fig.12** the roofing of their recess and of the room has been sketched as simply as possible. Walīd's architect could certainly have invented something more interesting. The "butler's pantry" was approached from outside.

19. Iṣfahānī (1905), iii, 93-96.

20. Reading *al-'uzl*, "the unarmed", which fits what follows. But it is also read as *al-'azl*, a place name. For the original text, see Appendix III, no.6.

Figure 12A. Outline reconstruction of the wine bath.

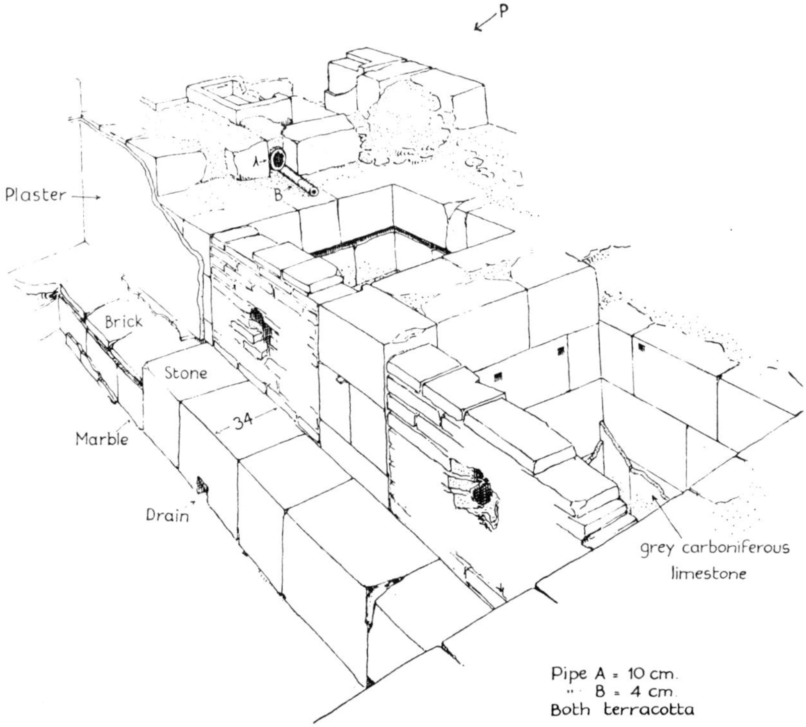

Figure 12B. The wine bath as excavated.

I sang that, and by God I had barely finished when he tore open a brocaded gown he was wearing, worth I know not what, flung it down in two halves, stripping himself naked as his mother bore him, and jumped into the *birka*; whence he drank until, God knows, the level was distinctly lowered. Then he was pulled out, laid down dead drunk and covered up. I took the gown and got up and no-one, by God, said to me either leave it or take it; so I went off to my lodging marvelling at what I had seen of his fine looks,[21] his behaviour and the violence of his emotion.

The next day his messenger came for me again. As I entered he said to me: '‘Uṭarrad!' I said: 'At your service, Commander of the Faithful.' He said to me: 'Sing me "Must life go on?"...' So I sang:

> Must life go on like this, that brings me none
> To heal the wounded heart of love?
> They said: Be doctor to yourself! In physic
> There's relief. I gave myself
> A double dose. But nothing came of it.[22]

I sang him that and he tore apart a brocaded gown gleaming with gold, beside which the first appeared as trash. Then he flung himself into the *birka* and drank from it until, I swear, the level was distinctly lowered. He was pulled out dead drunk, laid down, covered up and slept. I took the robe and went off; and no-one, by God, said to me either leave it or take it.

On the third day his messenger came and I was admitted to him in a *bahw* with a curtain lowered. Walīd spoke to me from behind the curtain and said: '‘Uṭarrad!' I said: 'At your service, Commander of the Faithful!' He said: 'Imagine me and you both now in Madīnah, and in some meeting or assembly you speak of me and say: "The Commander of the Faithful sent for me and I went into his presence, and he bade me sing and I sang to him and delighted him, and he tore his clothes and I took his spoils, and so on and so on". You son of a whore, I swear by God that if so much as a whisper of what happened passes your lips, and I hear of it, I'll have your head off! Boy! Give him a thousand *dīnārs*!' Then to me: 'Take them and be off with you to Madīnah.' So I said: 'Would the Commander of the Faithful not see fit to let me kiss his hand and grant me one more sight of him, and to sing him one more song?' 'No need for that,' said he, 'either for me or for you, so be off!' So I left him, and God knows I told no-one of what had happened until well after the end of the Umayyad[23] dynasty."

21. What impressed ‘Uṭarrad here was Walīd's *ẓarf*, perhaps, in the circumstances, physical rather than intellectual.

22. Iṣfahānī (1905), iii, 96. For the original text, see Appendix III, no.7.

23. Abū'l Faraj's text has "Hāshimite", which must be a slip of the pen.

The *Bahw*

So ends 'Uṭarrad's story. In its last act he is received not beside the wine bath but in what the writer calls a *bahw*—a sumptuous chamber where space and beauty were combined. There the Caliph sat screened by a curtain. If, as his story of the wine bath makes likely, 'Uṭarrad's adventure indeed took place in the Ghawr, we may confidently follow him to that *bahw*; for there it is, a few steps only from the wine bath, and we may describe what he saw there (**Fig.13**). He would have passed, on that third day, through the length of the music room and would have been ushered through a door in the far right-hand corner. There he found himself in a lavishly decorated, square chamber dimly lit from above by light passing through delicately pierced grilles in eight windows high up beneath a dome. On the floor before him was a close diamond-patterned mosaic carpet with a double border and on either side low benches with upper surfaces also coloured with patterned mosaic strips (**Fig.14**).

The walls of this chamber were encrusted throughout with crisply-carved white stucco, in which intricate floral and geometrical designs were disposed on either side in large square panels, all different, surmounted by a frieze of deeply-cut acanthus leaves. Overhead, four winged horses in high relief within circular wreaths of minutely-carved acanthus leaves flew upwards on pendentives to sustain a frieze of partridges which in close file encircled the base of a cylindrical wall containing the eight windows. Each window was fitted with a differently-patterned grille between decorated colonnettes (**Fig.15**). Above the windows the stucco encrustations converged upwards, between ribs of carved ornament hollowed out and tinted red, towards a ring of human heads, male and female, carved and painted in red, black and gold, which formed a radial frame to encircle a giant rosette of deeply-carved and boldly-projecting acanthus leaves. This was the spectacular crown of the *bahw* (**Fig.16**).

Facing 'Uṭarrad as he entered, at the far side of the room, there hung between decoratively carved columns that curtain which concealed from him what a later generation may now profanely inspect—the sanctum in which Walīd had chosen on that day to receive him. This was a deep apsidal recess, of which the walls and ceiling were clothed with the most exquisite of carved stucco panels artfully adapted to the form of the chamber (**Fig.17**). There Walīd sat on a floor or dais raised by a step above the near part of the room.

Figure 13. The *bahw*, seen restored in perspective.

Figure 14. The *bahw* as found.

Figure 15. A window from the *bahw*.

Figure 16. Dome cap of the *bahw*.

In this floor was embodied the chief wonder of the place—a mosaic carpet extending over the full area of the recess, which depicted in subtly blended colours a quince tree in fruit, beneath which, on the left side, two gazelles peacefully grazed, while on the right, a ferocious lion ravaged the crumpled body of a third (**Fig.18**). Had 'Uṭarrad seen this he would have conceived a more objective appreciation of Walīd's artistic discernment and, from the technical perfection of the composition, from the range of colouring and

Figure 17 A. Wall decoration in the *bahw*.

intensity of the scene depicted, would have perceived that for this floor Walīd had employed a supreme master in the art of mosaic painting of his time.[24]

'Uṭarrad's story suggests, what the withdrawn location and intimate scale of the wine-bath confirm, that its use was a luxury that Walīd chose to enjoy in private. His swimming pool, on the other hand, was a more public affair, occupying so conspicuous a place in the music room. But even there, Walīd could swim in private if he would; for curtains could be drawn round the pool from supports carrying rails between the piers. The two ends of the barrier were made broad enough for a man to recline on the top; and Walīd's place was at the far west end, where he could enter by a private door linked to the palace by a covered corridor. Beside that a flight of six steps led him to the top of the barrier (**Fig.10**). Here, when the curtains were drawn, was a waterside *majlis*, where, we may believe, he presided in his peculiar style over another musical occasion not unlike that with 'Uṭarrad.

Ma'bad ibn Wahb

This enables us to bring into the music room and into the present story that eminent and venerable teacher of Mālik already mentioned, Ma'bad ibn Wahb.[25] Ma'bad was a much older man than Walīd, for he had sung for Walīd's father and, in youth, for an even earlier generation. His father, Wahb,

24. There is a detailed account of this floor in Hamilton (1959), 337-39, and a coloured reproduction in the frontispiece of that book.

25. Iṣfahānī (1905), i, 18, 20-21.

Figure 17 B. Wall decoration in the *bahw*.

Figure 18. Mosaic floor in the *bahw*.

was black; and he himself a mulatto, tall and blind in one eye. While he began life as a slave, authorities differ as to what family he served. But he himself is quoted as saying that as a lad he was owned by the Qutun family, dependants of the Banū Makhzūm. They were merchants, and he would manage their trading in sheep, which he would meet and convoy in the Ḥarra. One night in the Ḥarra, while so engaged, he fell asleep leaning against a rock. There he dreamt that he heard a voice singing. Waking up he remembered the tune and sang it to himself. That was the start of his singing.

About that time, or perhaps before, it happened that Abū Yaḥyā 'Abd Allāh ibn Surayj and 'Abd al-Malik al-Gharīd, two early masters of song in the Ḥijāz, were approaching Madīnah on a visit from Makkah. As they passed a well near the city, where women would bring clothes to wash, they came on a lad who was catching birds with a snare. As he worked he sang a song:

> The palace and the palm trees and the Jammā' that's
> Between them
> Are dearer to my heart than the gates of Jayrūn.[26]

They were astonished by the beauty of the voice and the tune. They approached the boy, and asked him to sing the song again. He did so. They turned to each other and said: "If that is singing by a boy who snares birds, what will it be like in the city?"

The boy was Ma'bad, and his song like himself became famous. In the course of time, he came under tuition of the greatest of all teachers, a freedwoman of the Banū Sulaym called Jamīla, described as the "Fount and Origin of Song", amongst whose pupils were numbered many of the finest singers, men and women, of the Ḥijāz. Ma'bad, in his turn, became one of the greatest masters, both as a composer and as a performer, credited with an art unequalled by his predecessors and unsurpassed by his successors. He became naturally a great teacher to whom many younger singers, like Mālik, humbly acknowledged their debt.

At the outset of his career Ma'bad was esteemed in society not only for his voice, but also for his personal integrity, and was accepted by litigants as a witness on whom they could rely. It is likely that he became fleetingly acquainted with Walīd as a young lad in the life-time of his father Yazīd ibn 'Abd al-Malik; later in the long reign of Hishām, he found himself more frequently in Walīd's company, and his reputation suffered, not for any misbehaviour of his own, but for allowing himself to be associated with one whose way of life was generally disapproved of.[27]

26. Iṣfahānī (1905), i, 21. For the original text, see Appendix III, no.8.

27. Iṣfahānī (1905), v, 134.

It was during the reign of Hishām that Walīd built his music room and bath in the Ghawr. There one day, in a moment of passionate nostalgia, apparently after a gap in their association, Walīd resolved to hear the voice of Ma'bad again.[28] A courier was despatched to Madīnah to fetch him. The story goes back to one Qarī ibn 'Addī, who relates that on Ma'bad's arrival Walīd caused a pool that was before his reception room (the *bahw*, it would seem) to be filled with rose water mixed with musk and turmeric. It was there that Ma'bad was received. A place on the edge of it had been spread with rugs for his reception. There the chamberlain commanded him to sit. He was alone, and before him was a curtain hung across the pool. The chamberlain told him: "Greet the Prince,"[29] and from behind the curtain came Walīd's response: "God give you life, Ma'bad," said he: "do you know why I sent for you?" "God and the Prince alone know," said Ma'bad. Said Walīd: "I was reminded of you, and had a longing to hear you sing again." "What shall I sing," said Ma'bad, "something in my head, or will the Prince choose?" "Sing me: 'I mourn for youth'...," said Walīd. So Ma'bad sang:

> I mourn for youth whose years with self-sought blows
> Have brought them low.
> For fitful Time pursued them without rest
> Unto their mutual death; and fitful Time's
> A corsair.
> My eyes unsleeping filled with tears
> At their disunion;
> For tears and falling-out of friends are one.[30]

As the song ended slave girls appeared and lifted the curtain. There was Walīd, wearing a scented robe, which instantly he threw off and plunged into the water. He ducked himself, and climbed out to where the girls were waiting to dress him with a fresh robe which they censed and perfumed. Walīd then had a drink, and gave one to Ma'bad and said: "Sing again, Ma'bad." "What would you like, Prince?" said he. "Sing me 'What ails you, encampment?'...," So Ma'bad sang:

> What ails you, encampment, that you answer not
> To one distraught with love?
> Who turns aside to greet and visit you?
> From every cloud abundant rain
> Has showered upon you, till you seem to smile
> With flowers. Had you but known

28. Iṣfahānī (1905), i, 24-26.

29. The text quoted by Abū'l Faraj says *amīr al-mu'minīn*, but I think that is an anachronism, for by the time of Walīd's accession Ma'bad was infirm of the palsy and incapable of singing.

30. For the original text, see Appendix III, no.9.

Who called to you, you would have answered him,
And would have wept for him hot tears of blood.[31]

As Ma'bad finished, again the girls appeared and lifted the curtain. Out came Walīd as before and plunged into the pool, submerging himself. He got out and donned a new robe. Then he drank, gave Ma'bad a drink and said: "Sing, Ma'bad." "What shall I sing?" said he. "Sing me 'She wondered when she saw me mourn'..." So Ma'bad sang:

She wondered when she saw me mourn
The barren halting place.
Standing upon that ground I weep,
For I see only ruins.
How can you weep for those the trudge
Of camels wearies not?
Whene'er I said: "They've rest at home,"
They said: "March on!"[32]

As the song ended Walīd dived into the pool. Then, as he got out, they gave him back his clothes. Again he drank and had drink given to Ma'bad. Walīd then confronted Ma'bad and said: "Remember, Ma'bad, he who would gain in favour with kings must keep silence on their secrets." To which Ma'bad replied: "With me the Prince's command on that goes without saying." Walīd then dispatched Ma'bad to Madīnah with the mail, ordering ten thousand *dirhams* to be paid to him at his home and two thousand for his journey.[33]

Buildings and the Man, with a Digression on Walīd's Marshal of Pleasures

It may seem a commentary on Walīd's inclinations and character that, in his plans for the Ghawr, he gave priority to his music room and its bath, following them only in later stages with a palatial mansion, a mosque, a garden fountain and pavilion. Apart from the obvious implication of that sequence, the impression I have gained that idiosyncrasies of their owner show through features in the buildings, though doubtless subjective, can be substantiated by more examples than just the mosaic rebus and the bizarre stone chain above it (**Figs.4 & 11**). If it be hard to admit that a prince in the ruling family, holding the exalted status of heir to the Caliph, could give his

31. For the original text, see Appendix III, no.10.

32. For the original text, see Appendix III, no.11.

33. The text says *dinārs*; but that would be beyond even Walīd's extravagance, and must be a slip of the pen.

mind to details of architecture, one curious hint survives in the literary record which suggests how that might have come about. To introduce that a short digression is required.

Among the artists in Walīd's musical circle there was one intimate friend on whom he bestowed the unusual pet titles of "Marshal of my Pleasures" (*jāmi'u ladhdhātī*) and "Quickener of my Rapture" (*muḥyī ṭarabī*).[34] This was one 'Umar ibn Dā'ūd ibn Zādān, a distinguished singer and founder of a school of singers in his native valley, the Wādī'l-Qura. How Walīd got to know this man is not recorded; but their friendship was close and not impeded by the presence of older and more famous singers like Ma'bad and Mālik. 'Umar's special skill was in composition and extemporization. He had a fine voice but did not play an instrument. Walīd composed some verses in 'Umar's honour:

> When 'Umar speaks I ponder on his word.
> For seekers after light he is a moon
> That dims the lamps; and when he sings
> It is a master voice that tunes the song.
> The valley perfected his art within
> The heart of poesy, where it abides.[35]

Their encounters were not all as soulful as these lines suggest. 'Umar has a story set in a different mood.[36] "One day Walīd ibn Yazīd came to see me wearing a ruby seal ring that almost lit up the room with its radiance. He said to me: 'Marshal of my Pleasures, would you like me to give it to you?' I said: 'By God, I would, my Master!' He said: 'Sing me the lines I shall recite to you, but do your best, and if you hit the mark to my mind you shall have it.' 'I shall do my best,' said I, 'and hope to succeed.' This was Walīd's song:

> Don't first white hairs and mellow age
> Divert your mind from Salmā?
> Don't wavering doubts enquire: "Keep joined
> Or break it off?"
> No, no! By God the Lord! I find
> No fault in thee!
> A tender girl whose heart is kind,
> Can there be fault in her?[37]

I went off by myself and turned the piece over in my mind until it came out right. Then I went off to him and found him with a maidservant standing by

34. Iṣfahānī (1905), vi, 137.

35. For the original text, see Appendix III, no.12.

36. For the original text, see Appendix III, no.13.

37. Iṣfahānī (1905), vi, 138-39.

his head holding a cup. He was not drinking at the moment, having taken too much already. He said to me: 'What have you made of it?' I said: 'I have done as you ordered.' Then I sang the piece to him. He cried out: 'Well done, by God!' Then, leaping to his feet and seizing the cup, he called me up to him. Then, holding the cup in his right hand and supporting himself on me with his left, he said: 'Sing it again.' I repeated it for him, and he drank. Then, still standing, he called for a second and a third and a fourth, until he almost fell to the ground exhausted. He sat up then, pulled off the ring and the clothes he was wearing, and said: 'By God Almighty, you're not leaving just like that, until I'm drunk.' So I went on repeating the song for him, while he drank, until at last he toppled over on his side and fell fast asleep."

So much for 'Umar's musicianship and its impact on Walīd. But Abū'l-Faraj tells of another accomplishment which helps to explain the special intimacy that developed between them. In a tantalizingly bald statement he says: "'Umar was an architect" (*kāna 'Umaru muhandisan*). Nothing more is said of 'Umar's architectural activities, but I am tempted, by this unexpected and surely rare qualification in a professional singer, to believe that it was not only his voice, but also his sharing in the creation of luxurious buildings, that excited the raptures of Walīd. The Marshal of his Pleasures will have known his whims and tastes, and helped to plan their physical settings. Such a companionship could have led to what we have found in the Ghawr—an artistic centre, remote from secular cares, amid the haunts of game, wherein with music, wine and talk, ignoring the frowns of his contemporaries, the passionate mind of Walīd could find its satisfaction.

Adventures in Architecture

The link between Walīd's architectural extravagancies and his musical circle was well understood by Hishām, who cited them together in a letter of censure (to be quoted later in this story) sent to Walīd on his deprivation of an official stipend.[38] "First," wrote Hishām, "the Caliph is aware of those places of yours on which you used to spend the monies that he granted you. Secondly, he is fully informed of your companions...waltzing around with you in your follies..." It was as clear to Walīd's contemporaries as it is to us that his adventures in architecture were inspired by a lavish, but too deviant, devotion to the arts and their exponents.

After the music room and its bathing annex, the palace, as it may be called, was an equally ambitious project. In this, too, a taste for non-conformity and paradox can be seen at work. Basically, it embodied the ancient Sasanian convention, commonly followed by the Umayyads, for a

38. Iṣfahānī (1905), vi, 104-05. On Walīd's "places" see below, Appendix I.

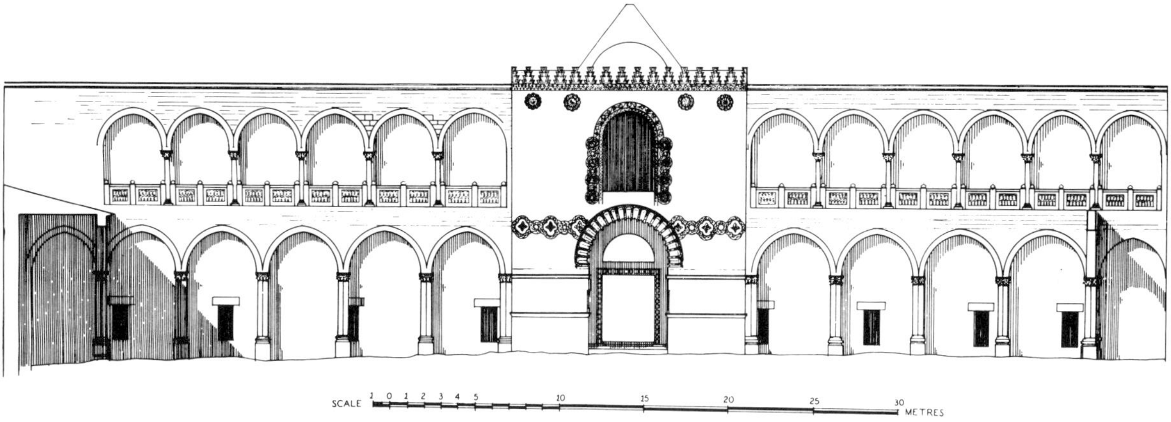

Figure 19. Front of the palace, restored.

castle or caravanserai—a square building fortified at the corners and along the sides by round towers.[39] But here this was disguised. By a sort of perversity, Walīd chose to hide the military aspect of a castle by ranges of graceful arcaded galleries in two storeys, giving to the front of the palace a welcoming expansive façade, which masked and, as it were, mocked the round towers behind them—outmoded emblems of an ancient theory of defence. What enhanced especially the elegance of the façade was an attractive range of balustrades enclosing the upper galleries. In each bay three posts supported two panels carved out of gypsum plaster with two ranges of miniature arcades pierced through on clustered columns (**Fig.19**).

At the centre of the same façade a flamboyant archway gave access to a hospitable open porch, equipped with benches, at the base of a central gate tower. The archivolt, carved with a fan of ornamental niches between radiating colonnettes, invited attention to what may be called, without overstraining the facts, an architectural joke. This lay in the cross-vaulting of the porch behind (**Fig.20**). For, by a *tour de force* which cannot be denied a touch of wit, the contours of the front ornament, half-round hollows between projecting half-cylinders, were turned inwards at the intrados, and transmitted horizontally along the surface of the inner vaulting. Since the porch was a short-armed cross its axial barrel-vault was intersected by another of narrower span, generating diagonal groins. Round these, by a teasing crazy

39. The accommodation provided on the ground floor of this building, augmented by single rooms along the periphery of the forecourt, suggested to me years ago an intention to provide hospitality, recalling the hospitality offered by Walīd as *walī'l 'ahd* at Zīzā' to returning pilgrims, Ṭabarī (1966), ii, 1754; and it may well be that here, too, in the Ghawr, Walīd was motivated by sentiments of hospitality not exclusively directed to his boon companions.

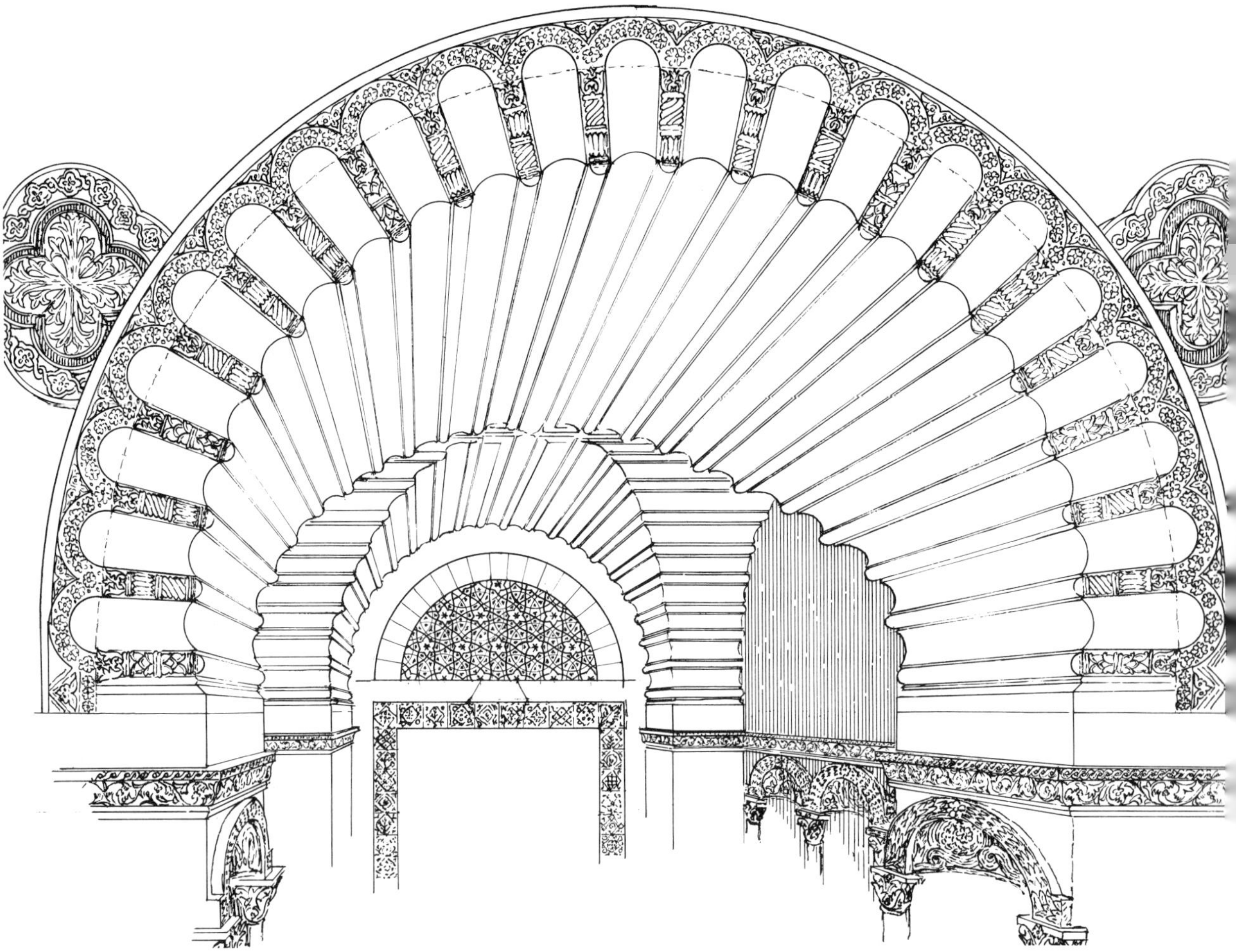

Figure 20. Cross-vaulting of the palace porch.

logic, the contours of the archivolt were perseveringly guided to the innermost recesses of the porch. **Fig.20** is an attempt to convey the curious effect of this device in which, whatever its aesthetic merit, Walīd or his architect appears to have experimented with a whimsical idea untried by earlier builders. Since for the construction of this vaulting the stones were correctly cut with radial beds and, for the groins, beds radial on both axes, the whole work, apart from the novelty of its intention, gives proof of impressive craftsmanship.

Visitors to the place sophisticated enough to notice that curiosity would have seen another in the doorway before them (**Fig.21**).[40] The jambs and

40. For this drawing I am grateful to my friend and former colleague in the excavations at al-Mafjar, Mr G.U.S. Corbett.

Figure 21. Doorway to the palace.

Figure 22. The palace waiting room.

lintel of this were decorated with carved square panels in continuous bands, worked without distinction of vertical from horizontal, and thus without relationship to structure. The lintel especially was surprising: it was composed of three stones, two long cantilevers with a hexagonal keystone between them. This arrangement, original but structurally without much merit, doubtless necessitated the relieving arch assumed in Mr. Corbett's drawing. That would have been filled, I think, with a carved plaster grille, as suggested in **Fig.20**.

In this doorway a double-leafed door opened to give access to an oblong waiting room, vaulted in two bays, and furnished with benches against both walls (**Fig.22**).[41] Entering here the newcomer encountered a further surprise, being greeted from niches in the walls by colourful sculptured girls proffering posies (**Fig.23**), and having sight of birds and beasts and little men in high relief animating the coils of vine trees carved across the vaults above his head. All this was worked in gypsum plaster, the girls' statues like those in the music room porch being painted, with posies of yellow and red flowers on red stalks in their hands.

The waiting room was open to the central courtyard of the palace, a stone-paved square overlooked on all sides by arcaded galleries in two storeys (**Fig.24**).[42] The principal difference in appearance between this and the atrium of a prosperous Christian monastery lay in the elegant variety of sculptured balustrades which closed the arches of the upper galleries (**Fig.25**). These again were in plaster, three panels between four posts in each bay, exhibiting a brilliant variety of intricate designs carved on both sides, always with different patterns.[43] Such lavish use of carved plaster seen in the palace

41. The drawing looks back toward the doorway. It can only remotely and inadequately suggest the impression of opulence that the form and decoration of this room must have made on the visitor or the entertainment he might derive from the vine-entangled fauna of the ceiling. For fragments of that see Hamilton (1959), pls. xxxv-xxxviii.

42. The drawing is a reconstruction of the south-east corner.

43. For these see Hamilton (1959), 241-81. Most of the designs, meticulously drawn out with ruler, cord or compass before carving, were based on the geometry of squares or hexagons. Of greatest interest, however, were two panels (ibid., figs.206 and 207) with concentric designs derived from the construction of a regular pentagon or of a ten-sided figure within a circle; showing, I believe, that the craftsman working with ruler and compass was aware of the arcane linkage between a circle and the golden section, necessary for this construction. I reproduce here as **Fig.25** photographs of the closely duplicated pentagonal design worked and being worked on two of the balustrade panels. Although on the half-finished slab the sculptor's guide-lines and compass marks are clearly seen, I cannot detect the construction by which he set out the points of the pentagonal figure. It is of interest, perhaps, to observe that in the music room, amongst thirty-eight diverse mosaic floors of geometrical design, there was just one which also incorporated the tenfold division of a circle; Hamilton (1959), pl.lxxxvii, 7. Of the hundreds of mosaic floors recorded from pre-Islamic Palestine I know of only one, a ten-pointed design in the late Byzantine or early Islamic mosaic floor of the monastery church of St. Euthymius at Khān al-Aḥmar, not far distant from al-Mafjar,

on walls, ceilings and balustrades, and in the music room on walls and domes, cannot necessarily be credited to the initiative of Walīd, since the medium was also used by his unloved uncle Hishām. We cannot say which of them was the first to exploit the virtues of this versatile material previously neglected by builders of Palestine and Syria, though familiar to earlier generations in Persia and Iraq. In those countries plaster was normally applied to wall surfaces in moulded slabs, a technique giving a singularly monotonous and wearisome effect. It was for the later Umayyads in Syria and Palestine, by handing the material to their native sculptors, to employ it with a brilliance of effect and in a variety of contexts never apparently attempted before their time in the countries of its origin.[44] Walīd's craftsmen can be seen to have played a leading part in that achievement.

One more conspicuous and curious feature remained for the notice of a stranger in the courtyard. High up in that façade which confronted him as he entered was a round window of stonework tracery which admitted fragmented shafts of light to some apartment at the centre of that side of the building (**Fig.26**).[45] To anyone considering the design with attention, remembering Walīd's other eccentricities, it must appear as another mild joke—a solid structure made to look like a cat's-cradle of ribbons. Its weight, of three tons or more, appears to rest on two sharp points at the bottom. In truth these are reinforced by inconspicuous pads further back; to the spectator only the points are visible.[46]

Before Walīd's palace and music room lay an enclosed area, one hundred and thirty yards long by forty yards wide, which I would willingly call a garden but have no particular evidence to do so (**Fig.27**). At the centre of this he caused to be placed a square pool fed by a fountain at its centre and surrounded by a paved walk. The pool was sheltered by a pavilion of solid build, the design of which once again reveals the originality of Walīd or his architect. Its structure can be described as composed of two parts: a central

which ventures, in the sphere of geometry, beyond the possible elaborations of square or hexagon. It may be that in these inconspicuous novelties we have another original contribution of local 8th-century or Umayyad craftsmen to the arts of their time. The floor at Khān al-Aḥmar seems not to have been published. For others at the same site see Avi-Yonah (1938), 180, item 172.

44. That carving, as against moulding, of plaster appeared also in Persia under the Umayyads is attested by examples identical in style to carved wall stuccoes at al-Mafjar; Thompson (1976).

45. The drawing of **Fig.26** shows the remains of this window (found in fragments but nearly complete) assembled by conjecture in the gable end of an upper floor feature, of whose cornice moulding remnants were found in the same area. The bull's head at the apex was sadly lost; but the two forelegs of the animal, unmistakably a bull, survived on a stone displaying the junction of the two raking mouldings. A distant glimpse of the feature is seen in **Fig.21**.

46. A more detailed discussion of the window may be found in Hamilton (1946) where the paradox it seems to present is given a different and at the time more conventional interpretation than mine today.

Figure 23. Plaster figure from the waiting room.

square of four L-shaped piers linked by arches, and carrying a clerestory and dome above the fountain, surrounded by a flat-roofed octagonal skirting carried by eight two-armed piers. The square was inscribed within the octagon, and the octagon within the square of the pool, leaving the corners of that open to the sky (**Fig.28**).

The interest of this pavilion is that not only did it give shade to the pool, and a spectacular centre to the garden, but also its octagonal roof was a promenade, furnished for the purpose with a decorative stone balustrade and a bridge linking it with the upper gallery of the palace front.[47]

Thirty years ago, knowing no parallel to this elegant but substantial building, I troubled myself to seek an ancestry for it, but without convincing success.[48] Today it seems enough to recognize that the Umayyads needed no

47. The scanty footings of the bridge do not reveal how this linkage was effected; nor has that problem been worked out for **Fig.27**.

48. Hamilton (1959), 120-21. My remarks there may be compared with those offered more recently by a distinguished art historian on the same pavilion: "...has no immediately known parallels but almost certainly reflects a classical tradition of *ciborium*-like pavilions in gardens. Once again Islamic evidence illustrates a lost architecture from earlier times. But one

Figure 24. In the palace courtyard.

Figure 25A. Pentagonal design on a balustrade panel.

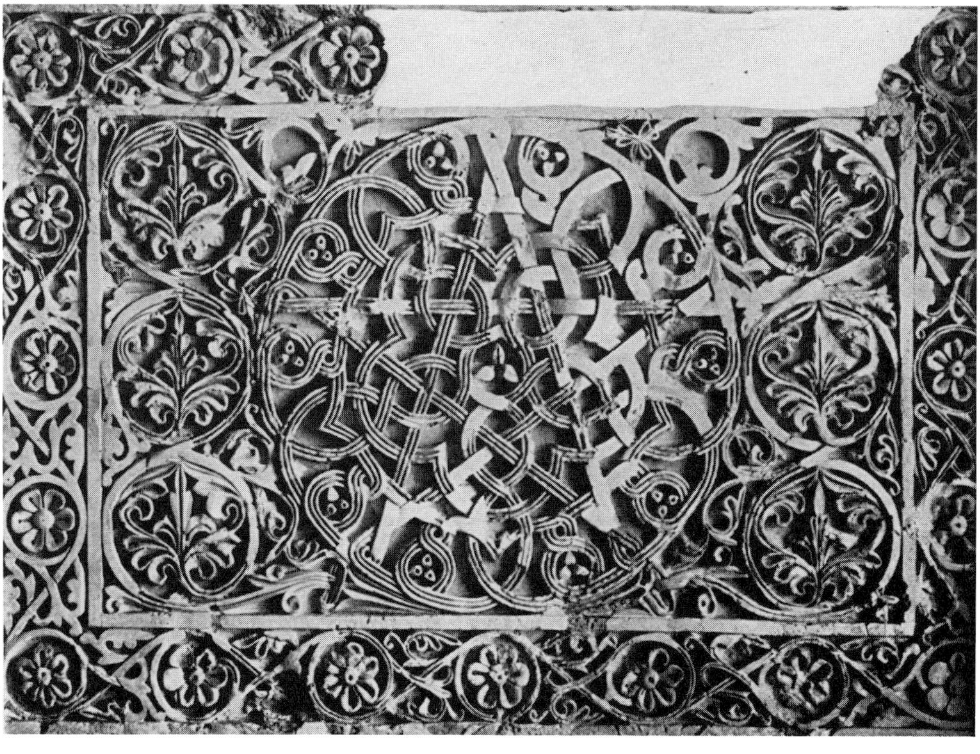

Figure 25B. A similar panel, unfinished.

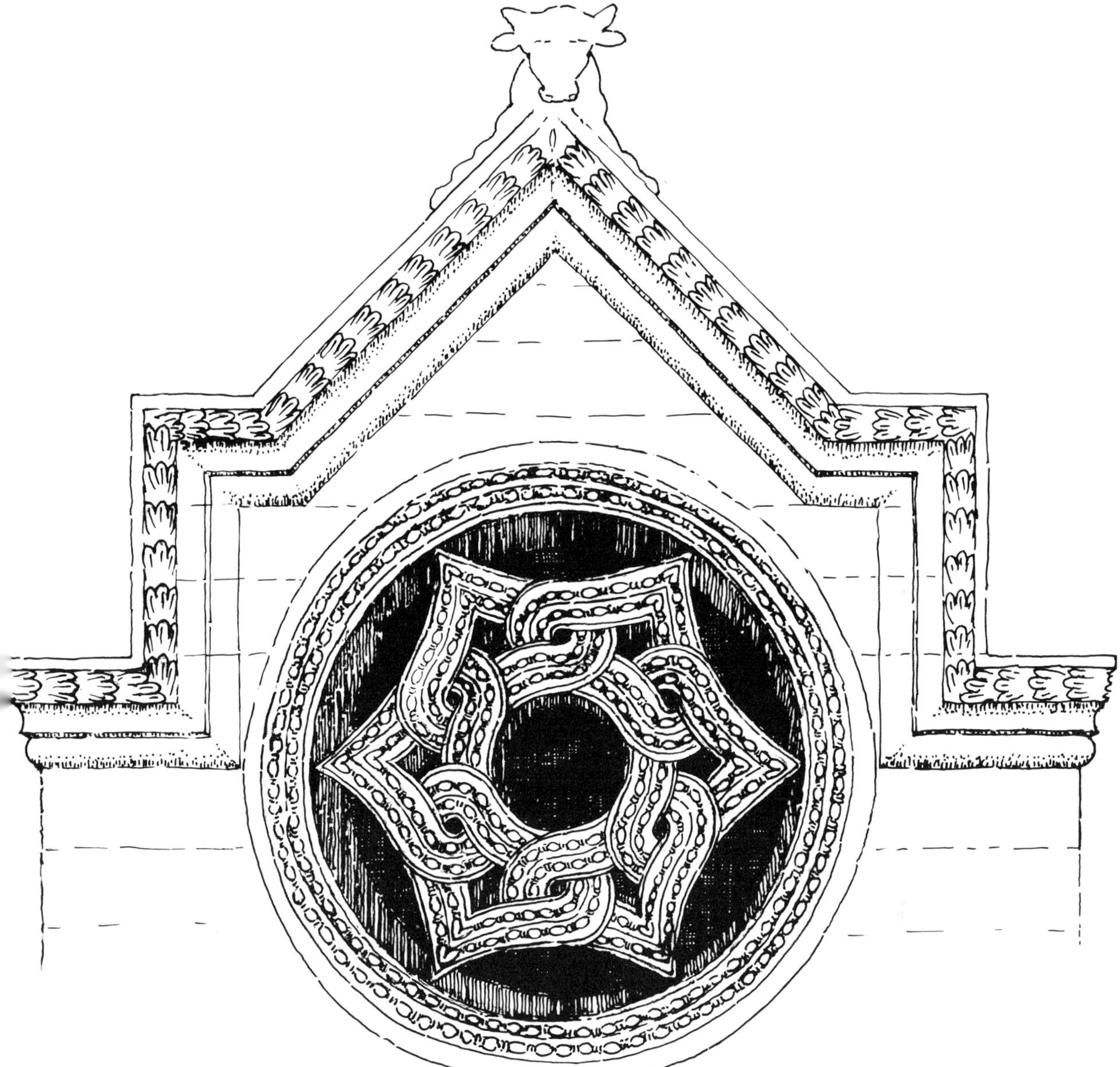

Figure 26. Stonework in a gable end.

Figure 27. Sketch of the palace front and pool pavilion.

Figure 28. Pool pavilion, restored, in elevation and section.

earlier examples to give guidance to their architects, but could rely on them to produce original buildings such as this and the music room (they have structural features in common) from their own fertile imaginations.

From Frivolity to Tragedy

Walīd's music room and bath in the Ghawr survive to show what contemporary critics and later historians meant when they denounced his addiction to *ladhdhah* and *lahw*. The congenial winter and spring climate of the site, well below sea level; the opulence of the buildings and their abundant supply of running water; the limitless scope for hunting and other modes of relaxation—all these, offering escape from public affairs, were an invitation to days of luxurious leisure which became with Walīd an obsession bringing him into conflict with more conventional members of his family.

Walīd was acknowledged as outstanding among his contemporaries for athletic and physical accomplishments, for good looks and personal charm, as well as for his poetical talent and music. But he combined these advantages with a contempt for social and religious conventions and a provocative humour which mortally offended influential relatives; and this, aggravated on his accession to the caliphate by acts of atrocious cruelty, led finally to his own political rejection and assassination. Thus Walīd's life ended in tragedy.

Yazīd, the Father of Walīd, with Digressions on Sallāmah al-Qass and al-Aḥwaṣ

The misfortunes of Walīd must be traced in great part to the contrasting characters of his father Yazīd and his uncle Hishām. The circumstances of his own upbringing cannot have been such as to prepare him for a responsible approach to public life. His father Yazīd ibn ʻAbd al-Malik ibn Marwān was about eighteen years old when Walīd was born. He became Caliph eleven years later in 101/719, as ill-equipped for the office as could be imagined: a pleasure-seeking idler, weak in will, uninterested and incompetent in public affairs, and irresolute even in pursuit of his own pleasures. In later years a critic of the Umayyad dynasty thus described him: "A weak and silly youth, who never grew up or became a man, and who was not fit to be trusted with any affair of the Muslims".[49]

cannot totally rule out an Umayyad invention." Grabar (1973), 159. A flick of Occam's razor will improve the argument: "...has no known parallels and is therefore an Umayyad invention".

49. Abū Ḥamzah al-Mukhtār in a sermon at Madīnah; Iṣfahānī (1905), xx, 106.

Nothing exposed more blatantly Yazīd's incapacity for office than his subjection to women. It happened some years after Walīd's birth, during the caliphate of Sulaymān ibn 'Abd al-Malik (97-99/715-17), that Yazīd was in the house of one Ibn Mīna, a freedman of Madīnah, when a slave girl was brought in and introduced to him. Her name was 'Āliyah.[50] She wore a veil with two long ends, and was a girl of conspicuous beauty and sweetness. She carried a tambourine with which she struck up and then in a lovely voice sang a song to this effect:

Mulayka loveliest! Her neck and breasts
With beauty crowned!
Give me a night when all men sleep, the dogs too
And their master.
A night invisible, no human eye but stars alone
To reck of us![51]

Yazīd was enchanted. He entered into agreement with 'Āliya's master to buy her for four thousand *dīnārs*. Now Yazīd had recently spent large sums on two additional wives after Walīd's mother, Umm al-Ḥajjāj: he had paid twenty thousand *dīnārs* for Sa'da ibnat 'Abd Allāh ibn 'Amr ibn 'Uthmān, and a similar sum for another lady, Rabīḥa ibnat Muḥammad ibn 'Alī ibn 'Ubayd Allāh. When news of the transaction for 'Āliya reached Yazīd's brother, the Caliph Sulaymān, a man no less self-indulgent than Yazīd, addicted equally to women and to food, his comment was: "I'll have the silly imbecile restrained!" Hearing of that Yazīd cancelled his contract. 'Āliya was bought by an Egyptian and carried by him to Ifrīqiyā.

Yazīd thus tamely gave up his prize, but did not forget her. The thwarting of his passion on this occasion was but one example of Yazīd's unhappy destiny to be bullied by his brothers. He had been similarly frustrated, but over a marriage, by Sulaymān's more distinguished predecessor, the Caliph Walīd ibn 'Abd al-Malik.[52] Yazīd was on pilgrimage when he proposed for a daughter of 'Awn ibn Muḥammad, a great-granddaughter of the fourth Caliph 'Alī ibn Abī Ṭālib. He had offered 'Awn a notably large sum as her price. Walīd ibn 'Abd al-Malik, as an Umayyad, took it ill that his brother should pay so much for a Hashimite girl, implying that her lineage was superior. He wrote accordingly to the governor of Makkah, Abū Bakr ibn Muḥammad ibn 'Amr ibn Ḥazm, and ordered him to summon 'Awn the father, recover the money and annul the marriage. If 'Awn refused he was to flog him until he paid up to the last farthing. Abū Bakr wrote and demanded the money. The unfortunate father replied that he had spent it all and was

50. Iṣfahānī (1905), xiii, 148-49; Ṭabarī (1966), ii, 1464. Ṭabarī names 'Āliya's owner as 'Uthmān ibn Sahl ibn Ḥunif.

51. For the original text, see Appendix III, no.14.

52. Iṣfahānī (1905), iv, 50-51.

penniless. Abū Bakr declared: "If you do not pay up I have to whip you until I have recovered the lot."

At that point Yazīd intervened. He sent for 'Awn and advised him not to risk his skin but to pay up. "I will reimburse you," he said, hoping that the money would find its way back, through Abū Bakr, to himself. So 'Awn paid up and Yazīd, bound by his promise, lost his money and his wife together.

Apart from his wives, 'Āliya was not the only woman on Yazīd's mind. Historians relate his subjection to another and earlier girl named Sallāmah. This was a ravishing creature born and bred in Madīnah, who became the darling of that city before she was Yazīd's. Her early years deserve a digression from the story of Yazīd.[53]

Sallāmah had been a pupil of all the greatest experts of the Ḥijāz in the art of song: of Ma'bad ibn Wahb, of Ibn 'Ā'ishah and of their great teacher Jamīla. She became in her turn a wonderful performer and captured the heart of one of the most sober of the citizens of Makkah, one 'Abd al-Raḥmān ibn Abī 'Ammār. So conspicuously devout was this worthy, and addicted to prayer, that he earned the sobriquet of *al-Qass*, "the Priest". And so devoted was he, not only to prayer but also to Sallāmah, that she in her turn became known as "Sallāmah al-Qass", as if his daughter or property. She had a sister Rayya, of similar attractions; and a doggerel of the time ran:

Rayya and Sallāmah
  Both enslaved the Qass.
They left the Qass with nothing,
  Neither sense nor breath.
Two girls: one the moon,
  The other like the sun—
Their secret, cheerful looks
  In lovely faces delicate,
And hennaed fingers sleek.[54]

It was Sallāmah more than her sister who caught the imagination of the citizens of Madīnah as well as of the Qass. Her story was that 'Abd al-Raḥmān one day accidentally heard a girl singing in a house at Makkah. Greatly moved, he stopped to listen. The owner of the house saw him and invited him in. 'Abd al-Raḥmān refused, but was at last persuaded to take a seat inside while the girl sang in another room. The owner then offered to bring her in to sing before him. Again 'Abd al-Raḥmān refused, but was persuaded by his host's persistence. Sallāmah was brought in and made to sit before the Qass and sing to him. Poor pious 'Abd al-Raḥmān fell instantly in passionate love with her, and she with him. A day came when they were able

53. Iṣfahānī (1905), viii, 5-7.

54. For the original text, see Appendix III, no. 15.

to exchange declarations: "I love you," said she. "And I, God knows, love you," the Qass replied. Said she: "I long to put my mouth on yours." "And I," said he, "would dearly love the same." "Then what prevents you," said the girl, "for here we are alone?" He said: "I have heard Almighty God to say: 'None is alone! There is no solitude! On That Day each is against his fellow—one as witness against the other, save only the righteous.' And I dread it that the true love that is between us should turn to enmity." With that the Qass got up and departed, reverting to his old ascetic ways. So ended the curious romance, perhaps curtailed in the telling, which gave Sallāmah her surname.[55]

It is not related how long after these events, or in what circumstances, Sallāmah came to the notice of Yazīd ibn 'Abd al-Malik. It is said to have been in the caliphate of Sulaymān. She belonged then to Suhayl ibn 'Abd al-Raḥmān, who lived in Makkah.[56] Yazīd, having been shown her and heard her sing, resolved to have her. He paid Suhayl three thousand *dīnār*s, and this time there was no interference from the Caliph; perhaps it was before the episode with 'Āliya.

There were tears and dismay in Madīnah at Sallāmah's impending departure, for she surpassed all the singers of her time, young or old. When Yazīd's emissaries arrived to fetch the girl, her people begged a few days' grace while they prepared the ornaments and the clothes, the cosmetics and the aromatics suited to her charms and station. But the emissaries replied: "Quite unnecessary! We have it all and need nothing more. Time now to set off." So Sallāmah left the city followed by a crowd of the inhabitants. When they reached the Fountain of Sulaymān, where there was a caravanserai, the party halted and Sallāmah told her escort that she must say goodbye properly to her friends. So the crowd was allowed to approach. Rushing forward it soon filled the yard of the caravanserai, where Sallāmah with her lute sang them a farewell song:

> They have forsaken me, and well I know
>   For one who's tasted death there's no return.
> The people of Ḥiṣāb have left me, one
>   Whose heart Ḥiṣāb had fired with ardent love.
> They've trooped toward their doom, the clan, and now
>   That they are gone no blame can fall on Time.
> The vale of Abū Mūsā's house was their
>   Abode, the vale that reached unto the palms.

55. In fact, Abū'l Faraj a little later, Iṣfahānī (1905), viii, 14, quotes a more passionate effusion exchanged by the two; with the same ending however.

56. Mas'ūdī (1830), ii, 175; Iṣfahānī (1905), viii, 8. Sallāmah appears at different times in both Makkah and Madīnah; and there is some confusion even about her owner or owners.

In yon Ḥajun how many lie who once
In youth or virtuous age lived worthily![57]

"I was in the crowd," says an eye-witness, "and she sang the song over and over again until she left; and as she rode off the people all fell to sobbing and I never thought to see such tears as I saw then."

Sallāmah had been in Yazīd's possession for some two years or more, during the brief caliphate of Sulaymān's successor, 'Umar ibn 'Abd al-'Azīz, when Yazīd himself became Caliph. The girl had by then quite subjugated his heart. But he still remembered that other girl in Africa. One day Yazīd's wife Sa'da said to him: "Commander of the Faithful, is there anything yet in the world that you desire and have not?" He answered: "Yes, 'Āliya." Sa'da then privately sent a man to Africa and bought 'Āliya from her owner for four thousand *dīnārs*.[58] When she arrived and had recovered from the fatigues of her journey, Sa'da made her up, and brought her to Yazīd's house, sat her behind a curtain, and again asked him if there was anything in the world that he desired. Yazīd, irritated, replied: "You have asked me that already, and I told you." Sa'da raised the curtain, and said: "Here is 'Āliya, and she is for you." Then she got up and left them together.

Yazīd's happiness was complete. He had complained earlier that the caliphate in itself would never satisfy him without the two girls.[59] Now he could say: "I feel as the poet says—'Down staff and rest at journey's end; thus peace of mind attends the traveller's return.'" Yazīd gave 'Āliya the pet name of Ḥababah, and so she has ever since been called.

It was Yazīd's supreme felicity now to be governed by the two girls. Ḥababah was the prettier but Sallāmah the better singer. Yazīd's affections were fairly divided between the two, favouring first one and then the other in turn. Between the girls themselves there was at first a brief estrangement; for Ḥababah, the newcomer, could perceive that Yazīd's devotion and love for Sallāmah were greater than for herself. She could not conceal her jealousy and began to treat Sallāmah with indifference. Sallāmah spoke out: "Are we not sisters? Do you forget that I love you? Have you forgotten our singing lessons with Jamīla, and the rule she gave us? How she spoke to you one day saying: 'Hold to what I have taught you about your sister Sallāmah and it will be well with you all your days, and you will always be friends'?" Ḥababah replied: "You are right, my dear, it has been hateful of me." They never quarrelled again, and although in the end Yazīd turned more toward the lovely Ḥababah, Sallāmah bore that with equanimity.

With the two charming and accomplished girls as his companions, the arts

57. Iṣfahānī (1905), viii, 10. Ḥajun in line 9 is a cemetery near Makkah. For the original text, see Appendix III, no. 16.

58. Ṭabarī (1966), ii, 1464-65.

59. Iṣfahānī (1905), xiii, 148.

of song and their exponents invaded Yazīd's life, driving out all thought of public affairs. He became known as the first of the Caliphs to admit singers into the court circle, an innovation that seemed the more scandalous by contrast with the strict manners and orthodox life of his immediate predecessor, the virtuous 'Umar ibn 'Abd al-'Azīz.

Not long after Ḥababah's arrival, one of his many half-brothers, Maslama ibn 'Abd al-Malik, confronted Yazīd, and reproved him for his neglect of duty and dedication to drink and frivolous amusements.[60] "You have succeeded to 'Umar," he said, "who died only yesterday, and was just and upright, as we all know; you ought to be following his example. But instead you let yourself be distracted from the people and their affairs. People suffering injuries call out to you; delegations are at your doors; but you ignore them all. Now give up these frivolities, which your governors have copied, as they have the rest of your acts and behaviour."

"You are right," said Yazīd; and thereupon resolved to give up drink and follow 'Umar's example. He even abstained from seeing or sending for Ḥababah, the present favourite, and stuck to that for a week. Ḥababah took this badly. She secretly got in touch with Aḥwaṣ, a poet lately rescued from an unpleasant predicament by Yazīd, and got him to write some lines on the subject: "If you can cure this whim of his," she said, "there is a thousand *dīnār*s for you."

Aḥwaṣ and the scrape from which Yazīd had rescued him require at this point a digression from the story of Yazīd.[61] Nick-named "Pinch-Eyes" for an oddity in his features, Aḥwaṣ was properly called 'Abd Allāh ibn Muḥammad. He could boast a long pedigree, and in it a great-grandfather named 'Āṣim Ḥami'l-Dabr who, having been slain by "polytheists"—that is, Christians—while on a mission for the True Prophet, had gained renown and a legendary name from a swarm of hornets which guarded his corpse, and kept it inviolate from the hands of his killers. Aḥwaṣ himself, though handicapped by an excessive humility, even self-abasement, in manner, enjoyed a high reputation as a poet amongst the people and professionals of the Ḥijāz. His literary style was distinguished by simplicity, clarity and correctness; his verses were unequalled in melodious brilliance and sweetness. Above all, fellow poets adjudged him pre-eminent in the accents of love and quoted amongst his verses a couplet:

> I had two nights and one a honeyed night.
> In it I met my love beneath a lucky star.
> A night to soothe my heart, as I were swung
> Beneath the Heavenly Twins until the morning.[62]

60. Iṣfahānī (1905), xiii, 150.
61. Iṣfahānī (1905), iv, 40; 43-44; 48-50.
62. For the original text, see Appendix III, no.17.

Alas, for all that excellence! The esteem it won him was sadly eroded by a deficiency in manly qualities, which earned for Aḥwaṣ the stigma of effeminacy and the scorn of his contemporaries. Worse, it got him into a painful scrape under the Caliph Walīd ibn ʻAbd al-Malik for whom the poet had recited a laudatory ode, thereby earning a grant of privileged status and access to the royal kitchen. This proved Aḥwaṣ's undoing; for in the kitchen he made amorous advances to some of the bakers, and was denounced by their chief to the Caliph. Walīd, incensed, commanded the governor of Madīnah, named Ibn Ḥazm, no friend of Aḥwaṣ, to award him a hundred strokes of the lash, pour oil on his head and have him stood on the *bulus*, or "sacks", a local form of pillory.

All this was done. And there, whatever his defects, Aḥwaṣ showed himself at least a man of spirit: exposed to the ridicule of the people, from his elevation on the "sacks", he recited lines of defiance and humour:

No wound of fortune puts me to the test but honours me
  And heightens my estate.
Let cowards hide: not I! You see me like the sun above,
  That nowhere hides his light.[63]

Sympathizers in time brought Aḥwaṣ release from his predicament: but in the subsequent caliphate—unless tradition has made two separate stories out of one and the same event—he was again in trouble with the same painful consequences. It was under Sulaymān ibn ʻAbd al-Malik, in the second story, that Aḥwaṣ rashly introduced the names of some women of good society into certain erotic verses he had written. The poet was reprimanded, but unfortunately his lines got into the repertoires of two of the most fashionable singers of the time, Maʻbad and Mālik, and so gained dangerous publicity. Complaints were made through the governor to the Caliph. Sulaymān, like his predecessor, ordered Aḥwaṣ to receive, as before, a hundred lashes, to be stood on the "sacks" and, furthermore, to be banished to the island of Daḥlak in the Red Sea, a dreary place inhabited by Ethiopian Christians.

The Caliph's orders were duly carried out, and Aḥwaṣ after his beating found himself among the Ethiopians and destined to stay there for the duration of Sulaymān's reign. When the caliphate passed to Sulaymān's successor, ʻUmar ibn ʻAbd al-ʻAzīz, a delegation from Madīnah waited on him to plead for the poet's rehabilitation. They reminded ʻUmar of the distinguished ancestry and artistic eminence of Aḥwaṣ, and begged for his release from the company of "polytheists", and readmittance to the home of his people and to the Ḥaram of the True Prophet. This was a subtle approach, but ʻUmar had a practical way of dealing with it. He quoted in succession a number of verse lines all of an amorous tendency and required

63. For the original text, see Appendix III, no.18.

the delegation, after each quotation, to name the poet. In each case they replied: "Aḥwaṣ." "The adulterer," said 'Umar, "he was not thinking of home or Ḥaram then! I will not have him back while I am Caliph."

So in Dahlak Aḥwaṣ remained for the rest of 'Umar's reign and for a short time after that under Yazīd ibn 'Abd al-Malik. How he came then to be released is the subject of differing stories. The most plausible is that he secretly conveyed to Ḥababah a flattering poem for her to recite to Yazīd.[64] One night as they sat together on the roof of Yazīd's house at Muwaqqar Ḥababah sang to him:

Noble of ancestry among Quraysh
  In beardless youth and manhood hailed as king!
Though bounteous his gift to you today
  He's not deterred when you come back tomorrow
    From doubling it.
  Paternal wealth he holds of low account;
His praise it is habitually to lead
    In virtue's path.
By sire and grandsire glorified, a tower
  Of lofty fame is his inheritance.[65]

"Why bless you, Ḥababah," exclaimed Yazīd, "who is this man of Quraysh?" "Who should it be," said she, "but you, Commander of the Faithful?" "And who is the poet?" said Yazīd. "It is Aḥwaṣ," Ḥababah replied; "he wrote it in praise of the Caliph." "Where is he?" Yazīd asked. "He has for a long time been imprisoned in Dahlak," she answered. "I wonder," said Yazīd, with wonderful naïvety, "I wonder at 'Umar so neglecting him." Whereupon he had Aḥwaṣ released, and ordered him a reward of money and a robe.

Thus Aḥwaṣ was a ready choice for Ḥababah as her ally in the task of curing Yazīd of his virtue. He got to work and Ḥababah arranged an audience. With Yazīd's permission Aḥwaṣ sang:

Ah! Cease today to scold the foolish-seeming heart
  Whose grief is past enduring.
I wept lost passion sore; so some abused while some
  Consoled and eased my tears.
In search of heart's content I'm called a fool, yet know
  I'm not alone in love.
You, if you have not loved or known what passion is,
  Then stay a block of hardest stone.

64. Iṣfahānī (1905), iv, 49-50.

65. For the original text, see Appendix III, no.19.

Cold hearts may scoff and scold; but life is what you love
And gives delight—that's all.[66]

For a week nothing happened, and still Yazīd kept off Ḥababah. Then, as Friday came, she told one of her maids: "When the Caliph goes out to prayers let me know." So it was: she met him, lute in hand, and sang Yazīd the first line. He covered his head and said: "Stop it! Don't!" Then she sang: "Life is what you love and gives delight—that's all!" Yazīd turned towards her and said: "You're right, by God! Damn him who blamed me for you! Boy, go and bid Maslamah to lead the prayers." So he went back to Ḥababah, and stayed with her, drinking while she sang, and so reverted to his old habits.

On one occasion dispute arose in front of Yazīd between Sallāmah and Ḥababah on the correct version of a line of song attributed to their old teacher Ma'bad. [67] "How comes this," said Yazīd, "when you both learnt the song from Ma'bad himself?" Each in turn then said: "That is how I learnt it." Yazīd said: "This is absurd, with Ma'bad still alive," and forthwith he sent to Madīnah for Ma'bad to be brought. When Ma'bad on enquiry heard what he had been sent for, he instantly asked which of the two girls was at present in favour. When he arrived, accordingly, Yazīd explained to him: "These two girls are disputing about a song of yours; you must adjudicate." Then to Ḥababah he said: "Sing." And she sang. The same with Sallāmah—she in turn sang it. "The right version is Ḥababah's," said Ma'bad. But Sallāmah would not have it. "You bastard," said she, "you know well that I was right, but you had found out which of us was in favour with the Caliph, and just answered to flatter his mood." Yazīd laughed, delighted. He seized a cushion, put it on his head and waltzed around the house crying at the top of his voice: "Fresh fish at the farrier's four *raṭl*s in season," until the whole house whirled around him. Then he returned to his place in the *majlis* and called for a song from Ma'bad. When the session broke up and Ma'bad had returned to his lodgings, Sallāmah sent the old man a pleasant message saying she forgave him for what he had done. Both girls were good to him and he enjoyed their kindnesses until Yazīd released him to return to his home in Madīnah.

Yazīd once said to Sallāmah and Ḥababah: "Whichever of you sings the song I have in my mind shall have a wish." So Sallāmah had first try but failed. Ḥababah then sang and got it right. "Make your wish," said Yazīd. "My wish," said Ḥababah, "is that you give me Sallāmah and all her belongings." "Ask for something else," Yazīd told her. But she refused, and he had to say: "Then she is yours." Sallāmah took this hard, but Ḥababah reassured her that all would be well. Yazīd then asked Ḥababah to sell Sallāmah back to him. She said, however: "I declare she is a free woman. You

66. Iṣfahānī (1905), xiii, 151. For the original text, see Appendix III, no.20.

67. Iṣfahānī (1905), xiii, 154-55.

must ask me for her in marriage, and I will marry you to my freedwoman." Sallāmah was upset at all this. But Ḥababah said: "Don't be upset, I was only teasing him."

Yazīd had ever found it hard to make up his mind or stick to his decisions. His servants knew his weakness. A ludicrous example of that is related by the singer Mālik ibn Abī Samḥ: "It was on our first appearance before Yazīd ibn 'Abd al-Malik, with Ma'bad and Ibn 'Ā'ishah. We had sung to him that night and he had been delighted. He ordered each of us a thousand *dīnār*s and wrote a warrant to that effect. Next morning we took the warrant along to the secretary, who when he saw it would have none of it. 'What,' said he, 'a thousand *dīnār*s each to the likes of you? No, by God, not for love or money.' So we went back to Yazīd and told him what had happened, repeating the man's words. Yazīd at first professed not to believe it; but we assured him it was true. 'Refuse!' said Yazīd, 'A fellow like that!'—and sent for the man. When the secretary appeared and saw us there he was embarrassed, but asked for Yazīd's instructions and then fell silent. 'Yes, I gave the order,' said Yazīd, 'and it would not look well to go back on my word; but, cut it down,' said he. Then, by God, Yazīd died and we got four hundred *dīnār*s each."[68]

Yazīd had about four years to enjoy the company of his girls. The fifth had hardly begun when it occurred to him to test the common saying that no man can enjoy a whole day and night of perfect happiness without some trouble intervening.[69] "I will try it," he said, and told his staff that next day no news and no letters were to be brought to him. Then, at a place named Bayt Ras in Syria, he shut himself away with Ḥababah, allowing only food and drink for the two of them to be brought in. There Ḥababah was eating a pomegranate, when she choked on one of the pips and died.

So Yazīd found by experiment that the popular belief was true. He abandoned himself to grief; and many were the stories—true or false—of the frenzied devices by which he tried in vain to prolong his enjoyment of her company, delaying her burial or even—according to one story—causing her body to be exhumed. On which occasion, although her face was sadly degraded, he is said to have declared: "I never saw her more beautiful!" A more probable story relates that his brother Maslamah intervened and, calling Yazīd to reason, said: "For God's sake! She was only a slave girl amongst others and now the earth has covered her."

So Yazīd in his misery took to him a little maid of Ḥababah's who would talk to him kindly about her. One day, going round the house with this girl, Yazīd said: "This is where we were together"; on which she quoted the verse:

68. Iṣfahānī (1905), iv, 170.
69. Iṣfahānī (1905), xiii, 157-58.

'Tis grief enough for desperate love to see
His love's abodes deserted, desolate.[70]

That little slave stayed with Yazīd and kept him company until, in only a few days, he too fell ill and died. He was buried beside Ḥababah. Sallāmah lived on; years later she was to be found in the household of her master's son, Walīd.

Hishām's Succession to Yazīd

Yazīd's irresolution played a part in the troubles of Walīd; which began when Yazīd, having in 101/719 lately succeeded to the caliphate, was induced to nominate a successor.[71] This proved an ill-fated step. No obligation compelled a Caliph in the first year of his reign to name the man who would succeed him. But affairs were unstable, and Yazīd on his accession was confronted by a dangerous revolt in Iraq, led by another Yazīd, the son of Muhallab, with which his own weak and dissolute character seemed little qualified to cope. It was a moment for intrigue and manoeuvre to get active.

To meet the revolt Yazīd had appointed Maslamah, another son of 'Abd al-Malik, to lead the main body of troops sent to Iraq; while a nephew, 'Abbās (son of the great Walīd ibn 'Abd al-Malik), was to command a Damascus contingent. These two prominent Umayyads in turn approached the Caliph—the nephew first. "Commander of the Faithful," said 'Abbās, "the people of Iraq are a treacherous lot and prone to false rumours. With us two sent by your order to the war anything may happen; they might well, I fear, start a rumour that you had died and had appointed no successor. That might in due course penetrate the Syrian contingent—and then what? Suppose you were now to nominate a successor—say 'Abd al-'Azīz ibn al-Walīd?" "Time enough tomorrow," said the Caliph, doubtless noting how his adviser recommended his own brother.

Word of this conversation reached Maslamah, who hastened to Yazīd. His approach was at once more devious and more subtle. "Whose son do you like the better," he asked, " 'Abd al-Malik's or Walīd's?" "Why, 'Abd al-Malik's," replied the Caliph. "Then who has the better right to succeed—your brother or your brother's son?" "Apart from my own son," said the harassed Yazīd, "my brother has the better right." "Your own son is a child," said Maslamah (he was, in fact, eleven at the time), "so proclaim Hishām first and your son after Hishām." "Tomorrow I'll proclaim it," said the Caliph. And so he did: Hishām to succeed and Walīd to follow him. He put Hishām on oath not to dispossess Walīd or cancel his succession.

70. For the original text, see Appendix III, no.21.

71. Iṣfahānī (1905), vi, 99.

So it came about that when four years later (105/724) Yazīd died Hishām succeeded to the caliphate. Young Walīd was then fifteen years old, married and full of independent spirit. Already he was resenting the long years that must elapse—Hishām being still in his prime—before he himself could succeed to the caliphate. Yazīd himself, before he died, had come to regret his deference to Maslamah's advice and had taught his son to harbour rebellious feelings. Seeing Walīd reach puberty he had once exclaimed in his presence: "God stands between me and him who put Hishām between me and you."[72]

Nevertheless, the arrangement was binding on all concerned: Hishām was Caliph and Walīd his recognized heir. All must abide by that and Walīd must just wait for Hishām to die. Clearly the seeds of trouble had been sown; they did not immediately germinate. For a time Hishām treated his nephew with affability and the respect due to his rank and status. Whether in Damascus or Ruṣāfah, where Hishām spent much of his time, Walīd had ready access to the Caliph and was welcomed at his receptions. But no love was lost between them; and nothing could reconcile Walīd to the prospect of long dependence on an uncle whom he despised. For no two men could have differed more in temperament. Hishām was serious-minded and conscientious—a good administrator: careful, pernickety, pedantic, sober, moralistic and intolerant of extravagance and sloth. He had a damaging reputation for stinginess. Walīd was the opposite of all those things: frivolous, impish, open-handed, hating public affairs, irreverent, artistic and licentious. He had a taste for wine, which Hishām proscribed from his court; and, perhaps worse, he indulged in a liking for the company of singers and composers of verse. He was himself a poet and amongst his contemporaries reputed a paragon of wit, sensibility, generosity and good looks. Hishām was rough-spoken with a harsh voice and a churlish manner.[73] He once caught a man in a musical symposium, with girls and wine, carrying a guitar (*barbaṭ*). Hishām said: "Break that 'banjo' on his head!" (the word he used was *ṭanbūr*, not exactly translated by 'banjo'). The man began to sob; a friend comforting him said: "Come, bear up!" Said the first: "Do you think it is my head I mind about? No! It's the insult to my guitar: he called it a 'banjo'!" Not knowing the difference between a *barbaṭ* and a *ṭanbūr*, and despising them both, Hishām was betrayed among Walīd's friends as a boor and a philistine.

Hishām the Umayyad Statesman

Later historians, when not concerned to lampoon him or castigate the Umayyads collectively, gave Hishām credit for a strict and incorruptible

72. Iṣfahānī (1905), vi, 99; Ṭabarī (1966), ii, 1741.

73. Mas'ūdī (1830), ii, 180; Ṭabarī (1966), ii, 1733.

administration. Authorities quoted by Mas'ūdī linked his name with those of Mu'āwiyah and 'Abd al-Malik as the three true statesmen amongst the Umayyads.[74] His career was even particularly studied by Abū Ja'far al-Manṣūr, founder of the 'Abbāsid dynasty, who was said to have taken Hishām's sound policies and virtuous life as models for his own administration.

Under Hishām the state became as rich as himself. It was related that from Khurāsān there came to him, either as revenue or as spoils of war, treasure beyond computation; likewise from Iraq, and all of it was put in store or brought meticulously to account.[75] Hishām was vigilant beyond all his predecessors in scrutinizing the public accounts and registers, and seeing that they were kept in impeccable order. Thus wealth was amassed on a scale never equalled before or after. Some of this was expended in public works, in the digging of canals and cultivation of the land. Reservoirs were built along the road to Makkah, and tracts of land beside them brought under cultivation. Hishām took steps also to strengthen the frontiers of Islam, instituted military training and kept bodies of troops under arms. He took particular interest in horses, and established a racing stable—a thing not heard of before—where as many as four thousand horses of his own and other people's were said to have been assembled.[76]

By a curious paradox in one so notorious for his rigid ideas of economy, Hishām was something of a dandy. According to Aṣbagh ibn al-Faraj, quoted by Ibn 'Abd Rabbihī, he was the best dressed of all the Umayyads and the most perfumed.[77] He was equally addicted to rich furnishings and rugs, and his reign was as noted for the production of silks and velvets as it was for frontier posts and canals. It took six hundred camels to carry his personal belongings on pilgrimage.

A further shadow of doubt falls on the legend of his parsimony if we accept the account by Ḥammād al-Rāwiyah, a literary encyclopaedist who enjoyed a high reputation amongst the Umayyads, of a chamber in which he was received by Hishām in Damascus. This Ḥammād, of whom more must be told in a later chapter of this story, had been a protégé of Hishām's predecessor, Yazīd ibn 'Abd al-Malik; and that won him the hostility of Hishām, the censorious younger brother, who alone of the Umayyads is said to have mistreated him. When Yazīd died and Hishām succeeded, Ḥammād was thrown into a state of alarm. For a year he stayed quietly at his home in Kūfah, never leaving the house except secretly to visit friends whom he could trust. But when a year had passed and no untoward rumour reached him, he ventured forth to attend the Friday mosque. Here let him report his own tale:

74. Mas'ūdī (1830), ii, 184.
75. Ṭabarī (1966), ii, 1732-33.
76. Mas'ūdī (1830), ii, 180-81.
77. Ibn 'Abd Rabbihī (1876), ii, 250.

"I was sitting by one of the gates, the Elephant Gate, when two security men stood before me and said: 'Report to Amīr Yūsuf ibn 'Umar.' I said to myself: 'This is the thing I feared.' I said to the two men: 'Can you allow me to go home and say a last farewell to my family from one whom they will never see again? Then I will come with you.' 'Impossible,' said they. So I put myself in their hands and went with them to Yūsuf ibn 'Umar in the Red Porch. I saluted him and he replied, throwing me a letter, where I read: 'From the Servant of God, Hishām, Commander of the Faithful, to Yūsuf ibn 'Umar, greetings. When you have read this letter you will send for Ḥammād al-Rāwiyah, and without threat or compulsion will send him with a riding camel and five hundred *dīnārs* to Damascus, to arrive there in twelve days time.' Well, I took the five hundred *dīnārs*, and lo and behold, there was a camel saddled. I put my foot in the stirrup and rode off, travelling continuously for twelve days and nights until I found myself at Hishām's door in Damascus. I was admitted to his presence and found him in a spacious house paved with marble; and he was in a *majlis* also paved with marble. There, between every slab of marble and its neighbour was a strip of gold; and so it was also on the walls. Hishām was sitting on a red carpet and his clothes were of red silk perfumed with musk and ambergris. In front of him were containers of gold filled with crushed musk, which he stirred with his hand to diffuse the scent."[78]

So much for Ḥammād's glimpse of palace life. Hishām had summoned him for a literary question. But of that I say no more now; for from this point the textual integrity of Ḥammād's narrative as transmitted is open to serious doubt. I shall return to it later in the story. For the present we may accept Ḥammād's picture of luxury in the palace as a cautionary comment on the popular image of Hishām, and conclude that some at least of his domestic comforts must have escaped the full rigour of his economic practice.

However that may be, it was certainly Hishām's financial austerity which caught and held the imagination of the general public and inspired a corpus of unflattering legends, many of them of very dubious authenticity, like that concerning an old cloak.[79] A certain 'Aqqāl ibn Shabba was summoned for a briefing on a mission to Khurāsān and found Hishām wearing a green fur cloak. Hishām noticed 'Aqqāl gazing at it in a particular way, and said: "What is the matter with you?" 'Aqqāl said: "Before you became Caliph I once saw you wearing a green fur cloak and I was wondering if this was the same one or another." "It is the very same," said Hishām: "as God the One God knows it is the only cloak I have." He went on: "This wealth you see me collecting and preserving, it is all for you people."

This altruistic posture may or may not have impressed 'Aqqāl; he later

78. Iṣfahānī (1905), v, 157-58.

79. Ṭabarī (1966), ii, 1730-31.

said: "I visited Hishām and found him a man stuffed full of intelligence!" Other contemporaries were more sceptical. They took Hishām's vigilance over the accounts and his careful expenditure as marks of plain meanness; and that lowest vice in Arab eyes was not only ascribed to him personally but was believed to have infected his subjects in general.[80] Mas'ūdī remarks on this: "The whole people in his days followed his way of life: men guarded their possessions, good works were rare and charity cut off. A harder time than his was never seen."

Hishām's careful economy dominated his own household as well as the public registers. His son Sulaymān once wrote to him: "My mule cannot carry me, would the Caliph perhaps see fit to order me a stronger beast?" Hishām wrote back: "The Caliph understands your letter and what you say of your animal's weakness. The Caliph believes that it is the result of your own inattention to his feeding: he is not getting enough. So you will in future attend personally to your animal's feeding, and the Caliph will look to your mounting for confirmation of his view."[81]

Another son got into trouble for laziness; he had missed Friday prayer, and Hishām demanded to know what had kept him. He said: "My animal died." "And were you too weak to walk?" said Hishām: and forbade him an animal for a year.

No detail was too trifling for Hishām's notice. He wrote to one of his workmen: "The Caliph has received the truffles you sent him, forty of them; but some arrived spoilt. That was simply because of the packing. In future when you send any of these things, make sure they are well packed with sand in the container, so that they cannot move or knock against each other."

Hishām was one day with a companion passing by an enclosure where there were olive trees.[82] Hearing someone shaking a tree he stopped and sent a man in to tell them to pick the fruit by hand, not shake the tree. "Or," said he, "they will be splitting the berries and smashing the branches."

One of Hishām's dependents was charged to take him two fine birds from one of his estates.[83] "I found Hishām in the courtyard of his house. 'Take them into the house,' said Hishām. I took them in and he went and inspected them. I said: 'Commander of the Faithful, my reward!' He said: 'Reward! Fie on you! What is the reward for two birds?' I said: 'As you wish.' 'You can take one of them,' said he. So I hurried back into the house. 'What's up with you?' said he. 'I'm choosing my bird,' I said. 'Ah! So you'll choose the better as well, will you, and leave the worse with me? Well, you can leave them both, and we'll give you forty *dirhams*, or perhaps fifty.' "

Akhṭal, the poet, according to Madā'inī, composed an ode in praise of

80. Mas'ūdī (1830), ii, 181.

81. Ṭabarī (1966), ii, 1734.

82. Ibn 'Abd Rabbihī (1876), ii, 250.

83. Ṭabarī (1966), ii, 1734.

Hishām, who rewarded him with a paltry five hundred *dirhams*.[84] Akhṭal was not pleased; he took the money to the market and bought apples, which he distributed amongst the small boys in the street. Hearing of it Hishām said: "God befoul him! He only hurt himself!"

Hishām resisted wage increases.[85] He put a freedman of his in charge of one of his estates. The man did a good job in two successive years and got bumper harvests. After the second year he sent his son to report and deliver the proceeds. Hishām rewarded him handsomely and seemed pleased. Encouraged by that the son said: "Commander of the Faithful, I have a request to make." "What is that?" said Hishām. "Another ten *dīnārs* to my allowance, please." "Ten *dīnārs*, indeed!" said Hishām. "Like all the rest of you, you think ten *dīnārs* mere peanuts! No, by God! I'll not have it!"

Another story, perhaps less credible but illustrating the bias of popular humour, describes the Caliph strolling one day with some companions through one of his orchards.[86] The others began to help themselves to fruit from the trees as they passed. "God's blessing on the Caliph," they said, "for these fruits." "Can God bless me," he said, "if you eat them all?" He then sent for the gardener and told him to uproot the fruit trees and plant olives in their place. "No one can eat those," he said.

Hishām did sometimes relax, but not so much as to forget altogether his sense of propriety. One day in a moment of leisure sitting with Abrash al-Kalbī, a brother-in-law, he noticed one of the maid-servants wearing a smart costume.[87] He said to Abrash: "Make her laugh." Abrash called to the maid: "Give me your dress." To which she retorted: "Greedy! You're worse than Ash'ab." "And who is Ash'ab?" said Hishām. She explained that he was a comic and notoriously acquisitive character in Madīnah; and she told them some of his stories. Hishām laughed and ordered Ash'ab to be summoned. When the despatch had been sealed he fell into an abstraction; at length, breaking the silence, he said to Abrash: "Can it be, Abrash, that Hishām should write to the city of the Prophet (God bless and preserve him) to fetch a buffoon? No, by God!" Then he quoted: "Comply with passion and find yourself where tongues will wag!" And he stopped the letter.

To complete the gratification derived from rich clothes and perfumes Hishām dyed his hair black; but he was disadvantaged by a severe squint. This pleased his nephew Walīd, but caused Hishām himself some considerable annoyance on occasions. One of these occurred during an inspection of troops at Ḥimṣ.[88] One of the local men was having trouble with a nervous horse. Hishām rebuked him: "What made you choose a jittery animal to train?" he said. "No, Commander of the Faithful," replied the fellow, "no, by God the

84. Iṣfahānī (1905), vii, 171.
85. Ṭabarī (1966), ii, 1732.
86. Mas'ūdī (1830), ii, 184.
87. Mas'ūdī (1830), ii, 183.
88. Mas'ūdī (1830), ii, 183.

Compassionate, I swear he's not in the least jittery. But he caught the roll in your eye and mistook it for Ghazwan the Farrier's." (Ghazwan was a Christian of Ḥimṣ who suffered from the same handicap). "Get on with you," said Hishām, "and God curse you and your horse, the pair of you together!"

Hishām's erratic eye was a sore subject. A certain Arab poet named Abū Najm, one of the best extemporizers of his day, committed a gaffe.[89] He was in attendance with some others on a day when the Caliph, in a relaxed mood, set them an exercise in imaginative description. They were to describe a scene of his choice in verses that would give him the illusion of seeing it all happen before his very eyes. The subject was to be a file of camels being smeared with pitch, then led down to water, then brought back again.

They recited their various versions of the scene until it came to the turn of Abū Najm, who decided to place the events in the context of a sunset. Unfortunately, he began by quoting another man's poem, which opened with the words: "Praise God the Bounteous Giver..." He continued, still quoting, until he reached a verse where it said: "The sun upon the horizon is as the eye..." at which point he stopped and fell speechless in confusion. For he had remembered, too late, that the next word had to be "of him who squints". "Go on," said Hishām, "finish the verse." Obediently Abū Najm resumed: "The sun upon the horizon is as the eye of him who squints," and continued to the end of the passage. He won no praise. Hishām ordered him to be expelled from Ruṣāfah. To the Chief of Police he said: "Look out for yourself if ever I see that man again." The Chief of Police in turn passed word to the notables of the city; and thereafter the unfortunate Abū Najm had to depend on the charity of one or two friends for his daily meals and on the mosques for nightly shelter.

In the sequel, however, Hishām showed the humane side of his character. It happened one evening that, suffering from boredom, he told one of his servants: "Go and find a story-teller, a *badawī* poet and reciter to come and divert me." So the servant went to the mosque and happened on Abū Najm. He poked him with his toe and said: "Get up. Go to the Caliph!" Abū Najm pleaded: "I'm only a *badawī* Arab stranger here." "You're the man I want," said the servant, "you can recite, can't you?" "Yes, I can," said he, and went with him. He was shown into the palace, the door was shut behind him and he feared the worst.

He was admitted to Hishām in a small room adjoining the women's quarters, with a light curtain between them, and lit by a candle. As he entered Hishām said: "Are you Abū Najm?" "Yes, Commander of the Faithful, it is I, your exile." "Sit down," said Hishām, "tell me where you have been sheltering and who took you in." Abū Najm told him and

89. Iṣfahānī (1905), ix, 75.

explained that he had slept in the mosque where the servant had found him. "And what about your possessions and your children?" asked Hishām. "I have no possessions," said Abū Najm, "but I have three daughters and a little son called Shaybān." "Have you married off any of your daughters?" said Hishām. "I have married two of them, and the third skips along to our songs like a little ostrich," said Abū Najm. "And what advice did you give your first daughter?" said Hishām. "She's called Innocent," said Abū Najm, "and I told her that temper was good in a dog but bad in a mother-in-law. 'She may dress you in gold and pearls,' I said, 'but God knows her nature is bad; but blows and tugs will turn the sweets of life for her to bitterness.'" (In all this Abū Najm expressed himself in verse). At which Hishām laughed, and said: "What did you tell the other one?" "I said: 'Don't spare with words and blows to thump his mother; her elbows, knees and ribs are where to aim.'" Hishām threw his head back and laughed aloud. "Fie on you," he said, "that's not the advice Jacob gave his sons." "I'm not like Jacob, Commander of the Faithful," said Abū Najm.

"And what is your advice to the third girl?" said Hishām. "My advice to you, my daughter," said Abū Najm, "what I believe is this: Let your kinsman praise you, and your neighbour and the hungry honoured guest. Turn not away the poor man who is destitute. Neglect not your long finger nails, wherewith to scribe your mother-in-law's face. As for a husband—a poor companion he." "How comes it," said Hishām, "that having spoken so you have not yet married her? How do you explain the delay?" "I say of her: 'Dhilāmah, Shaybān's sister, is an orphan with her father still alive. Her head is all lice and nits; her legs are just two strings. The Devil himself would run from her in fright.'"

At that Hishām laughed so heartily that the women behind the curtain laughed to hear him. He said to the chamberlain: "What is left in your cash?" He said: "Three hundred *dīnārs*." "Give it to him," said Hishām, "to put something better than string into Dhilāmah's legs."

Relaxations of Hishām

The malicious strain in popular legend must not be taken as good evidence that Hishām was in reality a philistine devoid of all humane and artistic instincts. Contrary indications, like the story of Abū Najm, have escaped the malice of detractors and give glimpses of Hishām as a patron of art like other aristocrats of his time, ready to hear not only versified praises of himself but also the genuine effusions of established poets and the art of those learned reciters whose long memories kept alive the store of ancient Arabic poetry and tradition.

It is related that once at the age of nineteen Hishām had with him the poetical triumvirate of Jarīr, Farazdaq and Akhṭal.[90] He sent for a she-camel of his and then pronounced the gnomic line: "I needs must make her kneel before I ride..." "Whichever of you," he continued, "completes the line to my liking shall have her—she is his."

So Jarīr said: "As it were an ostrich, runs across the steppe." "You fail," said Hishām. Farazdaq then spoke: "As one that halts weak-kneed upon the waste." "Nothing for you," said Hishām. Then Akhṭal spoke: "With soft lips loose and soft divided chins." "Mount her," said Hishām, "by God's gift she is yours."

On another occasion Hishām gave audience alone to a Nubian singer, Nuṣayb, a former protégé of 'Abd al-'Azīz ibn Marwān, Hishām's uncle.[91] Hishām bade him sing elegies on the dead of the Banū Umayya. Nuṣayb sang, and his singing ended with both of them in tears. Nuṣayb earlier had sung an ode in Hishām's praise which contained a line which—for what is was worth—gave the lie to popular calumny:

In honour's race your right hand wins the prize
For generosity; your left is runner up.[92]

Hishām addressed him: "Black man, yours is the highest praise; ask what you will." To which Nuṣayb returned: "Your hand is readier to give than my tongue to ask." "That is better, by God, than the poem itself," said Hishām; and—for what might seem a stock reply—rewarded him handsomely.

Hishām was once passionately in love with a slave girl from Madīnah whom he had bought for a generous sum. Her name was Ṣaduf.[93] One day he was annoyed with her for some reason, and, putting her aside, swore he would not be the first to renew their intercourse. It happened that the poet Kumayt ibn Zayd had admittance at that juncture and found the Caliph in a mood of grievous depression. "How is it, Commander of the Faithful," he said, "that I see you so depressed? May God relieve your sorrow!" Hishām told him what had happened. Kumayt fell silent for an hour and then spoke:

Was it Ṣaduf or you began the quarrel?
    Hard words from such as you do such as her an honour.
Don't sit in tedious self-reproach for her:
    'Tis only that your heart's too much in love.
The burden of detachment is for him
    Who's strong enough to bear it; and you're weak.

90. Iṣfahānī (1905), vii, 171.

91. Iṣfahānī (1905), i, 131.

92. For the original text, see Appendix III, no.22.

93. Iṣfahānī (1905), xv, 117. Iṣfahānī tells the same story of Walīd ibn Yazīd in Iṣfahānī (1905), vi, 119. The last two lines of the poem occur only there.

Love in a man is stronger than himself;
Submission is the customary path.[94]

"You are right, by God," said Hishām, and leaping to his feet went into Ṣaduf. She jumped up to him and threw her arms about his neck. Kumayt took his departure, and Hishām sent him a thousand *dīnārs*. The girl sent him an equal sum.

While still prince designate for the caliphate Hishām had once again with him the three popular poets: Farazdaq, Jarīr and Akhṭal.[95] Amongst those also present was one Subbah ibn 'Iqal, to whom Hishām thus addressed himself: "I need your advice; these three have been tearing each other's reputations to pieces, exposing their private lives and putting their kinsmen at each other's throat—all to no good or useful purpose. Now tell me, do, which of the three is the best poet?" Subbah replied: "Well, Jarīr draws from an ocean; Farazdaq hews from a rock; while in eulogy and glorification Akhṭal is supreme." Hishām said: "You have not made things clear to us at all; you must reach a conclusion." Said Subbah: "I have nothing else to say."

So Hishām turned to a more vocal and forthcoming member of his court, Khālid ibn Ṣafwān, and asked him to put the three in order of merit. Khālid thus began: "For grandest magniloquence, longest memory, greatest originality, most powerful sympathy; for least sensuality, for sweetest profusion—it's that river in spate, that lion who roars, who in eminence soars; dove or hawk, when he coos he pronounces, when he hovers he pounces; his oratory's plain, he wields a long rein—that's Farazdaq. But the best at narration and versification, most praised of them all and least prone to fall; who in satire brings low but lets eulogy flow—that's Akhṭal. But in learning the most copious, in verse the most refined; to expose his enemy the deadliest; in antithesis the most brilliant; who pursuing is not outrun, who pursued is not caught—that's Jarīr. All sage in mind, all lofty of purpose, they all strike fire from their steel."

Then spoke Hishām's brother, Maslamah ibn 'Abd al-Malik: "Good Khālid, from first to last we have not heard or seen the like of you. I declare that in the truth and sympathy, kindness, restraint and generosity of your portrayals you surpass them all." To which Khālid replied: "God fulfil his grace, and bestow his generous gifts upon you. May he befriend your goings out and dispel your anxieties. For well I know, Prince, that you are good soil to the saplings, knowing the people, generous in time of drought, giving largesse with a smile, forbearing with the flighty; the crown of Quraysh, the soul of 'Abd Shams; your today surpasses your yesterday."

Hishām smiled at that and said: "I never saw, Ibn Ṣafwān, a task so well

94. For the original text, see Appendix III, no.23.

95. Iṣfahānī (1905), vii, 69.

performed—the manner in which you portrayed and praised them all, and sent each one of them away contented."

This Khālid was indeed a spinner of words. He won the respect of Hishām and in a story of later years is revealed as a self-appointed arbiter of royal morals. The occasion arose when, being a resident of Iraq, Khālid was included in a delegation of persons from that country waiting on Hishām as Caliph.[96] They found Hishām with members of his court and household and relatives encamped in a picturesque encampment which Khālid, telling the story, describes in the language of eloquent enthusiasm. They had found a broad level site overlooking its surroundings, where first and second spring rains had fallen early, and had embellished the land with the many colours of blooming spring flowers and vegetation, and with the delightful scent of fresh rain asperging a soil redolent of flaked camphor grains. Here Hishām had pitched a great awning of striped cloth specially woven in Yaman, within which was a pavilion where four beds of red silk had been spread, with pillows to match. He himself was clothed in a shirt of red silk and a turban of the same.

The company had taken their places when Khālid from amongst them attracted Hishām's attention, and thus addressed him: "May God fulfil His grace upon you, Commander of the Faithful, and may He truly guide this kingship with which He has crowned you to a consummation that will redound to His praise. May He perfect it in the fear of God, and give it increase. And may nothing cloud with trouble what is clear in it, or mingle in its gladness any evil.

For the faithful confidence has now dawned. Reposing their lives on you, they moderate their transgressions and conduct themselves with godly fear. And I know nothing that can better promote the justice of your rule and the dignity of your councils, or better fulfil my own duty to Almighty God in attending on you, than that I should remind you of His benefits and your debt of gratitude therefore. And to that end I know nothing more wholesome than a story of one of the kings your predecessors; and if the Commander of the Faithful permits, I will tell it to him."

Hishām settled himself and reclining comfortably said: "Let us have it, Ibn al-Ahtam!" Khālid began his story: "There was once a king, Commander of the Faithful, from among the kings before you, who went out in a year like this of yours to Khawarnaq and Sadīr, a year when the first and second rains in succession had fallen early, and the earth had decked itself in all the diverse colours of its sweet spring flowers. And there was he in the loveliest site and surroundings, on high ground where the soil was full of flaked camphor grains. Gifted was he with youth and wealth and mastery and dominion. And he

96. Iṣfahānī (1905), ii, 33-34.

looked about him and said to his attendants: 'Did ever you see the like of my estate? Who ever had the same? To whom was ever given what fate has given to me?'

Now there was a man with him who had survived from the old pilgrim carriers, and still walked in the path of duty and right (for the earth was not then void of some to undertake for God the pilgrimage of His service), and he said: 'O king, you asked a question, do you permit an answer to it?' And he said: 'Yes.' Then said the man: 'What think you? Has this state in which you now are, been yours for ever, or did it come to you by inheritance? Is it a thing that will cease for you and, as it first came to you, even so will it pass to another?' He answered: 'It is so.' The man said: 'I perceive, then, that what you marvel at is a thing of small account, which for a short time you will enjoy, and from which for a long time you will be sundered; and for it you will tomorrow be called to account.' Then cried the king: 'Where then can refuge be found? What recourse is there?' The other said: 'Two ways. Either, on the one hand, you may keep your throne, and there labour in obedience to the Lord your God, whatever he may send of grief or joy, distress or burning pain; or, on the other, you may put aside your crown, put off your robes, put on a hair shirt, and serve your Lord until your end comes to you.' The king said: 'When day breaks knock on my door, and I shall have chosen one of the two ends. If I choose that on which now I am, you shall be my counsellor, whose word is law; and if I choose the desolate wastes of this world, you shall be my companion and governor.' So he spoke. And at daybreak the other knocked on the king's door; and he had put off his robes and his crown and was clothed in a hair shirt, and had chosen the ascetic life. And they two abode in the wilderness until death came to them. And it was as in the poem of 'Adī ibn Zayd of the Banū Tamīm:

> You who rejoice at others' ills, but rail
>   On Time yourself; are you, then, one immune
> From life's curtailment? Have you with the days
>   A solemn pact? Witless! You are deceived.
> Whom have you seen immortalized by Death?
>   What man from Time's oppression found defence?
> Where now is Kisrā, Kisrā of the kings,
>   Anūshīrwān? Or where Sāpūr before him?
> The pale-faced noble race of kings of Rūm—
>   Not one of them today is on men's tongues.
> And Hatrā's lord—to build it Tigris and
>   Khābūr he channeled there. With marble high
> He raised it, and with lime he made it smooth.
>   And in its pinnacles the birds had nests.

But Death inscrutable revered him not:
    His kingdom passed, his gate is desolate.
Khawarnaq's lord remember: riches and
    The wealth of his possessions gladdened him:
The lake, and eke Sadīr. Then, at his height,
    Upon a day reflection made him wise;
His heart was turned. He said: no happiness
    Will live till death.
Thereafter kingship, wealth, prosperity
    And all were hidden by the grave. And as
Dry leaves by south and east winds are despoiled
    So they became."[97]

Hishām at this was much affected; tears came to his eyes, and fell in such profusion that not his beard alone but his turban too was wetted. He ordered his pavilions to be dismantled and his family, relations, household, guests and all to depart. He himself retired to his palace and remained there.

The company then confronted Khālid ibn Ṣafwān: "What were you after with the Caliph?" they said. "You have spoilt his pleasure, and upset his way of life." "Let me be!" said Khālid. "I have sworn to God (glory and honour to Him) that I will never fail, in private discourse with a king, to remind him of God (glory and honour to Him). And in the story of Khawarnaq and its lord, and of Hatrā and its lord, I pointed to the better and the worse; for that is the wholesome and necessary lesson of the story. And one thing leads to another."

None will doubt that the pen which wrote this tale of Khālid and Hishām was dipped deep in the well of folklore; and so it must be read. It may nevertheless be allowed some link with truth as a fable or parable designed to reconcile two real sides of Hishām's personality: the pleasure-seeking sybarite of his early years and the austere administrator of his later prime.

Education of an Heir Apparent

While the reformed Hishām—if reform there was—conscientiously and efficiently governed the empire, Walīd was free to pursue his own education, in which he enjoyed the help of a tutor, one named 'Abd al-Ṣamad ibn 'Abd al-A'lā', whom Hishām detested.[98] For 'Abd al-Ṣamad was reputed a heretic and a sodomite. A certain Sa'īd 'Abd al-Raḥmān ibn Ḥassān, a handsome young man having, on his way to call upon Hishām, by chance encountered 'Abd al-Ṣamad, entered the Caliph's presence in a fury and

97. Iṣfahānī (1905), ii, 34. For the original text, see Appendix III, no.24.

98. Iṣfahānī (1905), ii, 76.

complained: "Commander of the Faithful, except for you, by God, that 'Abd al-Ṣamad would not have escaped from me unharmed." "Why so?" said Hishām. "He sought from me," said Sa'īd, "what no man ever sought from me before." "And what was that?" said Hishām. "Not knowing me or my father," said Sa'īd, "he fain would put the serpent in the lion's den." Hishām laughed and said: "Do what you will to him, I shall not object."[99]

Under that man's guidance Walīd's researches were directed to what could best contribute to the pleasures and elegance of life—poetry, song, girls, wine, horses, hunting and the clean air of desert and countryside. These were the immediate objects of Walīd's abundant energies; but the caliphate, which could lay the whole world of power and pleasure at his feet, remained the ultimate aim of his ambition. Walīd had a further particular interest not recognized or recorded by the historians, but now made manifest in his works: an interest in architecture. He had resolved to enhance and enlarge his enjoyment of the arts and comforts of life, and, at the same time, satisfy his notions of ancestral grandeur by construction of the most elegant and spectacular buildings possible for the containment of his pleasures. And he conceived of the Ghawr of Jordan as a winter and spring resort well suited by climate and landscape for his purposes. Accordingly, supplied with abundant material and human resources, enjoying the friendship of 'Umar al-Wādī and himself gifted with a flair and humour for architectural invention, he succeeded in planning, and over a period of years, elaborating in the Ghawr an agreeable setting for all those activities embraced in the concept of *lahw*—relaxation, sport and music—to which the critics deplored his addiction.

A Muslim concerned, in the early years of Islam, to explore the good things of life, could learn not only from the cities, made resplendent with their columned streets, public baths and popular churches, but also, more particularly and more to their taste, from the ancient Christian monasteries of Syria and Iraq. These places had special attractions for the Arabs: they liked the gardens, and the water the monks made sure they were supplied with; they admired the well-built and often brightly decorated churches; and in general they appreciated the secluded life and willing hospitality of the monks. Whatever purely architectural ideas they may have picked up from the monasteries, such as, in Syria, the grouping of living quarters round a colonnaded courtyard, they were above all charmed by the monastic gardens; and their writers enjoyed describing these pleasant retreats in terms of *nazh*, the notion of clean air and pleasurable remoteness from the common ills of every-day life. It was these qualities, reminding them perhaps of Khawarnaq and Sadīr, the fabulous but deserted palaces of the ancient kings, that the wealthy among the Umayyads sought to create when they built in the desert

99. Iṣfahānī (1905), vii, 158.

those castles for which they became famous, and the aqueducts that from distant springs supplied them with fresh water.

Walīd frequented a number of the monasteries, and learnt from them some of the pleasures he resolved to assemble in the balmy climate of the Ghawr. One of the most favoured of these places, for the extent of its gardens and the freshness of its water, was Dayr Ḥanna, an ancient foundation on the outskirts of the pre-Islamic city of Ḥīra, in an area known as Ukayrāḥ, "The Booths" or "Cells".[100] A singer and poet called Jaḥẓa describes a visit there: "I stayed three months at Kūfa with Ibrāhīm ibn al-Mudbir, who entertained me most kindly. One day the conversation touched on Dayr Ḥanna, and Ibrāhīm said he had heard it was a spot of beauty; there were many poems in its praise, he said, including one by Bakr ibn Khārija of Kūfa, which he recited:

A place beloved, by gardens fair embraced,
  From whence Khawarnaq's waters flow,
Dayr Ḥanna! Bless the days we passed in you,
  With wine's enchantment morn and eve;
The one of us with flowery garland crowned,
  The other's curls with saffron drenched.
As clouds are gilded by the lightning flash
  Your watery meads with flowers glow.
Trees in their ranks, as evening shadows fall,
  Are camels filing through the dusk.
Would you have pearls? The chamomile is there.
  Or rubies? See the anemones!"[101]

Ibrāhīm went on to say he would dearly like to see it, and to drink the wine; but he did not know exactly where it was. Jaḥẓa continues: "We were shown the way by Ḥusayn al-'Alawī, who said: 'This is the time to visit it, in the spring; while the gardens are in full bloom, and the pools are yet standing after the rain. The steppe is near at hand,' he said, 'and we shall not fail to hear the purest Arabic borne on the air to our ears. And they will bring us gifts of ostrich eggs and truffles.' So Ibn Mudbir set his servants to work getting ready the necessities and we set off. We found the Dayr indeed a beautiful building, encompassed by its gardens, with the river of Ḥīra, known as the Ghadīr, flowing near by. So there our tents were pitched. And the monks came out bringing us such gifts and favours as they had.

As we sat there eating and drinking there passed by us a lovely youth, with a cheek like the full moon on a bough, carrying one of the Christians' holy books. He was a lad of perfect intelligence and bewitching looks and

100. 'Umarī (1924), 312-34; 319-22.

101. 'Umarī (1924), 313. For the original text, see Appendix III, no.25.

voice. Seeing him Ibn Mudbir drank a *raṭl* straight off, and gave him a cup to drink. The boy then begged to be excused, for he said: 'I have here a book which the monks must have for their service, and the bell has been ringing for an hour.' Ibn Mudbir made him promise to return, and ordered him a gift of a hundred *dīnārs*."

Jaḥẓa continues his story: "I wrote Ibn Mudbir a song, with a tune to go with it, which he hardly stopped singing while we were there. This is it:

He hurried past us to the Dayr; their holy books
    Were in his hand.
His languorous eyelids dazzled me; his girdle's knot
    Ungirt the knot
Of my good sense. Him I redeemed, for him I served
    Their abbot well;
A very doctor of divinity was I. He warned
    Me of hell-fire,
But knew not of that other fire deep in my heart.[102]

We stayed there three days and then returned to Kūfa. On that I composed and sang a couplet:

Oh, the days we had in al-Ḥīra
    And al-Ukayrāḥ, so fine!
When the water got too much for us
    We mixed the wine with wine."[103]

With that we may leave Jaḥẓa.

Among the inhabitants of Dayr Ḥanna was a vintner renowned for the quality of his wine, and the high standard of his service. His name was Mar 'Abda, and it is he who tells us of the first visit of Walīd to the monastery: "The day was young, I had just opened my shop, and taken my seat by the church, when three horsemen came up the desert road from Samāwa and halted before me. Their faces were muffled in silk turbans, and their clothes were of gold-embroidered stuff. They greeted me and one of them, unwrapping his face, said: 'Are you Mar 'Abda and is this Dayr Ḥanna?' 'Yes.' He said: 'We were told of your excellent wine, and how clean your place is; give me a *raṭl*, will you?' I lost no time, washed my hands, tapped the jars, picked out the clearest and broached it. He drank, wiped his mouth and his hand with the napkin and said: 'Another, please.' I washed my hands, put aside that jar and that cup and that napkin, and tapped another jar. Having satisfied myself of its clarity, I drew a *raṭl* from that into a fresh cup, took a

102. 'Umarī (1924), 321. For the original text, see Appendix III, no.26.

103. For the original text, see Appendix III, no.27.

new napkin and served him. He drank from that in the same manner, and ordered another *raṭl*, which I dispensed for him with a new cup and new napkin as before. He drank that, wiped his mouth and hand, and said: 'Bless you! Your excellent wine, this immaculate place, and your own perfect manners! It is not my habit to drink more than three *raṭls*, but seeing all these perfections of yours my very soul invites me to a fourth; let us have it!'

So I served him in the same manner. Having drunk that he said: 'Nothing would please me more than to sit here with you all day, but things prevent it!' With that he turned away and set off on the road by which he had appeared. One of the other riders threw me a purse; but I said: 'By my faith as a Christian, I will not take it until I know who that is.' He said: 'That is Walīd ibn Yazīd ibn 'Abd al-Malik! He heard about you, so came from Damascus to see Ḥīra and your monastery and to drink your wine.' With that he went off and I opened the purse; it was of four hundred *dīnārs*."

Much nearer to Damascus were several monasteries in the Ghūṭa, the abundantly watered oasis encircling the city. Somewhere here, on a hillock at the foot of Mount Qasyūn, overlooking fields of saffron, stood Dayr Murrān, a monastery much favoured by the Arabs, which enjoyed some literary fame long after its fabric had fallen into ruin, and even its site was half forgotten. The monastery was surrounded by gardens abundantly supplied with water and shaded by many trees.[104]

It was once visited by Hārūn al-Rashīd, the 'Abbāsid Caliph. Liking the look of it, Rashīd halted and ordered a light picnic to be produced. The abbot, an ancient man, came out to greet the Caliph, and begged him to partake of the monastery's own food, which, he said, was clean and good. Rashīd accepted and asked the old man to sit down with them. As they talked, the subject of the Umayyads came up; and Rashīd asked if any of them had stayed there. "Yes," said the abbot, "Walīd ibn Yazīd stayed here with his brother Ghamr. This is the very place where they would sit, and where they would eat and drink and be sung to. One day, when the drink had begun to affect them, Walīd jumped up, went and filled that basin over there and drank it right off. Then he filled it again and gave it to his brother; and so they went on, turn and turn about, until they were both quite tipsy. Finally they filled it for me—with silver *dirhams*." Rashīd looked at the basin, a huge thing too big to lift or drink at a draught. He said: "I scorn the Umayyads, but must hand them one prize: in their pleasures they were unbeatable."

When they were not drinking, Walīd and his brother will have explored the church of Dayr Murrān, which was remembered in later years for its coloured stone pavements and, more particularly, for a curious painting in the

104. 'Umarī (1924), 353, 355-56; Yāqūt (1866-73), ii, 696-67. The floor of the monastery church is thus described: *wa akthar farshihi bi'l-balāṭ al-mulawwan wa kānā fī haykalihi ṣura 'ajība daqīqatu'l-ma'ānī.*

church described by 'Umarī and Yāqūt as a "marvellous picture of abstruse meaning"—presumably some sort of symbolic representation. It might have been that very picture, which had disappeared with the rest of the monastery by the time of Yāqūt, which put into Walīd's head the idea of a rebus when he came to record his name on the floor of his music room in the Ghawr.

Another haunt of Walīd's was a monastery also overlooking the Ghūṭa named Dayr Ṣalība.[105] It stood not far outside Bāb Farādīs, the Garden Gate, in a rural setting made delightful by walled gardens with trees and running water. In the minds of Muslims it was memorable as the camping ground of Khālid ibn al-Walīd, their commander at the siege of Damascus. The monastery itself was a notably fine building; and a convent of nuns stood close by. The poet Jarīr said of the two establishments: "When I remember the twin monasteries my heart melts to hear the clucking of chickens and the clanging of clappers."

Walīd would ride through Bāb Farādīs with his women and other companions and stay for a few days in the monastery, each day sitting for an hour in the courtyard and choosing one pleasant room or another to eat and drink in. On one of these days Walīd had called for a morning meal, and in the company was the singer Ḥunayn. They were sitting at the meal when Walīd said to Ḥunayn: "Ḥunayn, yesterday you sang me a poem of your friend 'Īsā ibn Zayd; but it was at the end of the session, and the drink had taken hold on me so that I did not fully enjoy your singing. I want you to sing it again to me now." So Ḥunayn took up his *zuqaq* or tabor, struck up and sang:

Lubayna, light the fire! He whom you love
  Has gone astray.
Many the fire I've watched by night that nibbled
  The aloe wood and laurel;
A faun beside it fans the flame,
  Knotting a girdle at his waist.[106]

Walīd was mightily thrilled; he got up from the meal, seized a tabor and set to thrumming upon it with Ḥunayn. Everyone else followed suit, grabbing an instrument and thrumming in like fashion. Walīd then made for the door of the entrance hall with Ḥunayn and the rest at his heels. The chamberlain was sitting there waiting for Walīd to begin receiving the public in audience—a number of Arab shaykhs were already gathered. Seeing the rout of Walīd's company and the state they were in, the chamberlain had the presence of mind to cry out to the people: "The women, the women! You must leave—out, out!" So the shaykhs retreated, leaving the chamberlain to

105. 'Umarī (1924), 349-50.

106. For the original text, see Appendix III, no.28.

expostulate to Walīd: "Commander of the Faithful, the delegates of the Arabs are waiting for your audience, and here you are coming out in that state!" To which Walīd cried: "You waif! Go in!" and ordered him a *raṭl*. The fellow swore he never touched strong drink. "By God, you'll drink with me," said Walīd, "until I'm drunk myself;" and had the poor wretch forced to drink with a pipe down his throat until he fell as one dead and was carried out.

Walīd was not always welcome at monasteries. He was riding one day in the Ghūṭa when he came across a small monastery called Dayr Bawanna. It contained only a few monks but was endowed with sunny gardens and rushing streams. It was said to be one of the most ancient of the monasteries, built not long after the birth of Christianity itself. Walīd passing was charmed by the look of it, and decided to stay there. That he did, and exhibited his worst behaviour, celebrating the occasion with a deplorable poem:

Hurrah for my night at the Dayr of Bawanna,
  For the drink we were served and the songs we were sung!
Our gyrations kept time with the glasses rotating
  Till the ignorant thought us possessed of the jinn.
Perfumed women we came by, with song and with wine;
  So what else could we do but to stay?
In our japing God's Caliph was made to play Peter,
  The Councillor likewise played John.
We took their communion and bowed to their crosses,
  And the tale of our doings was the talk of the town.[107]

Walīd and his Uncle Hishām

Walīd in the early days of Hishām's caliphate received an allowance from him of public funds. In later years Hishām came to regret this, for he watched with disapproval the vast sums Walīd was spending on what Hishām regarded as frivolities, including undoubtedly the extravagant buildings erected in the Ghawr.[108] In this and other respects the nephew was a constant irritant, and a quarrel was inevitable. One aggravation of Hishām's dislike was a friendship that grew up between Walīd and Hishām's second son, Maslama. Hishām was in fact unfortunate in both his eldest sons. The older, named Mu'āwiya, to whom he was much attached, died young in a fall from a horse.[109] The story is told by an eye-witness, Abū 'Āṣim al-Dabī: "I was baking bread," says he, "in the courtyard of Abū Sharīk, a Persian, when a young stranger rode up

107. 'Umarī (1924), 351; Yāqūt (1866-73), ii, 649. For the original text, see Appendix III, no.29.

108. Ṭabarī (1966), ii, 1747-8. Hishām's letter of Walīd quoted below.

109. Ṭabarī (1966), ii, 1738.

and stopped beside me. 'Breakfast!' said I, and he dismounted. I brought out the new loaf and dipped it in curds, which he ate. People came in then, and I asked who that was. They said: 'That is Mu'āwiya son of Hishām.' He ordered me a reward, then mounted and rode off. Just then a fox got up before him and he galloped after it. He had not gone a bowshot's distance when his horse bucked and he came off. They picked him up but he was dead." Hishām's comment, when he heard it, was: "I meant to train him for the caliphate, and, my God, he chases a fox!"

The next son was Maslama, commonly known by his *kunya* as Abū Shākir. To Hishām's disgust he became friendly with Walīd, and was drawn into some of his disreputable courses. This created an opening for a malicious jibe of Walīd's. Hishām had expostulated on Walīd's excessive and persistent indulgence in drink and other pleasures, and ended saying: "Fie on you, Walīd! Are you or are you not a Muslim? For the life of me I am at a loss to know." To which Walīd replied with a written couplet:

O you who ask about our faith,
 We are of Abū Shākir's faith.
We drink it neat, we drink it mixed;
 We drink it warm or sometimes cool.[110]

Pleased with this conceit, Walīd developed it in another couplet, which is recorded without context:

While others pace around the Holy Shrine
 We circumambulate a bin of wine.
For God all true believers touch the floor;
 With equal faith the bottle we adore![111]

Hishām was not a little vexed. He rebuked Abū Shākir: "Walīd uses you to mock me," he said, "and I was training you for the caliphate. Now be true to your breeding and keep your place in society!"

Digression on Umm Ḥakīm and her Cup

Maslama's mother was another source of embarrassment.[112] She was known as Umm Ḥakīm, "Mother of a Wise One", and was famous as a beauty and daughter of a beauty. Her mother, Zaynab ibnat 'Abd al-Raḥmān, whom she closely resembled, was reputed in face and figure the fairest of women. Her

110. Ṭabarī (1966), ii, 1742; Iṣfahānī (1905), vi, 99-100. For the original text see Appendix III, no.30.

111. Nawajī (1859), 79.

112. Iṣfahānī (1905), xv, 46; 48-50.

bodily perfection, in Arab eyes, was succinctly defined: "Above she is a wand; below, a swelling dune." Hishām was deeply in love with Umm Ḥakīm, and she bore him two sons: one, Maslama, was the friend of Walīd ibn Yazīd; the other, Yazīd ibn Hishām, was one of Walīd's many detractors. With all her charms Umm Ḥakīm had one defect, an insatiable addiction to drink; and in this she was encouraged by possession of a fabulous drinking cup which, besides acquiring historic fame, was to inspire Walīd to some verses calculated to annoy Hishām. The hostile son, Yazīd, had ventured on some lines lampooning Walīd on his wine-bibbing and drinking companions; Walīd retaliated:

Pure water fills the weakling's[113] cup, a cup
    Not like the cup of Umm Ḥakīm—
That mighty bowl of glass wherein she drinks
    Her nectar unadulterate.
'Twould knock a camel or an elephant
    That drank of it insensible.
She bore him drunk; so hardly he came forth,
    Instead of wise Ḥakīm—a Fool.

This and another poem of Walīd's extolling the cup in due course reached Hishām, who questioned his wife: "Is it true, what Walīd says about you?" She replied: "As if you would believe anything the scoundrel says! Do you really believe this? No! It is like any other of his lies."

The cup became a popular legend and had a subsequent history. In the time of the 'Abbāsid Caliph Ma'mūn it was found in the royal treasury of precious metals, and was described as being of green glass mounted with a gold handle weighing eighty *mithqāls*. Later, under Mu'tamid, when another survey of the treasury took place, the cup was still there but sadly despoiled of its gold, so that the surveyors asked themselves why so poor an object had ever been placed in the treasury. It was described then as round like a skull, with a capacity of three or four *raṭls*. Before that, in the reign of Hārūn al-Rashīd, while still an object of admiration, the cup had made a brief public appearance, for which I prolong this digression, since it involves the second of Walīd's poetical effusions on the cup; wherein he also declares his philosophy of good fellowship and names the great love of his life.

The tale originates with one Ibn al-Agharr, who relates: "We were in company with Muḥammad ibn Junayd al-Khatalī in the days of Rashīd. One night Muḥammad was drinking and singing, and his song was:

113. He uses the word *'ajūz*, "old woman" or "old man", but clearly alludes to Yazīd. For the original text, see Appendix III, no.31.

Another draught! The vineyard's eldest child!
    And pour it in the cup of Umm Ḥakīm!
She in a mighty bowl of glass doth drink
    Old wine unmixed. Preserve me from the taint
Of every stingy knave; for he's the worst
    Companion that I know. But if amongst
My fellow-drinkers there's a generous soul
    Than let him taste a touch of heavenly bliss!
Of women would that Salmā were my lot;
    For Salmā is my paradise and bliss!
Then spare to blame me for her; truly he
    Who blames me for her has a heart of stone.[114]

He went on singing that with variations and extensions the whole night long, drinking at the same time, until at dawn there came word from the palace that Rashīd would be riding. Now Muḥammad was in attendance on the Caliph and had the duty of taking him his horse. 'What shall I do?' he cried. 'The Caliph will never excuse me, and I am drunk.' We told him: 'You will just have to go.' So, drunk as he was, Muḥammad mounted, and took the horse to Rashīd. 'What state is this that I see you in, Muḥammad?' said the Caliph. 'Commander of the Faithful,' he replied, 'I did not know that you intended to ride, and I spent all last night drinking.' 'And what was your song?' asked Rashīd. Muḥammad told him. 'Well, now go home,' said the magnanimous Rashīd, 'I do not need you.' "

"So back he came," Ibn al-Agharr continues, "and told us what had happened. He begged us to stay by him in the circumstances. So we went up and seated ourselves on the roof. As the day advanced, one of the Caliph's servants appeared on a pony carrying in his hand something wrapped up in a long trailing cloth. He climbed up to us and addressed himself to Muḥammad: 'Muḥammad,' he said, 'the Caliph sends you his greeting and says: "We are sending you the cup of Umm Ḥakīm for you to drink out of it, and a thousand *dīnārs* to spend on your morning draught." ' Muḥammad stood up, took the cup from the servant's hand, kissed it and poured into it three *raṭls*, which he drank still standing. He poured then for us likewise, and gave to the servant two hundred *dīnārs*. Having then washed the cup and returned it with its wrapper to the servant, he proceeded to distribute the *dīnārs* among the rest of us, keeping less than half for himself." So much for Umm Ḥakīm and her cup.

114. Iṣfahānī (1905), xv, 48. For the original text, see Appendix III, no.32.

Walīd as a Pilgrim

It was no doubt true that Hishām had been training first Mu'āwiya and then Maslama for the caliphate; for he had hoped to persuade Walīd to resign the succession. But Walīd had no desire to please his uncle and no intention of abandoning the prizes that would accompany possession of supreme power. He refused flatly to resign.[115] Hishām then had the idea that popular pressure might have more effect; and in the year 116/734 he appointed Walīd to lead the *ḥajj*, hoping that he would disgrace himself sufficiently in the Holy Cities to be hounded out of his position by popular outrage. In the event Walīd's folly exceeded even Hishām's expectations. Ṭabarī recounts that he took with him not only a supply of wine but also dogs packed in crates, one of which, dog and all, fell from the camel. What happened to the dog we are not told; but the man who hired the camel got a painful whipping, and doubtless the whole episode was a gross scandal.

A more bizarre aberration of Walīd's was to take with him a domed canopy made to the measure of the Ka'ba, which he had the idea of erecting on top of the building as a belvedere from which he might watch the crowds. Fortunately, his attendants dissuaded him from such a folly, which would have aroused the fury of the populace. The scheme was abandoned; but Walīd gave offence enough by summoning the best-known singers of the Ḥijāz to sing for him and dispensing extravagant rewards for their performances.

It was during this pilgrimage,[116] according to Abū'l-Faraj, that chance brought to Walīd's acquaintance a singer and poet who later played a brief but decisive role at a critical moment in his domestic life. This was a man properly named 'Ubayd Allāh ibn Qāsim, generally better known by his nickname Abjar, or Pot-Belly. Born and bred in the cities of Makkah and Madīnah, Abjar was notably gifted with wit, personality and good looks. He made the best of these assets by wearing an expensive costume worth a hundred *dīnār*s, and riding a mare and possessing a litter both of the same value.

It happened on the seventh day of the pilgrimage that Abjar had found himself a place to pass the night at a spot called the Tan'īm beside one of the roads leading to Makkah. There, toward morning, he heard the approach of an armed convoy escorting a private caravan, in the midst of which was seen a black mare bearing a saddle ornamented with gold trappings. Abjar raised his voice and burst into song:

I saw the tribe's encampment bare and void;
Where, as I mused, it seemed a line was writ.

115. Iṣfahānī (1905), ii, 76; Balādhurī (1974), 7; Ṭabarī (1966), ii, 1742.

116. But see below, page 104, and note 134.

I stopped to hear what word the abode would give.
But it declared no tidings of its people.[117]

At the sound, occupants of the litters and palanquins called for a halt, and a voice was heard calling for a repeat of the song. "No, by God," replied Abjar, "except in exchange for the black mare and her saddle and bridle and four hundred *dīnārs*." "Who are you?" said the voice, "And where do you live?" "I am Abjar," he replied, "and I live at the entrance to the Street of the Cobblers." He then sang. When morning came, the mare and a chest of brocaded garments and four hundred *dīnārs* appeared with a messenger at Abjar's dwelling. The owner of the caravan had been Walīd ibn Yazīd; and the following day Walīd himself paid a visit in person to the singer; who subsequently followed him on his return to Damascus. We shall meet Abjar again.

Walīd's behaviour on the pilgrimage, revealing a contempt for the institutions and dignity of religion and family, was duly reported to Hishām; but it did not have the effect for which he had hoped. Hostility, however, now became open between them. Hishām would publicly castigate Walīd's way of life and choice of friends, and deride his conceit. Walīd responded with defiant insolence.

Rupture with Hishām and Disastrous Consequences of a Song

One day Walīd walked into Hishām's *majlis* at a moment when Hishām himself was out, and sat down in the Caliph's place.[118] A number of other Umayyads were present, all naturally known to Walīd. In a taunting and provocative fashion he began to ask each one in turn his name and origins, as if all were strangers. With the third person so provoked a quarrel broke out. Both stood up and were exchanging obscene insults when Hishām walked in. The two fell silent and sat down, Walīd still at the head of the room. Hishām moved up to take his seat, Walīd hardly making room for him. "How are you, Walīd?" said Hishām. "Quite well," said Walīd. "And what have you done with your people?" "They are all busy or keeping others busy," Walīd replied. "And what about your drinking friends?" said Hishām. "They are well enough," answered Walīd, "and God damn them if they are any worse than your lot here!" "Son of a whore," said Hishām, "Break his neck!" No one did that, but Walīd was gently pushed out of the room.

Walīd cherished grandiose ideas of his own ancestry, mingling semi-fabulous tribal origins with an actual but remote connection with the

117. For the original text, see Appendix III, no.33.

118. Iṣfahānī (1905), vi, 100.

Prophet. In fact his paternal grandmother, 'Ātika ibnat Yazīd ibn Mu'āwiyah, through her mother Umm Kulthūm ibnat 'Abd Allāh ibn 'Āmir, was a great-granddaughter of the Prophet's aunt, Umm Ḥakīm al-Bayḍā'. This just enabled him, with some poetical licence and more genealogical latitude, to boast:

I am a son of Abū'l-'Āṣī: and 'Uthmān is my sire.
    Marwān is my grandsire, a man of deeds and piety.
I am a son of the Great One, the glory of the Two Cities,
    Of Thaqīf and Fihr and of the Great Rebels.
The True Prophet is my uncle, and he whose uncle is
    The True Prophet in him outboasts the proudest.[119]

To genealogical bombast Walīd added fantasies of military prowess unknown to history. He sent a reciter with verses of his on these themes to Hishām, with apparent intent to tease:

Walīd am I, Abū'l-'Abbās; the great ones of Ma'add
    Have known the depth and daring of my charge.
By male and female ancestry proclaimed
    My lineage tops the highest peak of all.
My fame's a beacon tower, a landmark bright,
    Built by a builder not incapable.
My line is from the purest stocks distilled,
    Whose haughty eminence the whole world knows:
A mountain top, high, unattainable,
    In pride to rival with the Pleiades.[120]

Hishām was unimpressed and not amused: "His charge! His daring! The most Ma'add can have known of that is that once he drank with his uncle, Bakkār ibn 'Abd al-Malik, and had a quarrel with him and his slave girls. If that is what he means by 'charge' and 'daring'—so be it."

Beside his friend Maslamah, Hishām's son, Walīd had another champion with Hishām, an older man, also called Maslamah. This was a son of 'Abd al-Malik, and therefore a brother or half-brother of Hishām and uncle of Walīd. Maslamah would protest when Hishām was too hard on Walīd. Unfortunately, Maslamah died and Walīd was greatly upset. He wrote a lament:

Two couriers from Wāsiṭ pacing came
    With riddling words. No, Maslamah! I said,

119. Iṣfahānī (1905), vi, 100. For the original text, see Appendix III, no.34.

120. Iṣfahānī (1905), vi, 103. For the original text, see Appendix III, no.35.

No, do not part from us; for parting is
    But death! You were our light that lit the land
Which now is dark. We hushed the news, in fear
    To learn the truth; until the truth itself
Made plain what was obscure.
    How many an orphan child in hostile lands,
How many a widowed woman you took in!
    And you it was, when battle flowed with blood,
Who raised in it a standard all men knew![121]

On the same day Hishām was receiving visits of condolence at a military encampment when Walīd walked in, intoxicated according to an eye-witness, and confronted the Caliph: "Commander of the Faithful," he said, "he who remains behind is doomed to catch him up who has gone before. Without Maslamah the chase, for him with eyes to see, is void; the frontiers are deranged and like to fall; and in the steps of him who went before must he that follows tread! So get you ready; and the best provision is the fear of God."

Hishām turned from him without a word, and the company, stupefied, fell silent. Walīd seems to have seen in Maslamah a popular figure representing some sort of indictment of Hishām and his associates. This appears in another poem of his composition:

Are people silent now the day's far gone?
    Or do they talk in whispers? They have heard
A noble prophet's voice; and people's talk
    Is as a voice from God that does not err.
Now Maslamah has gone, who was our hope,
    We are as topers overcome by wine;
Or foster-mothers in a camel train
    That turn in longing for their foal. Would that
Thou hadst not died, but in your place a crowd
    Whose mindlessness the palaces protect
From us—malevolent and mean, and one
    Who visits not nor need be visited.[122]

As the hostility between them intensified, a time came when Walīd resolved to escape from harassment, and once for all to leave the circle of Hishām's court.[123] He moved away from Damascus and Ruṣāfah, and settled himself far to the south near Azraq in the Balqā', at a source of water known as

121. Iṣfahānī (1905), vi, 101. For the original text, see Appendix III, no.36.
122. Iṣfahānī (1905), vi, 101. For the original text, see Appendix III, no.37.
123. Ṭabarī (1966), ii, 1743.

Aghdaf, taking with him a company of personal friends and attendants, including his former tutor and instructor in pleasures, ʻAbd al-Ṣamad ibn al-Aʻlāʼ.

It is not recorded in what year exactly this move took place; but probably it was during the last five, or even three, years of Hishām's life; and certainly, as we know, after the death of Maslamah. By that time Walīd's establishment in the Ghawr must already have existed. For we may be sure that that extravagance had been achieved before the imminent rupture with Hishām, while the monies he received from central funds and all the human and material resources of the Umayyad realm were still at Walīd's disposal.

At Aghdaf, consequently, Walīd was neither obliged nor likely to spend the inclement months of winter on the windswept uplands of the Balqāʼ, but could from the first descend, as the cold advanced, into the Ghawr, and there with his companions enjoy the spring-like balmy air, the luxuries of bath and music, and the pursuit of game abounding in the thickets of Jordan. The traces of these visits both before and after the final break with Hishām may today be seen in the ashes that still blacken the flues and furnaces of the bath and in the lime that encrusts the water pipes.

Not to be cut off completely from the Caliph's circle Walīd had left behind him at Ruṣāfah his secretary, ʻIyāḍ ibn Muslim, with instructions to keep him informed of events there by letter. Meanwhile ʻAbd al-Ṣamad, accompanying Walīd in his exile, was to be the cause of the ultimate trouble. For it happened one day, during a sojourn in the Ghawr as it will appear, when the company had been drinking and were drawn to song, that Walīd called on ʻAbd al-Ṣamad to compose some verses. This is what he produced:

> Seven times saw you not how the Pleiades,
> In their round swift returning,
> Have strayed from their path to the Ghawr
> And there sought their rising?
> Their light shining gladdened my heart,
> So I spoke of my longing:
> Now perchance Walīd's kingship is near,
> And this is the eve of his fortune!
> Our hopes had been set on his kingship,
> As the drought-stricken hope for green pasture.
> To his rule we have sworn our obedience,
> And worthy is he to receive it.[124]

ʻAbd al-Ṣamad's allusion to the Pleiades rising over the Ghawr, as if that were a portent, could be enigmatic, but is explicable if the poem was recited

124. Iṣfahānī (1905), vi, 102. For the original text, see Appendix III, no.38.

while Walīd and his company were actually staying there, and the stars' appearance could be represented in playful flattery as a happy omen. One of the party present was 'Umar al-Wādī, and it was he whom Walīd called upon to sing the verses.

In Arab society a song on men's mouths would spread swiftly, and however private the occasion may have been, whether by chance or by malice, it was not long before 'Abd al-Ṣamad's verses reached the ears of Hishām. For him they amounted to treason. He reacted swiftly, cutting off Walīd's allowance and stopping monies previously paid to his dependents and guards. At the same time he wrote saying: "I hear you have taken on 'Abd al-Ṣamad as friend and companion. I am also reliably informed that he is no Muslim, and his poem about you confirms it. I cannot absolve you from complicity in his mischief. So you are to dismiss 'Abd al-Ṣamad forthwith and send him to me with my messenger."

Walīd had no choice but to obey. He wrote to Hishām saying he had done so, but asked if another of his adherents, a Yamanite, Ibn Suhayl, might be allowed to join him. Hishām's response was to flog and banish Ibn Suhayl. Then, hearing of Walīd's commission to 'Iyāḍ ibn Muslim at Ruṣāfah, he had him, too, severely flogged and imprisoned in irons and sack-cloth. 'Abd al-Ṣamad, in his turn, having been brought to Hishām, was brutally punished. Hishām handed him and a brother of his over to an agent, Yūsuf ibn 'Umar, who incarcerated them both in a specially built prison where he had the door cemented up and their food thrown down through a skylight. There eventually both died, one of thirst, the other of leprosy.

Walīd was bitterly aggrieved at these developments: "Whom can one trust?" he said, "To whom can one do a favour? This cross-eyed obscenity! My father preferred him to his own family, and made him his heir—and you see what he does to me! I dismissed 'Abd al-Ṣamad as he wanted, and only asked for Ibn Suhayl; so he beats and banishes him, knowing my regard for him. Then he hears that 'Iyāḍ ibn Muslim is attached to me; so he beats and imprisons him—all just to injure me. O God, rid me of him!"[125] He exploded then in verse:

Be warned by me who would be kind to low-born cads,
    Not having learnt their rottenness.
Show them regard, you'll find them insolent; disdain
    Them and you'll find they crawl to you.
You're proud? And all your fortune came from us! That you
    Will learn when Fortune turns our way!
Just look at them! And if the only likeness you

125. Ṭabarī (1966), ii, 1745; Iṣfahānī (1905), vi, 102; Balādhurī (1974), 13.

Can find is to a dog, try that!
Awhile his master feeds him up to hunt, until
The skinny brute that was gets strong.
Then it flies at him; and although it fails to hurt,
It would devour him if it could.[126]

Walīd then wrote to Hishām a letter alluding both to his present grievances and also to Hishām's fixed desire to disinherit him from the caliphate. He said: "I have heard of the cuts and cancellations the Commander of the Faithful has imposed on me and my companions and household. It had never entered my thoughts or my fears that God would use me thus to try out the Caliph. My asking for Ibn Suhayl and my concern for him do not merit the steps taken against me. And whatever Ibn Suhayl may, according to the Caliph, have been up to, it would be like the ass against the wolf. But if it is something against me in particular that the Caliph has in his mind, then let him know that it was God who ordained my succession, and God who set His hand and seal on my life and substance. Those no man beneath Him (blessed and exalted be He) can take from me nor diminish nor change one whit. Like them or not, God's decrees run; slow or swift they can neither be hastened nor retarded. So men's crimes under God are committed against themselves, and provoke their own punishment. It is right for the Commander of the Faithful to keep that in his mind and in his care. And may God strengthen him in his obedience and by His power enlighten his judgment of affairs." Walīd appended to his letter some verses:

A wondrous thing!
To see them daily watering at your reservoirs
And coming back rewarded!
But I, though laudable my hope
Of sharing at that watering place, return rebuffed,
My thirst unsatisfied!
Not all men's hopes are met
And where are mine of you? I'm here like one
Who clutches at a puff of dust, and in
His clenching finger-tips
Finds nothing![127]

This posture of disappointed client, clearly insincere and incompatible with the lofty tone and substance of the letter, reveals Walīd as in a mocking and ironical mood. The verses Hishām presumably ignored; the letter he took more seriously and answered in detail. But before that there was a

126. For the original text, see Appendix III, no.39.

127. Iṣfahānī (1905), vi, 104. For the original text, see Appendix III, no.40.

conversation, recorded by Ṭabarī, which began with Hishām questioning his friend, Nasṭās Abū Zubayr: "Nasṭās," he said, "if anything happens to me, do you think the people will accept Walīd?" "May God prolong your days, Commander of the Faithful," was all Nasṭās was able to reply at first. "Come, come, Nasṭās!" said Hishām. "One must die! Just tell me: Do you think the people will accept Walīd?" "The fact is, Commander of the Faithful," said Abū Zubayr, "that Walīd's succession is already laid on their necks." To which Hishām replied: "If people really accept him, then I can only think that popular saying is false which claims that three days as Caliph will save a man from hell-fire."[128]

Hishām's reply to Walīd is recorded with slight variations by Ṭabarī, Abū'l-Faraj and Balādhurī. Here is the substance of it: "The Caliph has understood what you write about the cuts he has imposed and other matters. He asks God's pardon for the pension he used to grant you, and has no misgivings of guilt for the step he has taken of cutting you off and removing your companions. This for two reasons: first, the Caliph is well aware of those places of yours on which you spent the monies he granted you, and of your attitude to him and your way of life that is not his. Second, he is fully informed of your companions and their lavish allowances. Not for them the set-backs experienced year by year by other Muslims when their campaigns break off. For there they are, your friends, with you waltzing around in your follies. The Caliph prays that God will overlook his former liberality toward you, now that he has stopped it. As for Ibn Suhayl, I ask you—by your excellent father!—what is Ibn Suhayl but a jackanapes singer of egregious silliness? And yet he is no worse than any other of your chosen companions in those affairs that are taboo with the Caliph and—by my life—damnable in you! As for that which you say God ordained for you, it was God who installed the Caliph therein and elected him thereto; and God's command prevails. And the Caliph is firm in his belief that it is not for himself that he holds what God in his goodness has given him—more to his hurt than to his enjoyment—and that it is a trust from God which one day he must give up. And God has too much pity and compassion for His servants to entrust their government to any but one acceptable to Him. The dearest hope of the Caliph, in his high esteem for his Lord, is that He may empower him to bring that about in one deemed worthy as acceptable both to Him and to them. God's concern far surpasses the Caliph's power of speaking of it or expressing thanks for it, except with His help. And if God's destiny for the Caliph is an early death, then to be sure, in that end to which he is travelling, and where he will arrive, there is by God's grace a replacement of this world. On my life, your letter to the Caliph is in keeping with your stupid folly. So spare yourself: temper your excesses and pity your weaknesses. Vengeance and might are

128. Ṭabarī (1966), ii, 1747.

God's, and He wreaks them on whomsoever He wills of His servants. The Caliph asks God's protection and succour in those things that are dearest and most pleasing to Him. Farewell."[129]

Hishām appears, as he wrote, to have known that his death was not far off. So did Walīd. He replied with some unpleasant verses made more sinister by this knowledge:

I see you strive to build on my disowning.
  If you were wise you'd pull down what you build.
Alas, for them your death will leave behind!
  A bitter crop you sow for them to reap!
I hear them cry: "If only...", "Would that we...";
  But in those days "If only..." will not help.
You scorned the hand of kindness; had you taken it
  The God of grace and mercy had rewarded you.[130]

What can have been the "hand of kindness" proffered by Walīd and rejected by Hishām? There is no intimation of that from our informants, who offer no relief from the record of ill will. Hishām in fact died—as I would surmise and as he, I think, foresaw—very soon after the correspondence with Walīd. He succumbed to diphtheria in the year 125/743. His hope of finding a worthier successor had failed; and Walīd became Caliph, very soon bringing to pass the miseries threatened in his verses. These things, however, belong to a later chapter in this story; now we may return to happier scenes enacted in the long years preceding the final quarrel with Hishām.

Affairs of the Heart

Walīd was fifteen years old when his father died in the year 105/723. He had already at that time a wife named Sa'dah, the daughter of Sa'īd ibn Khālid, a descendant of 'Uthmān ibn 'Affān, the third Caliph. Sa'īd ibn Khālid owned a desert castle at a place called Fudayn; Walīd's father Yazīd had a place there too. On one occasion at Fudayn Sa'īd fell sick and Walīd came several times to visit him. It chanced on one of these days that Walīd entering the house caught a glimpse of his wife's sister, a tall girl called Salmā. The maids and another sister tried to keep her out of sight; but as Walīd passed by they all stood up and Walīd saw her, for she was taller than the rest. Then, as the story was told, Salmā "dropped straight into his heart".[131] That was the

129. Ṭabarī (1966), ii, 1747-78; Iṣfahānī (1905), vi, 104; Balādhurī (1974), 13.
130. Ṭabarī (1966), ii, 1749-50; Iṣfahānī (1905), vi, 101. For the original text, see Appendix III, no.41
131. Iṣfahānī (1905), vi, 110.

beginning of trouble. As later events showed, Walīd was still in a way fond of his wife; but his obsession with her sister did not escape Sa'dah, and there were rows between them. Walīd's companions, the singers and poets, with whom he had already surrounded himself, soon noticed that something was wrong, and were not slow to discover the reason. One of them tells the story: "We singers had been sent for and each in turn sang, in every mode and rhythm, but Walīd sat glum and bored. Then Abjar, more cunning than the rest of us, went out as if for the privy, and asked a servant what had happened to Walīd to turn him sour. 'It is trouble between him and his wife,' the servant told him. 'She is angry, for he has fallen in love with her sister. He has sworn not to speak to his wife again or even send her messages; and now he has left her, and that is how things are.' "[132]

So Abjar went in again and sat down. Then he began to sing:

> Scorn me, and know that I'll not care.
> Burn high or low your lingering love,
> Know, when my friend was angry without cause,
> My heart turned cold.[133]

Walīd saw the poet had read his mind, and was delighted. He cheered up, wine flowed, and Abjar departed with ten thousand *dirhams* in his pocket.

It has been related above how Walīd had met Abjar on a visit to Makkah during the pilgrimage. For the biographer it would be a bonus to know if that was the pilgrimage, as stated by Abū'l-Faraj, on which Walīd had been sent by Hishām in the year 116/734; for that would establish that he was still married to Sa'dah in that year, and had therefore been faithful to her for at least eleven years. Unfortunately, there is no assurance that Walīd had not made the pilgrimage in some earlier year, when the meeting might have taken place; and in a later chapter Abū'l-Faraj seems to suggest that the quarrel with Sa'dah happened much earlier and not long after the death of Walīd's father in 105/723.[134] We had better assume, then, that all the parties were still quite young.

However that may be, encouraged by Abjar's song Walīd went ahead with Sa'dah's divorce and asked Sa'īd for Salmā. He got an unpleasant answer. It happened that Hishām, the Caliph, was married to another of Sa'īd's daughters, Umm 'Uthmān; he heard of Walīd's proceedings and sent Sa'īd a message: "Will you send your daughters to stud with Walīd, to divorce this and marry that?" So Walīd was snubbed. But he was not abashed. He was determined to see Salmā again, and set off for Fudayn.

132. Iṣfahānī (1905), iii, 113-34.

133. For the original text, see Appendix III, no.42.

134. He writes: "So when his father died he divorced his wife Umm 'Abd al-Malik, and proposed to her father for Salmā"; Iṣfahānī (1905), vi, 110.

On the way there he met a man driving a donkey loaded with jars of oil. Walīd accosted him: "Would you like to take this horse of mine," he said, "and give me your donkey in exchange, with his load? And give me your clothes in exchange for mine?" The oil man agreed and they made the exchanges. Walīd went on his way, driving the donkey before him, until they came to Sa'īd's castle. They entered the yard, Walīd crying out: "Who'll buy my oil?" One of the maids, looking out into the yard, saw him and went in to Salmā. She said: "There's an oil seller at the door who is the very double of Walīd—come out and see!" So Salmā went, had one look and turned back quickly saying: "That's him all right; and he saw me, the rascal! You tell him to be off—we don't want his oil." But Walīd had got all that he wanted—a glimpse of Salmā. He retreated happily and broke into song:

I saw a handsome goodly shaykh
Not too well dressed in shaggy cloth and cloak.
We sell our oil dirt cheap; it brings
Us nothing in. A dead loss there![135]

The high spirits that seem to inspire this little comedy were a thin and temporary disguise for Walīd's real disappointment. His true feelings were expressed in another short poem uttered at this time:

No wine twice tinged with musk, no honeyed milk,
No purest water cooled, for me is more
Desired than nectar sucked from Salmā's tongue.
No, never in my life, by God, shall I
Forget the bolted door with me shut out.[136]

After a short time, as nothing changed, he wrote to her father:

Abū 'Uthmān, would you not wish to grant
A boon to set you on the path of right?
Your gift would earn my thanks, Abū 'Uthmān,
And bring to life two hearts that died of love.[137]

The ingratiating tone of this left Sa'īd unmoved. Nor was he better disposed toward the lover when one day Walīd, intoxicated, addressed him: "Abū 'Uthmān, can you refuse me Salmā when if I had succeeded to the caliphate you would have offered her to me?" To which Sa'īd replied: "A man who gave his treasured daughter to one like you would need a better price than

135. Iṣfahānī (1905), vi, 111; Balādhurī (1974), 17, with slight variations. For the original text, see Appendix III, no.43.

136. Iṣfahānī (1905), vi, 112. For the original text, see Appendix III, no.44.

137. For the original text, see Appendix III, no.45.

you offer." Walīd at that broke into violent abuse, and a noisy exchange of insults followed until the two separated. Salmā was upset to hear of it; she burst into tears and roundly abused Walīd. He commented:

Salmā was cross with me, the silly girl,
  That I abused her father for her sake.
Good people! It is I who should be cross,
  Not her. My heart be pledged for her! And though
My heart agreed, for Salmā's father's sake,
  To disobey my love, so that today
I am bereft of her, yet Salmā still
  Fills my whole earth and firmament alike.
But I believe an enemy has come
  With hatred in his heart, to her despite.
I owe her good for ill, but little that
  Can be until she gives me her consent.[138]

Disappointed for the present over Salmā, Walīd never ceased to think of her or lost desire for her; at the same time he began to regret having lost Sa'dah. He tried corresponding with her, but that was no good, for she had married again. He persevered, nevertheless, and sent for Ash'ab ibn Jubayr, a singer of Madīnah, who for years had been a byword in Muslim society as a champion scrounger and buffoon.

It might be better, as Hishām had once on second thoughts decided, to say and hear no more of Ash'ab; but since Walīd was not above employing him, his introduction into the story can hardly be avoided. Popular folklore had assembled round Ash'ab a whole corpus of ludicrous tales which, if authentic, would have required him to have lived from the time of 'Uthmān to that of Mahdī—well over a century.[139] He seems to have become within his own lifetime a stock character on whom any incident of sufficient vulgarity or absurdity might be pinned. He once said to his mother: "I dreamt that you were smeared with honey and I was smeared with dung." Said she: "That was your naughtiness God dressed you in." "But there was something else in my dream," said Ash'ab. "What was that?" said she. "I dreamt I was licking you and you were licking me." "God curse you, you rascal," said his mother.

A woman friend of Ash'ab said to him: "Give me your ring to remind me of you." He said: "Remember me as refusing it to you; I love it better."

On one occasion Walīd ibn Yazīd sent for Ash'ab and made him put on a pair of breeches made of monkey skin, with the tail still attached. He told him to dance and then to sing: "If I like it," he said, "there's a thousand *dirhams* for

138. Iṣfahānī (1905), vi, 114. For the original text, see Appendix III, no.46.

139. For Iṣfahānī's biography of Ash'ab see Iṣfahānī (1905), xvii, 83-105. His longevity seems attested on p.95.

you." So Ash'ab sang and got his thousand. "One day," Ash'ab relates, "I went in to Walīd. When he saw me he raised his skirt and revealed his weapon at full cock—like a painted ebony flute. 'Did you ever see the like of it?' said Walīd. 'Never, my master,' said I. 'Then prostrate yourself,' he said. So I performed three prostrations. 'What's all this?' said he. 'I only said once.' 'No, master,' said I, 'one for the sceptre and one each for the orbs.' At which he laughed and ordered me a reward. "[140]

Many stories of equal or greater silliness were current about Ash'ab, the majority portraying him as persistently and shamelessly acquisitive. It was his boundless impudence and resource that Walīd now resolved to use in his pursuit of Sa'dah.[141]

"Ash'ab," he said, "I have ten thousand *dirhams* here for you if you will deliver a message for me to Sa'dah." "Let me see the ten thousand," said the ever-grasping Ash'ab. The money was produced. "Give me your message," said he. "Tell her," said Walīd, "Walīd says to you:

O Sa'dah, leads no road from me to you?
Shall we not meet till kingdom come? Time yet
May bring your husband's death or your divorce,
To my delight, and peace of mind, the end
Of separation, reuniting us!"[142]

Ash'ab found his way to Sa'dah's place and was announced. Sa'dah had a carpet spread and composed herself upon it; then she ordered Ash'ab to be admitted. He recited Walīd's piece. "Seize the rascal!" said Sa'dah to her servants. "How dare you bring me such a message?" "But, my mistress," he pleaded, "it was worth ten thousand *dirhams* to me!" "It is costing you your life, by God," said she. "Or—no! You'll take my message back to him, as you brought me his." "And what will you give me?" said Ash'ab. She said: "This rug I'm sitting on." He said: "Get up, then." She rose, and he folded it up and put it under his arm. Then he said: "Give me your message by all means." She said, "Tell him:

So you're crying now for Lubna!
And who was it that left her? You!
Well, now it's Lubna who has gone;
And what is left for you to do?"[143]

Ash'ab returned to Walīd and sang him Sa'dah's verses. "Son of a whore!" cried Walīd, "You've killed me! 'What is left for me to do' indeed? I'll tell you:

140. Iṣfahānī (1905), vi, 120.
141. Iṣfahānī (1905), vi, 110-11.
142. For the original text, see Appendix III, no.47.
143. For the original text, see Appendix III, no.48.

three things, and you can choose. Either I drop you head down into that well, or throw you from the roof of the palace, or break your head with my club here! That's what I'll do, and you can choose!" Ash'ab replied: "You can do none of those things." "How so, son of a whore?" said Walīd. "You'll never harm the head whose eyes have looked on Sa'dah," said Ash'ab. "You're right, whoreson," said Walīd laughing; and let him go.

The failure of Ash'ab's mission was the end of Walīd's concern for Sa'dah. For the rest of his life his thoughts were turned to Salmā. Nor did he lose all hope; fancying even divine intervention, he said:

May God not yet make me and Salmā one?
  Does He not do whatever pleases Him?
He'll bring her out and lay her on the ground
  And make her sleep; and, look, her wrap is down!
Then He'll bring me and lay me down on her,
  And waken me: and see, the thing is done!
And God will send on us a bounteous rain
  To wash us, and we'll know no weariness.[144]

A pleasant dream for Walīd; but years had to pass before anything like it came true. In the meantime, whether in Damascus or Ruṣāfah, in the Ghawr, at Aghdaf or in any other of the country resorts he may have visited from time to time, the record of his activities depicts him mostly in the company of singers and poets, the class of society looked on by Hishām in his mature years with disfavour. Many stories told of this period are nevertheless worth recounting for such light as they throw, authentic or distorted by prejudice, on the interests and practices of Walīd and his friends.

Walīd and Ḥammād al-Rāwiyah

There lived in Kūfah, in Iraq, three friends all called Ḥammād—Ḥammād al-Ajrad, the Naked; Ḥammād al-Rāwiyah, the Reciter; and Ḥammād ibn Zibarqan, the Bald.[145] They were known by their friends as the Three Ḥammāds, and they shared not only their name but also an addiction to compotations and heretical views. They all sang, and they all enjoyed hearing each other sing and drinking together. In short they were godless fellows, and the best of all possible friends. Of the three, Ajrad had the greatest reputation for heresy, and Rāwiyah for learning in ancient Arabic history, genealogy, poetry and language. In this he surpassed all his contemporaries and, in

144. Ibn 'Abd Rabbihī (1876), ii, 342. For the original text, see Appendix III, no.49.

145. Iṣfahānī (1905), v, 156-68.

particular, was esteemed as the infallible authority on the provenance of any poem or part of a poem that you chose to name.

Ḥammād al-Rāwiyah was in consequence a favourite of the Umayyad Caliphs. They would consult him on questions of Arab antiquity and pre-Islamic poetry; and would welcome him at their receptions. Thus he acquired a reputation throughout Syria, Iraq and the Ḥijāz as a prodigy of science and memory. It was this reputation that brought him into my story; for it aroused the curiosity of Walīd ibn Yazīd, and gave rise to a remarkable interview between them. Ḥammād himself tells us about it: "The Amīr of Kūfah sent for me, and showed me a letter from Walīd ibn Yazīd bidding him to send me to him. I was given a mount and in due course came to his place. I had to wait, for he was out hunting. When he returned I was admitted to a room where he was sitting entirely surrounded by Armenian rugs and hangings, which covered the walls and floor. He said: 'Are you Ḥammād al-Rāwiyah?' 'That is what they call me,' I replied. 'How do you come by that name,' he said, 'can you justify it?' 'I can recite from any poet known to you, Commander of the Faithful, or any of whom you have heard, or indeed of whom you may know and have heard nothing. Furthermore, I never quote a poem or saying, ancient or modern, without first identifying and separating out the original from the more recent accretions.' 'Fine!' said Walīd. 'But what about quantity? What does your repertoire amount to?' 'It is large,' said I. 'For every letter of the alphabet I can sing you a hundred full length poems as well as shorter pieces from pre-Islamic times, quite apart from Islamic verse.' 'That is indeed a repertory,' said Walīd, 'I shall examine you on that.'"

There we may leave Ḥammād's own narrative and continue the story in the words of his editor. But first the compiler must be corrected when he quotes Ḥammād as calling Walīd "Commander of the Faithful". For Ḥammād had been a favourite of Walīd's father Yazīd, and it is not to be thought that the four years of Yazīd and twenty-four years of Hishām's caliphate had passed before Walīd met him. Walīd was therefore Amīr at the time, not Amīr al-Mu'minīn.

"I must certainly examine you," said Walīd, and ordered him to sing. Ḥammād proceeded to do so and continued singing without intermission, and with such pertinacity that at last Walīd's endurance broke down, and he abandoned his part in the trial. Not to be defeated, however, he delegated its completion to a victim under oath, who was compelled to hear faithfully to the end the full consummation of Ḥammād's boast. Thus Walīd at last received a certified statement from the examiner of two thousand nine hundred full length poems, all of pre-Islamic date. He ordered Ḥammād a reward of one hundred thousand *dirhams*. As to the examiner, nothing more is heard of him.

Some time must have passed before the next recorded interview between Walīd and Ḥammād, and it is possible that it was during that interval that that conversation with Hishām took place of which I described the beginning above. But since both interviews concerned the same poem, it is apparent that the record of them has become confused in the telling, and must now somehow be separated.

This is how Ḥammād relates his second summons to Walīd: "I was summoned by Walīd ibn Yazīd who ordered me two thousand *dirhams* for my expenses and two thousand for my family. When I entered his house, the servant said to me: 'The Caliph is behind the red curtain.' I saluted him formally, and he said to me: 'Ḥammād!' 'At your service, Commander of the Faithful,' said I. He said: 'Then up they rose...!' I did not know what he meant. 'Confound you, Ḥammād!' said he: 'Then up they rose...!' I was still baffled to know what he wanted. Then, feeling that the honour of Iraq lay in my memory, it came to me and I said:

> Then up they rose to take the morning draught;
> And there stood forth a girl that held
> In her right hand a jug..."

It was for the very same verse that Hishām had summoned Ḥammād some time before; and for my story, I change the scene back to that earlier interview with Hishām that I interrupted before. It went forward thus, Ḥammād again speaking: "I approached until I could kiss his foot. At that moment there appeared two servant girls the like of whom I had never seen before. Each had in her ears golden earrings set with gleaming pearls. Hishām said: 'How are you, Ḥammād?' 'I am well, Commander of the Faithful,' said I. 'Do you know why I have sent for you?' 'No,' I said. 'I sent for you,' said Hishām, 'concerning a verse that has been in my head and I cannot recall the author; it goes like this: "They called on a day for the morning draught; and a maid stepped forth that held in her hand a jug..." '

'That is a verse from an ode of 'Adī ibn Zayd,' I said. 'It begins:

> At crack of dawn fault-finders cry: Wake up!
> What is my fault? It's thee, 'Abd Allāh's child,
> By whom my heart's ensnared. In their abuse,
> I ask, is he who blames me friend or foe?
> I cannot say. In beauty she's arrayed,
> Her hair piled up luxuriant. Her brow
> Is broad and full of grace. Her teeth well spaced
> And sweet; not short they seem, nor yet too prominent.'

'It goes on,' I said, 'with the line you quoted, and continues:

> . . .in her right hand a jug
> That's caught the ruby wine, fragrant as musk,
> Fresh vintage, clear as cock's eye from one straining,
> Tempered with heaven's pellucid dew, delicious.
> And as she pours, the leaping bubbles float
> As tiny pearls about the brim.' "[146]

There Ḥammād's recitation ended; and at this point the candid historian must pause and seek to disentangle the memories of two very different conversations, not clearly sorted out by Abū'l-Faraj. It is agreed by all that Hishām neither drank intoxicating liquors himself nor permitted others to be given them in his presence. The best authorities conclude, therefore, that the sequel to Ḥammād's recitation, appended by Abū'l-Faraj to the interview with Hishām, cannot belong there. The truth must be that the sequel derives from a quite different session with Walīd, to whose presence we must once more in imagination now return. This is how Ḥammād's story continues: " 'Well sung, Ḥammād, well sung, by God!' said he, 'Girl, give him to drink.' So she gave me a drink which took away the third of my mind. He said: 'Sing it again!' And I sang it again. In his delight, enraptured, he fell from his couch. Then he said to the second girl: 'Give him a drink.' And she gave me a drink which took away the second third of my senses. I said to myself: 'Another will disgrace me.' Then he said: 'Ask whatsoever you will!' I said: 'Really anything?' 'Yes,' he said. 'Then,' said I, 'one of the two girls.' He said: 'They are both yours, with everything on them and all that they possess.' Then he said to the first girl: 'Give him a drink.' And she gave me a drink which knocked me insensible to the ground. I knew no more till next morning, when there at my head were the two girls and some servants, one of whom handed me a purse of ten thousand *dirhams*, saying: 'The Caliph sends you greetings and says: "Take this and use it." ' I took the purse with the two girls, and made my departure."

Having distinguished himself at his first meeting by the prodigious extent of his repertory, and again by his rendering of the poem of 'Adī ibn Zayd, Ḥammād became one of Walīd's circle of favourite singers. He relates an incident when they were all present and he again distinguished himself: "I went in to Walīd and found him reclining at ease, with Ma'bad and Mālik and Ibn 'Ā'ishah and Abū Kāmil and Ḥakam al-Wādī and 'Umar al-Wādī all present with him.[147] They had been singing; and at his head, filling his cup, was a girl of accomplished perfection and beauty beyond all my experience.

146. Iṣfahānī (1905), v, 158. For the original text, see Appendix III, no.50.

147. Iṣfahānī (1905), xix, 92-93.

He said to me: 'Ḥammād, I have told these people to sing an air to match the quality of this girl; and I am making a present of her to anyone who can do it. None of them has so far succeeded; so you now sing me something to equal her perfection.' So I sang him the words of Rabīʿa ibn Maqrūm al-Ḍabbī:

Fine nose between soft cheeks, fair as full moon
  Revealed through parting clouds. Sweet is the air
About her as the scent of cloves or wine-
  Drenched lavender. Her mouth at slumber time's
A cup of purest water mixed with wine.
  Descrying her from his cliff-high retreat
The ascetic anchorite, grey-headed, through
  Unsleeping hours beseeching of his lord,
Until his suppliant flesh is withered up,
  Yearns for her beauty and her pleasant talk;
And soon resolves to leave his mountain den."[148]

The passage was well chosen; for just such anchorites, from inaccessible caves on Mount Quruntul to the west, could look down on Walīd's establishment in the Ghawr below. Walīd cried out: "That's her! You've hit the mark! And you may choose: take her or a thousand *dīnārs*!" Unpredictably, it seems, and even while Ḥammād was singing, Walīd had changed the terms of the competition; and, with the image in our minds of feminine perfection, it is distressing to hear of Ḥammād's choice. He tells us bluntly: "I chose the thousand *dīnārs*, and took the money." So Walīd ordered the girl away to his women.

We owe to Ḥammād the account of how Walīd acquired another of his life-long friends. It occurred at Bakhrā', a remote settlement in the region of Tadmur (Palmyra) where the Umayyads had found a castle built by the Persians in the days before Islam and had made it habitable. This was another of Walīd's haunts, to which he would repair with parties of friends to hunt and to sing. It was here that he was staying when on an impulse he sent for Ḥammād al-Rāwiyah to join him. Riding from Kūfah on an animal of the mail, Ḥammād arrived at Bakhrā' and thus describes what happened: "I was admitted," he says, "and found him on a settee wearing two yellow garments, a cloak and waistband, both having been dipped in saffron. He had with him Maʿbad and Mālik and Abū Kāmil, his *mawla*. He gave me time for my agitation to subside, then said: 'Let me hear "Do death and its caprice write sorrow on thy brow...?"' I recited him the poem to the end, when he said to the cup-bearer: 'Sibra, give him a drink.' Sibra gave me three cups of what numbed my senses from crown to sole."

148. For the original text, see Appendix III, no.51.

We turn, accordingly, to Abū'l-Faraj the Compiler, to take up the story. Walīd then, having bid Ma'bad sing him three different songs in succession, called for Sibra to give him of the wine called Pharaoh's Beard; of which he took twenty draughts from a little cup fitted with ivory.

At that moment the chamberlain announced that a man the Prince had sent for was at the door. "Let him come in," said Walīd. There came in a lad who had a deformity in one ankle but, according to Ḥammād, the loveliest face he had ever seen. "Give him a drink, Sibra," said Walīd. And Sibra handed him a cup. Then Walīd said to him: "Sing me 'And she was wearing at that time a veil...'" The lad sang the song, which went:

She found me as I was, a growing boy,
    Heedless, thick wavy-haired with slender belly,
A boy of boys, my waist-band hanging loose;
    Just ten, a little gold ring in my ear.
And she was wearing at that time a veil,
    And had a family of slave-girl toys.[149]

Walīd flung from him the two garments he was wearing, and said: "Now sing 'It was only a dream, but welcome a thousand times for any sight of Zaynab...'" At that point Ma'bad lost his temper: "Here are we," he said, "attending on you, with all our years and our standing, and you turn to this boy and leave us in the dog house!" Walīd took the outburst with good humour and replied mildly: "Before God, Abū 'Abbād, I do not for a minute forget your age or your standing; but the fire in this lad's song had me like a pot on the boil."

Walīd and Ibn 'Ā'ishah

The name of the lad was Muḥammad ibn 'Ā'ishah.[150] His mother 'Ā'ishah was a hairdresser; she bore him out of wedlock, and thus it was from her that he took his common name. From his earliest years Ibn 'Ā'ishah had plenty of self-confidence, which was increased beyond measure by possession of a marvellous singing voice. We are told that his singing ravished the ears of all who heard him; the youth of Madīnah, where he was born, would fight to speak or sit with him. He learnt singing from Ma'bad and Mālik, and had become their equal before they died.

It was not long before the compliments he received from important people

149. Iṣfahānī (1905), ii, 63-64. The "slave-girl toys" are reminiscent of Hishām's mother 'Ā'ishah, who would make dolls out of chewed gum and give them girls' names, Ṭabarī (1966), ii, 1466. For the original text, see Appendix III, no.52.

150. Iṣfahānī (1905), ii, 59-62.

turned Ibn 'Ā'ishah's head, and he became too proud for one of his humble origins. Once during the pilgrimage, when Hishām was Caliph, a friend of Ibn 'Ā'ishah found him standing vaguely at a spot by the road used by pilgrims; he asked him what kept him there. Ibn 'Ā'ishah replied: "I know a man who has only to open his mouth and all movement stops; people are held fast." The man said: "Who can that be?" "Me!" said Ibn 'Ā'ishah. Whereupon he began to sing:

> She sped past to the right—is not that luck?
> I said to her: Good-bye!
> Quick go! Quick come again!
> But when?
> The memory is sickness in my heart.
> I nurse my pain:
> But then the cure itself is pain.[151]

Lo and behold, everything came to a halt; caravans fell into confusion; camels stretched out their necks, and there was nearly a riot. Who should come up at that moment but the Caliph himself, Hishām ibn 'Abd al-Malik. "God's enemy!" said he. "Would you start a fight?" Ibn 'Ā'ishah stopped singing at that, but did not lose countenance. Seeing that, Hishām said: "Go easy with your conceit!" To which Ibn 'Ā'ishah said: "A man with that power over men's hearts has a right to be conceited." Hishām laughed at that and let him go his way.

That kind of thing gave Ibn 'Ā'ishah an insufferable pride. He was flattered to be held the most knowledgeable amongst the singers of Madīnah, and the best fitted by wit and social aplomb to keep company with kings and caliphs. Amongst lesser men his air was disagreeably haughty, and he would refuse to sing for common people or anyone not much grander than himself. When someone said to him "Well sung!" he retorted: "Is 'well sung' a thing to say to such as I?"

Attempts were made to suppress him, but not always with success. A sudden flood in one of the valleys once drew a crowd to see water filling the courtyard of Sa'īd ibn al-'Aṣī; and Ibn 'Ā'ishah was amongst them. He found a seat on the elevated corner of a well-head. As he sat there, there came up no less a person than Ḥasan ibn al-Ḥasan, grandson of 'Alī ibn Abī Ṭālib the Prophet's son-in-law, riding on a mule and followed by two young slaves as black as the devil. To these two Ḥasan gave the order to go forward quietly and place themselves at the foot of Ibn 'Ā'ishah's perch. As they reached their position Ḥasan called out: "How are you this morning, Ibn

151. For the original text, see Appendix III, no.53.

ʻĀ'ishah?" "Well, thank you," said Ibn ʻĀ'ishah; "my father's and mother's blessing on you!" "Look who is beside you," said Ḥasan. Ibn ʻĀ'ishah looked down and saw the two blacks. "Do you know them?" said Ḥasan. "Yes," said Ibn ʻĀ'ishah. "Well then, you have a choice: either here and now you sing me a hundred songs, or they have my order to pitch you into that well, or have their hands cut off if they fail."

Ibn ʻĀ'ishah without hesitation burst into song with an elegy by Abū'l-ʻAyyāl to a tune of Maʻbad's:

> Praise God for thee, the people's tower
> Of strength to stand in danger's hour.
> Who'll be our watch and guard, they say,
> And go before us to the fray?
> Why, you were he who, called by war,
> Leapt up and led them to the fore.
> Brother, as I remember thee,
> Sickness of heart returns to me;
> As, after dummy comfort brief,[152]
> Returns the stricken mother's grief.
> Thinking of Zuhra's son this night
> My sobs endure till morning light.

Whereafter he kept singing until he reached his hundredth piece:

> Say to the halting-places in Ẓahrān:
> Articulate!
> It's time you made your message crystal clear!
> They said: And who are you? Tell us!
> I said: One sick at heart, whose grief
> At love's vicissitudes you've stirred.[153]

At that Ibn ʻĀ'ishah fell silent; and it was said that never before had people heard so much of him, or heard the like of that singing. Not a soul grew weary or left to finish his own affairs. By the time Ibn ʻĀ'ishah had reached the end of that last song a crowd had hurried up from all directions, such as had never before been seen at that isolated spot. All raised their voices in applause. "Well sung, by God, well sung!" they cried, and escorted Ibn ʻĀ'ishah back in triumph to the city.

A story was told of Ibn ʻĀ'ishah after a visit to Walīd ibn Yazīd, whom he had pleased by his singing of a song on the theme:

152. "Dummy comfort" is the stuffed skin of her calf hung round the neck of a bereaved mother camel. For the original text, see Appendix III, no.54.

153. For the original text, see Appendix III, no.55.

When you are gone, what hope have I
    Of refuge or defence?
Defended refuges till now have baffled me to find.[154]

Walīd had ordered him thirty thousand *dirhams* and enough clothes to fill a laundryman's bundle. Ibn 'Ā'ishah was making his way back on horseback when he was noticed, as he passed, by a man of Wādī'l-Qura, whose name we are not told, only that he was a wine-drinker and passionate lover of song. This man asked his servant: "Who was that passing by?" Hearing that it was Ibn 'Ā'ishah the singer, the man approached him and said: "Are you indeed, I beg, a son of that 'Ā'ishah who was the Mother of Islam?" He said: "No, I belong to Quraysh, and my mother's name was 'Ā'ishah. That's enough for you and more." "What is that great purse and all that finery I see you have?" persisted the man. "I sang something to the Caliph," said Ibn 'Ā'ishah, "which so excited him that God and prayer dropped from his mind and he ordered me the purse and the clothes that you see." Said the other then: "I'd give my soul if you would but let me hear what you sang him." "God damn you, sir," said Ibn 'Ā'ishah, "am I a person to be accosted so on the road?" "Then what shall I do?" said the man. "You can follow me to the gate," said Ibn 'Ā'ishah, spurring the roan mule he was riding, hoping to shake the man off. But he kept up with him running so that they reached the gate together like race horses in a dead heat. Ibn 'Ā'ishah went in and waited a good long time, hoping the man would weary and go away. But he did nothing of the kind. At last Ibn 'Ā'ishah got tired and told his servant to let him in. Then: "For the love of God," he said, "where are you from to pursue me thus?" "I come from Wādī'l-Qura," said the man, "and I have a passionate desire to hear that song." "Are you interested in something that will be more useful to you?" said Ibn 'Ā'ishah. "What do you mean?" said he. "I mean two hundred *dīnārs* and ten sets of clothes for you to go back to your people." The man then replied: "I have a little daughter, who has not so much as a silver earring, God knows—let alone gold—to put in her ear; and I have a wife without a shirt to her back; so I'm utterly destitute. But if you gave the whole of what the Caliph ordered you, and doubled it, I would still rather have that song."

Now, for all his pride and reluctance to sing for anyone not a Caliph or man of great eminence, Ibn 'Ā'ishah was so astonished that he took compassion on the fellow and sent for writing materials. Then he began to sing—first extempore and then giving him the song. The man in a paroxysm of joy began to shake his head with such violence that Ibn 'Ā'ishah feared it

154. Iṣfahānī (1905), ii, 70. For the original text, see Appendix III, no.56.

would come off. The fellow then, finally satisfied and refusing to accept anything more, left the house.

The story reached Walīd ibn Yazīd. Having ascertained the full facts from Ibn ʻĀ'ishah, he had the man found and brought to him. He ordered him a pension and made him one of his circle, putting him in charge of the cellars. And so he remained until Walīd's death.

Ibn ʻĀ'ishah's associates, knowing him as a curmudgeon unwilling to sing to ordinary people, learnt by experience that he could be lured into singing of his own accord if his interest was sufficiently aroused in conversation. There was an occasion, described by Yūnus al-Kātib, when a group of Quraysh had gathered for a picnic at a beauty spot near Madīnah called al-ʻAqīq, the "Red Gorge".[155] They were joined there by Ibn ʻĀ'ishah, walking and supporting himself on the hand of a young companion. "I was singing," says Yūnus, "when Ibn ʻĀ'ishah came up, saluted us and sat down and talked. We all knew his touchiness and how it annoyed him to be asked to sing, so we told each other stories of Kuthayr and Jamīl and other poets, hoping to excite his enthusiasm and get him to sing in that way. But it did not work. Eventually I remarked that earlier on that day I had heard from a *badawī* Arab a story that beat all the others, and I offered to tell it if they liked. They all said: 'Let us have it.' This is the story the Arab had told me: 'I was passing near Rubdhah when I came upon some boys diving against each other into a pool. Sitting there watching them was another youth, pretty enough but physically emaciated and showing all the signs of sickness and consumption in his body. I greeted him and he returned my greeting and said: "Whence cometh the rider?" I said: "From Ḥamī." He said: "When came you there?" I said: "In the evening." "Where did you pass the night?" I named the tribe. He cried out: "Awah!" and threw himself backwards to the ground panting so violently that I thought his heart would burst. Then he opened his mouth and sang:

That place be green with heaven's life-giving showers
    Wherein at eve Sulaymah sets her foot.
And though I am no dweller there, yet one
    Therein alights who's very dear to me.
How excellent that close and constant friend,
    Though far his dwelling, gracious in my eyes.
What loving friend would censure me on him
    That loving friend in wrath shall be rebuked![156]

As the song ended, he fell silent in a faint. I called to the other lads, and they

155. Iṣfahānī (1905), ii, 72-73.
156. For the original text, see Appendix III, no.57.

brought water, which I poured on his face. He woke up and sang again:

The unknown lover, seeing me abased
  And sighing, wears
My sighs and my abasement as his own.
  The valleys draw my gaze and blind my eyes
With flowing tears.
  And as the stranger, welcomed by the tribe,
Finds friendship, so my heart
  Through you finds friendship in the solitudes.[157]

I said to him: "Shall I not stay and help you? Or go back to Ḥamī for anything you may need? Or take any message?" He said: "Your good friendship has been health and wealth to me. Go on your way, and finish your journey. Had I thought you could do me any good, I would have submitted to your desire and justified your endeavour. But you have found me at my life's last feeble ebb." So I left him, and I cannot think he lived to see that night.'

The company all marvelled at the tale, and Ibn 'Ā'ishah struck up and sang both the sick lad's songs complete, and spent the rest of the day with us in good spirits, drinking and singing until we left."

A shaykh of Tanūkh tells a story of Ibn 'Ā'ishah with Walīd ibn Yazīd. He says: "I was curtain-master to Walīd ibn Yazīd and saw Ibn 'Ā'ishah with him. He sang a song of a man of Quraysh which began:

I saw them as a gleam of stars
  That rise to ring the moon at night.
Such bright-eyed beauties as dispelled
  Resolves of abstinence.
It was the Day of Sacrifice;[158]
  I went forth seeking virtue's wage;
What I came back with was a load
  Of unpremeditated sin.

Walīd was enraptured, transported by the song beyond the bounds of faith or morals. He called to the servant: 'Boy, bring me a drink of the Fourth Heaven!' Then to Ibn 'Ā'ishah: 'Well sung, by God, my Prince! Again, for 'Abd Shams!' And he sang it again. 'Well sung, by God,' said Walīd:

157. For the original text, see Appendix III, no.58.

158. Iṣfahānī (1905), ii, 70; Mas'ūdī (1830), ii, 187. "Day of Sacrifice" (l.5) reading with Mas'ūdī *ṣabīḥat al-naḥr*, 10th Dhū'l-Ḥijjah. Iṣfahānī has *al-nafr*, 12th of the month, departure from Minā. For the original text, see Appendix III, no.59.

'Again, for Umayya!' So he sang it again. And Walīd persisted making him sing for one famous name after another repeatedly until, running through all the 'kings' he came to himself and said: 'For my own life, once again!' And he sang it again. And Walīd stood up and bent over him, kissing every one of his limbs in turn until he came to his 'thing', when Ibn ʿĀ'ishah crossed his legs against him. 'By God Almighty,' said Walīd, 'you will not leave until I've kissed it.' So Ibn ʿĀ'ishah let him. And Walīd kissed his head, then tossed him all his clothes, leaving himself bare until they brought him another set. Then he gave him a present of a thousand *dīnār*s and set him on a mule, saying: 'Ride off with you! You and your singing have left me like a pan on the boil!' So Ibn ʿĀ'ishah rode off, mule, saddle cloth and all."

One day Walīd received a crowded assembly of singers, amongst them Maʿbad and Ibn ʿĀ'ishah. Walīd called to Ibn ʿĀ'ishah: "Muḥammad," he said, "I have composed a poem; I want you to sing it." He recited the words and Ibn ʿĀ'ishah then sang:

Another cup! Another drop! Of the wine of Iṣfahān!
  Of the wine of the Old Man Kisra, or the wine of Qayrawān!
There's a fragrance in the cup, or on the hands of him who pours;
  Or is it just a lingering trace of musk from filling of the jars?
A wreath, a garland for my head! And take my poem for your song!
  Here's my rope to let me loose and here to bind me take my thong!
Spring time's only in the cup that's handed with the finger tips.
  And now the ardour of the cup has crept between my feet and lips![159]

Everyone present applauded Ibn ʿĀ'ishah for his rendering; but he, not content, turned to Maʿbad: "Abū ʿAbbās," he said, "how did you find it?" Maʿbad replied: "You've spoilt your singing by your bragging." "By God, you squint-eye," said Ibn ʿĀ'ishah, "if you were not our elder, and in the Caliph's presence, I would have taught you who it was that spoilt his singing—I with my bragging or you with your ugly face!" Walīd noticed the commotion and said: "What's going on?" "It's all right, Commander of the Faithful," said Ibn ʿĀ'ishah; "only a line Maʿbad was teaching me—I had forgotten how it went, and asked him so that I might sing it to you." "What was it?" said Walīd; then to Maʿbad: "Let us have it, Maʿbad." Ibn ʿĀ'ishah thinking quickly had quoted a line and Maʿbad sang it. Walīd congratulated him and said: "Maʿbad, you are the master of singers." Thus the quarrel was suppressed.

Ibn ʿĀ'ishah got into trouble with Walīd, but thanks to Maʿbad, got out

159. Iṣfahānī (1905), viii, 84. For the original text, see Appendix III, no.60.

of it again. When Walīd acceded to the caliphate he had no intention of dropping his association with singing friends; but he decided to keep quiet about it. While sending to Makkah and Madīnah for them to join him in Syria, he gave instructions that they were to separate and join him inconspicuously by night. Ibn 'Ā'ishah, unfortunately, made the mistake of arriving before the others and boldly presenting himself at Walīd's place in the daytime, thus drawing attention to what was going on. Walīd had him put in irons and imprisoned. There he stayed while the other singers, amongst them Ma'bad, turned up singly as instructed, and were admitted one by one at night.

They were all assembled, and as usual sang in their turns. When it seemed that Walīd was pleased with their gathering and was in a good mood, Ma'bad, being now an old man, remembered Ibn 'Ā'ishah in his misfortune, and, after a word with his companions, asked Walīd how he found their performance. "Good, delightful!" said Walīd. "How would it be," said Ma'bad, "if you had Ibn 'Ā'ishah here before you and heard what he could offer?" "Send for him," said Walīd. Ibn 'Ā'ishah appeared, hobbling in his fetters. As Walīd eyed him, Ibn 'Ā'ishah broke into song, with a flattering poem by Ibn Ṭurayḥ:

Broad valley levels are your ancestry;
  No bends or flexures trouble thee.
Happy your branches twain—this side and that;
  Happy your tangled roots entwined.
If you should bid the torrent leave its course,
  With mountainous conflicting waves,
It would subside, turn back, or at your word
  Would turn aside to other tracts.[160]

Walīd instantly ordered the shackles to be struck off and friendship was restored. It cannot have been for long; for at his accession Walīd himself had only fifteen months to live, and Ibn 'Ā'ishah is said to have died before him.

Various accounts are given of Ibn 'Ā'ishah's death; but most agree that he fell from the roof of the castle of Dhū'l Khashab, one stage out on the long road north from Madīnah to Damascus. By one story Ibn 'Ā'ishah was travelling with Ghamr ibn Yazīd, Walīd's younger brother, bound for Damascus. They halted on their first day out at Dhū'l Khashab, and were drinking on the roof of the castle, when Ibn 'Ā'ishah gave a song which particularly pleased Ghamr. He asked him to sing it again. In a fit of petulance Ibn 'Ā'ishah refused. Ghamr, annoyed and probably drunk, had him pushed off the roof.

160. Iṣfahānī (1905), iv, 80. For the original text, see Appendix III, no.61.

Others say that the governor of the castle had caused slave girls to join them, and Ibn ʻĀ'ishah was caught ogling one of them. Others deny all that and say that he merely got up to "relieve nature" and in a drunken lurch fell to his death.

A fuller and pleasanter account of what happened was told in later years by one of the older inhabitants of Madīnah: Ibn ʻĀ'ishah was returning home to Madīnah from the direction of Damascus, after a profitable spell in the company of Walīd ibn Yazīd, who had rewarded him for his art with unprecedented generosity.[161] He was travelling with baggage laden with rich garments, perfumes and cash, himself in high spirits. Approaching the city, he arrived at Dhū'l Khashab, where the governor of Madīnah at the time, Ibrāhīm ibn Hishām ibn Ismāʻīl al-Makhzūmī, an uncle of the Caliph Hishām, was residing in the castle. Word came that Ibn ʻĀ'ishah the singer was there, and if bidden to stay the night might give them some pleasure. So Ibn ʻĀ'ishah was brought in. As the day advanced, the company moved up to the roof of the castle. They had been drinking, and it happened that Ibn ʻĀ'ishah, admiring the view, perceived a party of women walking in the valley below. Turning to the others he said: "Are you interested in them?" They replied: "How should we be?" At which Ibn ʻĀ'ishah sprang up, donned a scented gown, and leaping on to a battlement broke into song with some verses of Ibn Udhayna well known for lines put into the mouth of a sprightly maiden called Sulaymah:

> Come hither, come hither, said she to her comrades!
> How good is our life, nature smiles on our meeting![162]

The women inevitably came up; thrilled, Ibn ʻĀ'ishah, did a pirouette, overbalanced and fell to expire at their feet. Such was the end of Ibn ʻĀ'ishah, the carefree ending of a famous life. His tomb at Dhū'l Khashab was still known a hundred years later.

Walīd and Abū Kāmil

Amongst the company present at Ibn ʻĀ'ishah's introduction to Walīd was a freedman and favourite to whom he was much attached, named Abū Kāmil al-Ghazīl. This was another excellent singer and an amusing person as well. As a mark of his affection Walīd is said to have brought him into a number of his poems, as when he said:

161. Iṣfahānī (1905), ii, 74-75.
162. For the original text, see Appendix III, no.62.

For Abū Kāmil golden wine of Babylon I poured;
For Ma'bad too, and every seasoned youth.
I have their love unmixed, and them my bounty overflows.
None blames me for them but the envious dunce.[163]

Abū Kāmil enjoyed a rare favour from Walīd. He had sung him a song which so pleased the prince that he gave him as a reward not only the clothes he was wearing but also his expensive headdress, a gold brocaded *qalansuwa*, a cap in the Persian style. This became an object of veneration with Abū Kāmil. Cherishing it with devoted care, he would wear it only at festivals, as they came round in the year, and then, wiping it with his sleeve and raising it to his head, with tears in his eyes, he would say: "I put it on only for the smell I sense in it of my master."

This is one of Walīd's drinking songs sung to him by Abū Kāmil at a lunch party described by Ḥammād al-Rāwiyah:

Pass the cup round to the right
Don't pass it to the left.
Pour first for him, and then for him,
You of the silver lute.
Dark wine long aged in earthen jars,
Sealed up with camphor, spice and pitch.
So my hereafter's sure: no fire for me! I'll teach
The folk to ride an ass's pizzle!
Tell him who looks for heaven to run along to hell![164]

Walīd and Ḥakam al-Wādī

The school of singers in Wādī'l-Qura, of which the founder and most distinguished member was 'Umar al-Wādī, Walīd's "Marshal of Pleasures", bred another of Walīd's friends. This was a pupil of 'Umar's named Ḥakam al-Wādī, commonly known by his *kunyah* as Abū Yaḥyā. He was the son of a barber, by name Maymūn, of Persian descent, who as a slave had the distinction of shaving the head of the great Caliph Walīd ibn 'Abd al-Malik, from whom he gained his freedom. The son Ḥakam, was tall, one-eyed and endowed with a hump back. Nevertheless, trained by 'Umar, he was unmatched in his day as an extempore singer and a skilful performer on the *daff*, the little drum on which he tapped accompaniment to his songs.

Ḥakam had traded as a camel-owner, hiring his services as a carrier of oil

163. Iṣfahānī (1905), vi, 139-40, For the original text, see Appendix III, no.63.

164. Iṣfahānī (1905), vi, 119-20. For the original text, see Appendix III, no.64.

from Syria and other sources to Madīnah. He is said to have lived to a great age and died in the reign of Harūn al-Rashīd. But a statement that he sang for the first Walīd ibn 'Abd al-Malik must be a mistake, for he is in fact represented as a young man when first introduced to Walīd ibn Yazīd.

It was 'Umar al-Wādī who introduced him. Ḥakam himself describes the scene: "Walīd was riding an ass; he had on him a gown and cloak both of figured brocade and soft boots to match. In his hand," says Ḥakam, "he held a string of gems and in the pocket of his sleeve was something I could not see to identify. Walīd said: 'Whoever sings me the thing my heart desires shall have what is in my sleeve and all that is on me and below me.' The others all sang, and nothing pleased him; so he turned to me and said: 'You sing, young man.' So I sang:

Her garland's all colours; her face a seduction.
  The mole on her cheek is without a companion.
Shimmering, swaying, she moves like a serpent;
  She's a cord round my heart, and I'm caught in her bridle.[165]

Walīd was delighted, pulled out the thing in his sleeve—it was a purse of a thousand *dīnārs*—and threw it to me with the string of gems. Later, when he had gone in, his messenger brought me the clothes he had worn and the ass." Ḥakam was then quite young, and he had long to live before achieving real fame. Muṭī' ibn Iyyās in a couplet says of him:

Abū Yaḥyā the singer of loves,
  Discerner of grave and gay.
When he sings to the lute he excels;
  He excels when he speaks to the drum.[166]

Ḥakam had an unequalled skill in varying, developing or abbreviating tunes he had once heard. When asked about this he explained: "I don't drink. Another man drinks, and when he drinks his singing suffers." His speciality was said to be the high thrilling style known as *hazaj*; but there is a story that he only took to this in his old age during the reign of the 'Abbāsid Caliph Manṣūr, when he was patronized by Muḥammad, son of Abū'l-'Abbās the first Caliph of the dynasty. When Abū Yaḥyā's son reproved him for singing "like a eunuch", his reply was: "Silence! You know nothing. For sixty years I sang deep and made barely enough to eat; now for a few years I have sung *hazaj* and you never saw the like of my takings."

165. Iṣfahānī (1905), vi, 62-64. The fourth line of "Her garland's all colours", quoted here from Iṣfahānī (1905), xii, 77, is often omitted. My translation is undoubtedly too free; nearer to the original would be: "tight-twisted she comes, as if she were a bridle." For the original text, see Appendix III, no.65.

166. For the original text, see Appendix III, no.66.

Literary Discourse with a Connoisseur

Walīd once heard of the exceptional social and conversational talents of one Shurā'ah ibn Zindabūd. He sent for him. On Shurā'ah's arrival a conversation took place:

Walīd: I did not ask you here for your views or pronouncements on philosophy or jurisprudence. You are not to lecture or read to me from the Qur'ān.
Shurā'ah: If you had asked me to do that, you would have found me an ass.
Walīd: What do you know about drink?
Shurā'ah: Let the Caliph ask me any question he likes.
Walīd: What do you say of water?
Shurā'ah: It is life. I share it with the ass and the mule.
Walīd: What about milk?
Shurā'ah: I cannot see it without remembering my mother and blushing.
Walīd: What do you think of raisin wine?
Shurā'ah: A noxious intoxicant.
Walīd: And date wine?
Shurā'ah: All flatulence.
Walīd: What about the wine of the grapes?
Shurā'ah: It is the joy that cools the heart, the companion of my soul and the drink of paradise.
Walīd: Good man! And where is it best to drink?
Shurā'ah: Where you can see the sky and be sheltered from heat and cold. No man could choose otherwise.
Walīd: Now what do you say of listening to music and song?
Shurā'ah: It gently wakens the remembrance of sadness; at times of sorrow it renews relief; it cheers the lonely and gladdens the solitary lover. It cools the vengeful heart; and from deep in the mind evokes pacific thoughts. It quickly spreads contentment through the body; it stirs the heart and strengthens tenderness.
Walīd: What say you of food?
Shurā'ah: He that loves drink cares not what he eats.[167]

Walīd will have shared Shurā'ah's feelings on song; but he could see another side to it, of which he warned his kinsmen: "You sons of Umayya, beware of song. It takes from modesty and adds to desire. It is the ruin of chastity and excites to drink; its effect is that of drunkenness. If you must by all means have it, keep the women away! For truly song bewitches unto fornication. And this

167. Iṣfahānī (1905), vi, 121; Mas'ūdī (1830), ii, 186.

I say albeit it is the greatest of all my pleasures, dearer to me than is cold water to him that dies of thirst. But the truth had better be told."[168] Later in the night of Shurā'ah's conversation, according to Iṣfahānī's informants, Walīd sent for a Qur'ān. Opening it, he saw before him the words: "Frustrate are all the stubborn proud, whom hell awaits; they shall be given to drink the waters of bitterness." "Abracadabra! Mumbo-jumbo!" said Walīd. Then: "Hang it up!" And, taking a bow, he shot the book to pieces. He then recited:

You threaten all the stubborn proud?
The stubborn proud—that's me!
So at the final gathering,
If you should meet your Lord,
Just say to God: my spoiler was Walīd![169]

There may be detected a note of desperation in these lines, echoed in some short lines on drink:

A drink! Yazīd! Pour out the gurgling wine!
My heart is ravished by the plaintive flute.
Pour, pour again! My sins encompass me,
And cannot be atoned.[170]

Daḥman and the Singing Girl

This is the story of how Walīd acquired a singing girl.[171] Daḥman, properly called 'Abd al-Raḥmān ibn 'Amr, was a camel owner and prosperous merchant of Madīnah. Furthermore, he was the possessor of conspicuous virtues, an inveterate pilgrim much addicted to prayer, who enjoyed a reputation in the city for reliability as a witness and integrity outstanding among his contemporaries. With all that he was a renowned singer, and was heard to say that of all vanities singing was the one that came nearest to righteousness.

168. Iṣfahānī (1905), vi, 130.

169. Iṣfahānī (1905), vi, 121. For the original text, see Appendix III, no.67.

170. Mas'ūdī (1830), ii, 186. Walīd used a variant on these lines as a tribute to his wine merchant in Damascus, a lady named Hushaymah, reputed as the greatest expert on wines and owner of the cleanest winery. Walīd entrusted her with the maintenance of his cellar. The lines are quoted by 'Umarī (1924), 398: "We've drunk; the plaintive reed has moaned./ Pour me a draught, Budayḥ (sic), of gurgling wine;/ Wine that's been aged in sage Hushaymah's jars;/ Wine flowing dark as blood of young gazelle./ Pour, pour again! My sins encompass me and cannot be redeemed." For the original text, see Appendix III, no.68.

171. Iṣfahānī (1905), v, 133-36.

Daḥman would hire out camels for mercantile journeys and accompany them himself. This took him round and about the world, particularly, I suppose, along the roads to Damascus and Aleppo. On one of his journeys a certain noise attracted him to a spot where he found a girl crying outside a house. He asked her what was the trouble and she replied that it was something between herself and the lady of the house. "Are you a slave, then?" asked Daḥman. "Yes," she replied, and mentioned the name of her owner. "Would she sell you?" said he. "She will indeed," said the girl, and disappeared inside to tell her mistress: "There's a man, outside, who wants to buy me." "Show him in," said the woman. So Daḥman was admitted and, after negotiation, paid down two hundred *dīnārs* in cash and continued his journey with the girl.

"She lived with me for a time," says Daḥman taking up the story, "and besides teaching her myself I put her under Ma'bad and Abjar and others of their quality until she became an accomplished singer. After that I always took her on my travels. Going to Damascus, she in her litter, we would stop at a place to rest. We would pile up some of the luggage to give a shade. I would get out something to eat and a bottle of something to drink, and there we would sit together, she and I, eating and drinking and singing until it was time to move on. And so it was, day after day, until we came to our destination."

The story continues. It was on the last of these pleasant halts, one day, the halt before Damascus, that the idyll came to an end. Daḥman had given the girl a tune of his own to learn, which went with the words of a short elegy by Kuthayr for 'Abd al-'Azīz ibn Marwān:

> If pity could have turned back mortal Fate,
> Mine would have turned it back from Marwān's son,
> 'Abd al-'Azīz.
> God blessed you from the womb; amid the tombs
> Night-hawk and owl are now your company.[172]

Twice or three times he sang it over until she knew it well and could start to sing. Just then a man rode up and greeted them. He asked if he might share their little shelter for an hour. They said: "Yes," and he dismounted. They bade him join them in their meal; and all ate and drank together. When they had finished the stranger asked the girl to sing once again the tune he had heard at the first; and then he asked if she had ever sung anything of Daḥman's. She said: "Yes." "Then let me hear you," said he.

172. For the original text, see Appendix III, no.69.

Daḥman now takes up the story: "I signalled her to keep quiet about me, and she sang a few of my songs. The stranger was delighted and drank a few more cups while she sang on. When the time came for us to leave, he turned to me and asked if I would sell the girl. I said 'Yes.' 'For how much?' said he. I said, joking: 'Ten thousand *dīnār*s.' 'I'll take her,' he said, 'bring ink and paper.' There and then, with graceful compliments, he wrote and sealed an order to pay the bearer ten thousand *dīnār*s, and gave me an address. Then he said: 'Will you give me the girl now, or bring her with you until you get your money?' I said: 'I give her to you now.' So he took her, saying: 'You will go to Bakhrā', ask for so and so, hand him my letter and take your money.' Thereupon the stranger and the girl departed."

So much for Daḥman's account of that episode. He went on his way, along with his camels, and in the course of time found his way to Bakhrā', remote in the Syrian desert. There he asked for the person named by the stranger and found him, to his surprise, at what was more like a palace than an ordinary house. The man received the letter with profound reverence; kissed it, placed it on his eyes and instantly paid up the ten thousand *dīnār*s. "This letter comes from the Caliph," said he; "sit down while I tell him you are here." Whereupon he ordered a meal to be served and departed.

Dismayed to find his chance acquaintance had been none other than the Caliph Walīd ibn Yazīd, Daḥman thought quickly and decided to make off. Whether he distrusted the friendship of one notorious for scandalous living and irreligion or for some other reason he does not tell us; only he remarks that the hospitality offered him by the servant was stingy and he took the opportunity to escape. When the steward returned Daḥman had vanished, and no-one knew either his name or his whereabouts. Walīd himself could only say: "He had fifteen camels; find them!" But Daḥman had lost two camels on the way, and having now only thirteen escaped identification.

In the meantime the girl remained in Walīd's household, apparently forgotten. But when her month was up she was summoned to spend the day with him. As the day drew to an end, Walīd said: "Now sing me something of Daḥman's." She did so, and Walīd said: "Sing some more." And so she did. Then the girl rose and stood before him and said: "Commander of the Faithful, have you not heard Daḥman himself singing his songs?" He said: "No." "But yes, you have," said she. "I tell you 'no'," said Walīd; "do you contradict me?" The girl said: "I swear by God that you have indeed heard Daḥman." "Confound you," said Walīd, "how can that be?" She said: "The man you bought me from was Daḥman." "Is that so indeed," said Walīd, "then how came it about that I was unaware of it?" "Because he signed to me not to let you know," said the girl.

Walīd forthwith sent to the governor of Madīnah with orders to send Daḥman to him. So Daḥman was brought, and remained with Walīd virtually a prisoner.

Walīd and Sindī

Amongst Walīd's friends must be counted his horse Sindī. Not only was this animal credited with having helped to frustrate an attempted assassination of his master, but also his purchase gave Walīd an opportunity to score a point off Hishām.[175]

Walīd and Hishām had one thing in common, a passionate interest in horses and racing. Hishām possessed a stable unequalled by any of his contemporaries or predecessors; it was numbered in thousands. Walīd, too, had a stable. One day he got word of a dealer bringing a collection of horses to Ruṣāfah for Hishām's inspection. Amongst these animals was a stocky colt approaching rideable age which caught Walīd's eye. Before Hishām knew anything about it, Walīd intercepted the man and began to abuse him, saying: "How dare you approach the Caliph with all this rubbish? Turn him off," he said. So they turned the fellow away. No sooner had he left the premises than Walīd sent him a purse of thirty thousand *dirhams* and bought the horse, which thereafter became famous with the name of Sindī. Sindī proved one of the fastest horses of his time and the chief rival on the course of Hishām's champion, named Zā'id; each of these two from time to time ran first to the other's second.

Walīd would take Sindī out hunting, and enjoyed some notable chases with him. He was particularly pleased once to catch and bring down a wild ass. On this exploit he caused a triumphal ode to be sung, with Sindī the hero ("fast as the wind and quick on the turn as a spinning top", with every other imaginable virtue in a horse). Out alone on one such occasion Walīd became aware of a man on a horse following him; either he knew or he suspected this to be an agent of Hishām sent against him with felonious intent. Iṣfahānī's informant says that Walīd turned and caused Sindī to trample the man to death. This may be an improvement on the true story, for Walīd's own versified account of the incident is different. He says:

> Imagine me without a care on Sindī
> Ambling at ease across an arid waste,
> When looking from a hollow I descried
> A horseman, and conceived a menace in
> His seeing me. Then, when I saw he rode
> Alone, I stopped for him. Till he came near
> And shot, and shot at me three times.
> But then 'twas I who struck
> And slaked in him my lance's thirsty blade.[176]

175. Mas'ūdī (1830), ii, 88.

176. Iṣfahānī (1905), vi, 128. For the original text, see Appendix III, no.70

At one of the race meetings at Ruṣāfah Walīd brought off a feat of horsemanship which made history. There was a field on that day numbering—if we may believe Mas'ūdī—a thousand five- year-olds. Walīd was watching on horseback. Near him, also watching, was Sa'īd ibn 'Amr ibn Sa'īd al-'Aṣ, who had a horse running named Miṣbaḥ, "Lantern". One of Walīd's sons was in the race with a horse named Waḍḍaḥ, "Daylight". As the field approached, "Daylight" was seen to be leading; but then its rider fell. Sa'īd's "Lantern" was close behind, and its rider was keeping his seat. Sa'īd, seeing victory imminent, cried out in triumph:

> Today God giveth us the prize;
> We beat the carpers' team,
> As through the ages we have led
> In honour and esteem.[177]

Walīd laughed—the lines echoed a couplet he had uttered himself earlier in the race. Now, fearing Sa'īd's horse might indeed be winning, he put spurs to his own, caught up "Daylight", leapt across onto her and won the race.

Walīd, according to Mas'ūdī, was the first to bring off this particular feat and made it legitimate within the rules. So it remained into 'Abbāsid times, when it was even repeated.

Two Passing Incidents

Jawharī tells a story about a poet, born a Persian, named Ismā'īl ibn Yasār al-Nisā'ī, who had moved in Umayyad society during the reigns of 'Abd al-Malik and his four sons, Walīd, Sulaymān, Yazīd and Hishām.[178] This man was a fervent partisan of Persian manners and traditions, as against those of the Arabs, particularly contrasting their treatment of women. This made him sometimes a figure of fun with his Arab associates, who could retort that it reflected their differing attitudes towards chastity and licence.

During the caliphate of Hishām, Ismā'īl got into the circle of Walīd ibn Yazīd, then *walī'l-'ahd* or "heir apparent". The incident of Jawharī's description took place by a pool, which we may imagine as perhaps the square pool in the garden of Walīd's establishment in the Ghawr, where the company could have sat round the edge of the water watching the fountain play beneath its octagonal pavilion.

Ismā'īl must then have been a man of mature years; but that did not protect him from a mischievous prank of Walīd's. At a certain moment Walīd

177. Mas'ūdī (1830), ii, 188. For the original text, see Appendix III, no.71.

178. Iṣfahānī (1905), iv, 118, 120.

signalled to his rather unpleasant and unpopular former tutor, ʻAbd al-Ṣamad, to tip Ismāʻīl, fully clothed into the water. He was fished out, by Walīd's order again, and expressed his feelings in verse to this effect:

Say to the Heir Apparent,
　If you should happen to meet him,
(And of all men the Heir Apparent
　Is deserving of proper direction);
"Had it not been for you ʻAbd al-Ṣamad
　Would not have escaped from me scatheless.
He has chosen to do to my honour
　What no-one has ventured before him.
So he's like one who chasing a partridge[179]
　Finds himself in the den of a lion."

Walīd made some amends for his unkindness by giving Ismāʻīl a splendid robe and a sufficient gift of money to content him.

A story was told in Kūfah that Walīd was sent a bowl filled with ancient Egyptian glass bottles, the like of which the narrator had never seen.[180] "It was the fourteenth day of the month," he says, "and that evening, as night came on, we were assembled outside with the full moon rising above our heads, and the bowl was brought out to hold the wine.

Walīd began the conversation by asking which of the constellations the moon was riding in. One of the company said: 'It is in the Ram.' Others made each his own guess—in this, that or the other of the Signs—until someone said: 'The moon is in the bowl.' 'Devil take you,' said Walīd, 'you have spoken my own very thought! You shall drink the *hafnajannah*!' 'And what is the "*hafnajannah*"?' asked someone. 'Amongst the Persians,' said Walīd, 'he who drank the *hafnajannah* must drink every day of the week for seven weeks—forty-nine days on end; that is the *hafnajannah*, and he shall drink it.' "

Private Sorrows of Walīd

It was related on the testimony of Madāʼinī that Walīd had gone to stay at what is described as a "hunting lodge" of his—whether that was the establishment in the Ghawr or somewhere else it is impossible to say. While he

179. Reading *durrāj*, some kind of bird, perhaps a sandgrouse rather than a partridge. Reading *darrāj* would give the more picturesque image of "chasing a hedgehog"; but Abyarī cites a current proverb to favour the other. For the original text, see Appendix III, no.72.

180. Iṣfahānī (1905), vi, 126.

was there it happened that one of his sons, named Mu'min, died.[181] No-one dared bring him the bad news; until, at a moment when Walīd had drunk well, a certain Sinān in his company, who was a writer as well as a singer, told him of the death. Walīd uttered his feelings in some lines of verse which survived him long enough to be sung in later years to the 'Abbāsid Caliphs Rāshid and Wāthiq. He said:

There came Sinān to me from Mu'min, bearing his farewell.
  I said to him: "I have recourse to God.
You who pour dust upon his bones, are not you, too, bereaved?
  Are not the fingers withered on your hands?"
They say "Conceal your grief! Show you are strong!" But what
  If that within my breast be stronger?[182]

The death of Mu'min left Walīd grieved, but blameless: his loss was unmixed with guilt. Another of his sorrows was embittered with remorse, for it was the consequence of his own folly. The story is told in a tradition heavily loaded with the dogmatic censure of his way of life which became habitual with future historians.[183] When Walīd, they say, persisted in his drinking and his pleasures, casting behind him all thought of the next world and turning his face only toward revelling and violence, with singers like Mālik and Ma'bad and Ibn 'Ā'ishah and the rest, one of his companions was Qāsim ibn al-Ṭawīl al-'Abbādī, a poet well bred and intelligent, from whom at that time Walīd felt himself inseparable.

Now, one day Ma'bad had been singing them that poem of 'Adī ibn Zayd which begins "At crack of dawn fault-finders cry: Wake up!...", which particularly pleased and inspired Walīd, so that he began to drink and ended by passing out asleep where he was reclining. Ibn Ṭawīl at that point went home. When Walīd woke up, still drunk, he asked for Ibn Ṭawīl and was furious to hear he had left. In a rage he cried to his servant Sibra: "Bring me his head!" Sibra went off and after a time reappeared with a dish bearing the severed head of Ibn Ṭawīl, which he presented to his master. Overwhelmed with shock at the horrible sight Walīd, now sober, asked what had happened. Being told the story he fell into a paroxysm of misery and remorse. Rocking his head in his hands, he uttered a lament:

Mourn, mourn, my eyes, the noble youth![184]
  Your tears as spring rains flow!
Weep, weep, you tears of mine! For that
  May quench the soul's torment.

181. Iṣfahānī (1905), vi, 130.
182. For the original text, see Appendix III, no.73.
183. Iṣfahānī (1905), vi, 128-29.
184. For the original text, see Appendix III, no.74.

God bless that tomb wherein are laid
    The bones of Ibn Ṭawīl.
How fine the gentle heart it penned
    When he was buried there.
Awhile from love of thee I hid
    Within a shadowy cave.
Now thou art gone I wake forlorn
    And lonely in the torrent bed.

Resorting then to his slave girls Walīd, it was said, confessed that, with Ibn Ṭawīl no more, he cared not when his own death might come. He had not long to wait.

Walīd's artistic circle suffered two further grievous losses during his brief caliphate. The death of Ibn 'Ā'ishah was one.[185] The second was the death of its oldest and most distinguished member, Ma'bad ibn Wahb.[186] Ma'bad had by this time long passed his seventieth year, for he could be called a "lad"—*ghulām*—in the time of Muslim ibn 'Uqba, who died in 64/683, twenty-six years before Walīd was born and sixty-one before his accession. Ma'bad was in Walīd's *'askar*, or retinue, when he died. His son, Kardam, was there too, and was looking on at the funeral. He relates how he saw Walīd, having acceded to the caliphate, and his brother Ghamr, each wearing just a shirt and a shawl, walking before the bier as it was carried out of Walīd's house and taken to the place of burial.

What interested the spectators more than the sight of the Caliph and his brother was the appearance of Sallāmah al-Qass, the girl in olden days of Walīd's father, Yazīd ibn 'Abd al-Malik, who was holding one of the poles on which the bier was carried. She was in tears, and as she walked sang a lament—the same that she had sung long ago at the burial of her former master, Yazīd:

Sickness and pain, God knows, were brother to my night;
    And sorrow, whispering, lay closest in my arms.
As I beheld the empty house my tears ran down—
    Empty of him who was our never-failing lord.
Don't blame us if our hearts are bowed, wasted and cast down.[187]

All eyes were on Sallāmah as she sang. Twenty years had passed since Yazīd

185. This may not be correct; for there is another tradition that Ibn 'Ā'ishah died in the reign of Hishām. And that is consistent with the story that his fall from the roof of the castle at Dhū'l-Khashab happened while Muḥammad ibn 'Abd Allāh al-Makhzūmī was governor of Madīnah. That would have been in Hishām's time.

186. Iṣfahānī (1905), i, 18.

187. For the original text, see Appendix III, no.75.

had died. How she spent those years we know not; probably in the household of Walīd, for there she was at Ma'bad's funeral. It was a charge against Walīd, during the revolt against him, that he had made love to his father's women; and it was said that Sallāmah was one of them.[188] Certainly Walīd admired her, and there is a pathetic tale which confirms it. It concerns the very same lament that she had sung at Yazīd's death. Walīd had asked her to sing it to him; she had shaken her head and wept to be asked. But Walīd persisted until she consented to sing. And that she did most beautifully. Walīd said: "God's mercy on my father, Sallāmah; and may He give me life, too, to enjoy the beauty of your voice. How could my father have preferred Ḥabāba to you?" "Indeed I know not," said she. "But I know, by God," said Walīd piously; "it was God's decree for her!" "It may be so, my lord," said Sallāmah.

Death of the Caliph Hishām

The death of Ma'bad has moved my story geographically northward to Damascus and forward in time to some moment in the fifteen months of Walīd's reign, passing over events at the time of his accession and immediately before that. To regain the thread of recorded events we must revert to that southern retreat where Walīd was to be found with his friends during the last months, or perhaps few years, of Hishām's life.

The thought of death was already on Hishām's mind at the time of his correspondence with Walīd, and was giving urgency to his misgivings on the future of the caliphate. It was early in the year 125/743 that he knew for certain that his end was near.[189] It was related by Sālim Abū'l-A'lā' that Hishām was seen one day leaving his house in a state of manifest dejection; his clothes were hanging loose about him and the reins of his horse were slack in his hands. It seemed an hour before he came to himself, grasped the reins and gathered his clothes about him. He told someone then to send for his friend and brother-in-law, Abrash al-Kalbī. Abrash arrived and said to Hishām: "Commander of the Faithful, there was something I saw about you this morning which distressed me." "And what was that?" said Hishām. "I was distressed by the state you came out in," said he. "Why, bless you, Abrash," said Hishām, "I am distressed myself; and how should I not be, when those who know have told me that in thirty-three days' time I shall be dead?" Sālim, overhearing the conversation, made a note of the remark and of the time. Precisely thirty-three days later, he tells us, there was a knock on his door. It was a servant bidding him wait on the Caliph and to take with him a medicine for diphtheria which had been effective with Hishām once before.

188. Iṣfahānī (1905), viii, 5.

189. Ṭabari (1966), ii, 1729-30.

Sālim went along with the medicine, and Hishām gargled. At first he was suffering great pain, but after a while said he felt better. He told Sālim to go home but leave the medicine. An hour later Sālim heard cries signifying that the Caliph was dead.

Far away to the south, meanwhile, Walīd in "that desert" (as Ṭabarī describes it) was still able somehow to keep informed of events in Ruṣāfah; he was consequently not without his anxieties and hopes.[190] He had with him some of his singing friends and, as secretary, one Mundhir ibn Abī 'Amr Abū Zubayr, who gives an account of events at the time of Hishām's death. "It was on that morning," he relates, "that Walīd sent for me. He said: 'Abū Zubayr, never since I can remember have I passed so long a night as last night, such troubles and such forebodings of that man's designs against me filled my mind. Come, ride with me and let us take some air.' "

So they rode together, until after a couple of miles they came to a sand hill. There Walīd halted his horse. He had begun talking in abuse of Hishām when he saw approaching in the distance a cloud of dust. He said: "Here come Hishām's messengers; pray God it is well." There was heard then the clatter of hooves and two men appeared on post horses. As they came near they saw Walīd and dismounted. Both came running up and saluted him as Caliph. Walīd at first could not utter a word. One of the men repeated his salute, and Walīd said: "Is Hishām dead, then?" He replied: "Yes." Walīd said: "Welcome to you both; what have you brought?" They said: "A letter from the master of posts, your man Sālim ibn 'Abd al-Raḥmān." Walīd read the letter and the men turned to go; but Walīd called one of them back and asked about his former secretary, 'Iyaḍ ibn Muslim, whom Hishām had imprisoned. The messenger told him that 'Iyaḍ had stayed shut in prison up to the time of Hishām's death, when he had been released.

Abū'l-Faraj, Ṭabarī and others tell the story of what had happened at Ruṣāfah before and after that. They say that when Hishām's life had ebbed to a point beyond recall, 'Iyaḍ, still in prison, was able to send word to the storekeepers to keep a hold on everything in their charge, and on no account let anything be moved. So when Hishām, temporarily recovering consciousness, asked for something he was refused. He had time to say: "So we have become storekeepers to Walīd!" and instantly expired.[191]

So began Walīd's reign as Caliph. For himself he remained for two nights (according to Mas'ūdī) in the south, celebrating with wine and song the death

190. Ṭabari (1966), ii, 1750.

191. Iṣfahānī (1905), vi, 105; Ṭabari (1966), ii, 1750-51. The story of Hishām being refused something from the store is suspect; for it can hardly be reconciled with the account of Hishām's death by Sālim Abū'l-A'lā'; and it conflicts with an earlier account by Ṭabari, of events at Ruṣāfah, which put the closure of the stores not before but after the death of Hishām, when they wanted a container to heat water for washing his body.

of "him of Ruṣāfah", and the change in his own affairs. To him while thus engaged, according to Ḥakam al-Wādī, who was in the company, there came a eunuch bringing condolences on the death of his uncle and carrying the symbols of office—rod, ring and scroll. His memory of these events Walīd transmitted to posterity in some brief verses:

How good was the day and how sweet the choice wine
  When they said that the man in Ruṣāfah was gone!
And the post brought us news that Hishām was no more;
  And it brought us the seal that the Caliph must wear.
So we toasted the morning with 'Ana drunk neat;
  And a girl made us merry with songs to her lute.[192]

After his second night of song, Walīd returned to Ruṣāfah and set about completing measures already begun on his behalf by the officious Ibn Muslim. He summoned his cousin 'Abbās ibn al-Walīd ibn 'Abd al-Malik to come and inventory the possessions of Hishām and his sons at Ruṣāfah.[193] He ordered Hishām's family and household to be arrested; but made careful exception in all this for Maslamah, his friend and former drinking companion, who had stood up for him against Hishām. Maslamah was not to be interfered with and his house not to be entered.

'Abbās was a man of moderation and good sense, but he was obliged to comply with Walīd's order. In due course he reported that he had Hishām's household in custody and the survey of property completed. This all appealed to Walīd's sense of humour. He wrote a little poem:

He should have lived, Hishām, to see
  His cornucopia filled up.
We used the bushel that he used himself,
  Fair measure, not a finger short.
And all was strictly orthodox,
  By holy writ legitimized.[194]

A less agreeable story was told how, enquiring about a certain noise at Ruṣāfah, Walīd was told it came from Hishām's house, where the bereaved daughters were weeping. He said:

It was Ruṣāfah whence one night
  I heard the sound of tears.
Approaching near with stately tread

192. Iṣfahānī (1905), vi, 105. For the original text, see Appendix III, no.76.

193. Ṭabari (1966), ii, 1751-52.

194. For the original text, see Appendix III, no.77.

I asked: "What ails the dears?"
It is the daughters of Hishām
Lamenting for their lord.
A noble chieftain they lament,
Who was their strength and ward.
Now "woe!" and "misery!" they cry;
For woe has them in thrall.
And I? Why, I'm not half a man
If I don't bed them all.[195]

The threat in the last lines was assuredly jocular, as was the rest of the poem; for amongst the offences later charged against Walīd the debauching of Hishām's womenfolk was never mentioned, only of his own father's.

Political Adjustments by a New Caliph

Having assured the safety of his friend amongst Hishām's sons, Walīd turned his mind to those who were not his friends. His particular dislike, fully reciprocated, was of Sulaymān ibn Hishām, who was known to have been the most relentless advocate of Walīd's disinheritance or assassination. Walīd now summoned Sulaymān and challenged him to deny having been his worst enemy.[196] Sulaymān gave him a rough and abusive reply. Walīd had him severely flogged, caused his head and beard to be shaved and incarcerated him in irons in 'Ammān, where he remained imprisoned until Walīd himself next year was assassinated.

Other advocates with Hishām of Walīd's disinheritance had been two brothers, Muḥammad and Ibrāhīm, sons of Hishām ibn Ismā'īl al-Makhzūmī. Muḥammad was an uncle of Hishām and had been his governor of Makkah and Madīnah at the time of Walīd's scandalous leadership of the *ḥajj*; and it was he, too, by whose order, according to one account of the event, Walīd's friend Ibn 'Ā'ishah had been pushed to his death from the roof of Dhū'l-Khashab. Walīd had another reason for disliking him. For, as a governor of Makkah, he had flogged, shackled and imprisoned until his death a well-known poet of amorous bent, a glutton for hunting and sport, and so a kindred spirit of Walīd's, named 'Abd Allāh al-'Arajī. All this put the Makhzūmī brothers in danger.

Walīd on his accession had appointed his uncle Yūsuf ibn Muḥammad

195. Mas'ūdī (1830), ii, 186; Iṣfahānī (1905), vi, 106. For the original text, see Appendix III, no.78.

196. Balādhurī (1974), 45. Balādhurī implies that Walīd acted against Sulaymān soon after his accession in 125/743. Ṭabari, however, puts the event in the following year, 126/744; Ṭabari (1966), ii. 1776.

al-Thaqafī to be governor of Madīnah, Makkah and Ṭa'if. He ordered the two brothers to be carried bound to Madīnah and handed over to this Yūsuf. He, as a first step, stood them on the "sacks" for public exhibition. Walīd then had them transported to Iraq, where in the course of time his agent, Yūsuf ibn 'Umar, on a charge brought against them of peculation, flogged them both to death.

That is the stark but sufficiently shocking tale related by Ṭabarī.[197] Iṣfahānī had access to further details, and had learnt also of a personal confrontation with Walīd not recorded by Ṭabarī.[198] When Walīd, he tells us, succeeded to the caliphate, he had both Muḥammad and his brother Ibrāhīm arrested and brought to him in Syria. There he called for the lashes. Muḥammad pleaded with him: "I beg of you as a kinsman!" "And what kinship is there between us?" said Walīd; "What is your kin but Ashja'?" "I beg you as 'Abd al-Malik's brother-in-law!" "But you were not faithful to that," said Walīd. Muḥammad then said: "Commander of the Faithful, the Prophet (God bless him) forbade the lashing of Quraysh, except by judicial decree!" "It is by judicial decree," said Walīd, "and in retribution that I shall lash you. For you it was yourself who first made that lawful, on 'Arajī; and he was my cousin, and was grandson to the Caliph 'Uthmān. You recked not then of his grandfather nor of his kinship with Hishām; nor did you then remember the Prophet's word. Now I am heir to his vengeance. Boy, lash him!"

So he lashed them both grievously, then despatched them in chains to Yūsuf ibn 'Umar in Kūfah, with orders to beat the skin off them. "Look out for yourself," he wrote, "if either of them survives." Thereafter, not sparing the feelings of a reader, Iṣfahānī describes in chilling detail how both brothers died, flayed, in a heap together. Walīd celebrated in verse his vengeance on Muḥammad:

> He's headed for Iraq, in streams of blood.[199]
> His journey ends in gaol, and after that
> The wooden horse.
> In shame he'll ride, all hell around. For him
> No saddle, nor a head-rope in his hand.
> If you should pass a black-eyed girl, you'll say:

197. Ṭabari (1966), ii, 1768.

198. Iṣfahānī (1905), i, 159-60. In the exchange with Muḥammad Walīd calls 'Arajī his cousin. In fact 'Arajī's father, 'Umar, was third cousin of Walīd's father Yazīd and of Hishām, having a common great-great-grandfather in Abū'l-'Aṣī. 'Arajī himself was the great-grandson of the Caliph 'Uthmān and fourth cousin of Walīd; Iṣfahānī (1905), i, 147.

199. For the original text, see Appendix III, no.79.

> "He cannot soften God who seeks to fly
> From his revenge." Hedgehog! you won first time,
> But now God gives the victory to us!

Walīd appended to these lines a genealogical gibe, in Arabian invective not to be thought irrelevant, although to modern ears the impact, in a murderous confrontation, may seem to lack pungency. He continued:

> Who was your father? Ask not him that gilds
> The lie: ask Kalb! Not Hāshim, he will say;
> Not Asad, Nawfal, Ḥajab—none of these,
> But only Ashja' has begotten you!

So much for the most conspicuous opponents of Walīd's elevation to the caliphate. The tale of their humiliation will soon have been carried to the outermost parts of the empire and caused all men of consequence to consider their own situation and security. Among the letters and delegations that converged on Walīd from the regions there came a gratifying message of support from a cousin of Walīd's father, Marwān ibn Muḥammad ibn Marwān, who had served Hishām as governor and military commander in Armenia and the northern frontiers of Islam and was destined to be the last Caliph of the Umayyad dynasty. Marwān's letter, revealing something of men's thoughts, and of the postures they adopt at a moment of critical change, deserves a brief digression, which I extract from versions of the text variously recorded by Balādhurī and Ṭabarī: "God's blessing on the Caliph in his appointment to command God's servants and inherit his realm. It was the deep waters and anxieties of government which submerged Hishām and led him to seek the diminishing of what God had magnified—the rights of the Commander of the Faithful... But what Hishām desired he found too hard for him, and he was restrained by God's ineluctable decree. For the Commander held his place from God, and God preserved him until the day He girt him in the most excellent raiment of the caliphate.

Thus he has assumed that which God deemed him fitted for, and stands in sovereign command of the charge that has been laid upon him...And praise be to God who has elected to His caliphate the Commander of the Faithful; whom God has defended from the designs of the wicked, raising him up and putting them down; humbling them and magnifying him. Whosoever essayed those vile courses destroyed himself and angered his Lord; while he who, repenting, abstained from wrong and turned to right found his Lord compassionate and forgiving.

Now I inform the Commander of the Faithful that when it reached me that he had assumed the office of God's caliphate, I mounted my *minbar* wearing two swords in readiness for the dissemblers; and I made known to those before me the favour God had bestowed on them in appointing the Commander of the Faithful. They rejoiced thereat, and said: 'No appointment of a Caliph has ever come to us for which we had more ardently hoped, or which gave us greater joy, than this of the Commander of the Faithful.' And I stretched forth my hands to proclaim you; and confirming that repeatedly, I bound them to it with weighty oaths and pledges. And all the people gave an excellent and obedient response.

So now, Commander of the Faithful, do you reward their obedience from the wealth that God has sent you; for truly you are the most generous and open-handed of men, and they have been waiting in hopeful expectation of your merciful bounty toward them. So let your largesse be greater than his who was before you, so that your superiority may be known and your bounty to them and all your subjects be made manifest.

Now, were it not for my anxious guard on the frontier where now I am, my love for the Commander of the Faithful would have led me to wait upon him face to face; for that would be the greatest possible pleasure to me. But without the Caliph's order I dare not appoint an agent. So if the Commander of the Faithful will permit me to travel to him, let him do so; and I shall speak in his ear of matters that I do not like to write."[200]

Marwān, from a close kindred branch of the Marwānid family, was a genuine supporter of Walīd, or at least an opponent of family dissension and revolt. And revolt was the secret matter he feared to mention in a letter. Whether Marwān made that journey to Syria, or made it in time to impart in Walīd's ear the murmurs of rebellion that he had heard, is doubtful; for he was still in Armenia, and tied by his duties there, when a correspondence reported by Balādhurī and Ṭabarī passed between him and an uncle of Walīd's, Sa'īd ibn 'Abd al-Malik. This good man is described by both historians (knowing the Deity was directly concerned in any dispute about the caliphate), as a "true worshipper of God."[201] "To every family", wrote Marwān to Sa'īd, "there are vouchsafed by God pillars of support, their shield in whom they trust. You, praise be to God, are a pillar of your family. Now I hear that a group of the foolish among your kinsmen have started an affair which, if carried through, will break their allegiance and open a floodgate of bloodshed not to be stopped. I myself am fully occupied in this vital and perilous frontier of Islam; but if you had confronted me with those people I would have spoken and acted to repair their mischief. For I know the mischief for religion and society that follows from dissension. Revolution in a nation means the break-up of discourse; and the breaking of discourse is temptation to the enemy.

200. Ṭabari (1966), ii, 1752; Balādhurī (1974), 25.

201. Ṭabari (1966), ii, 1786; Balādhurī (1974), 50.

You are nearer to these people than I am, so find out what they are up to and who are their followers; then threaten them with exposure. Talk to them and put them in fear; perhaps God will restore them to their senses and to the religion that has deserted them. What they have started means the ruin of all well-being and government. You must act, while the bonds of friendship still hold, the people are quiet and the frontiers secure." Marwān ended on a philosophical note: "In this world," he continued, "men's fortunes, for better or worse, change overnight. For years our family has enjoyed a succession of blessings, sneered at by the envious and all enemies of the fortunate. Satan's envy it was that drove Adam from the garden. These people pin their hopes on strife; it may be themselves will perish by it. In every house malignant souls there are who cause God to withdraw His favour; may God be your protection there! So let me know of their plans. And may God preserve your own faith, and may he save you from the predicament he has put you in and make your soul master of its own straight path."

Sa'īd took Marwān's letter seriously. He knew well the identity of the chief conspirator, a cousin of Walīd's named Yazīd, one of the sons of the former Caliph Walīd ibn 'Abd al-Malik. However inauspicious the beginning of Walīd's reign, Sa'īd agreed that acceptance of the new Caliph was preferable to civil war. He forwarded Marwān's letter to his cousin 'Abbās ibn Walīd, a wiser brother of the rebel and the most respected member of the Umayyad family. 'Abbās sent for Yazīd, rebuked him and threatened him with exposure. Yazīd's reply was to dismiss the charges against him as a canard devised by envious trouble-makers; and he swore obedience. 'Abbās for the time being believed him.

Another would-be upholder of the status quo, who nevertheless was fatally misunderstood by Walīd, was Khālid ibn 'Abd Allāh al-Qasrī, a former governor of Iraq under Hishām. Khālid had been sacked by Hishām for building up too rich and too proud an empire for himself in his province; but he had shown no hostility to Walīd. After Walīd's accession Khālid had been approached in Damascus by a group of Yamanis and others, described by Ṭabarī as "scum", who tried to persuade him to be their leader in a conspiracy to assassinate Walīd. Khālid refused, but agreed not to betray them.[202]

Walīd meanwhile, having reason to know that important members of the family were accepting his succession to Hishām, and perhaps therefore underestimating the extent and depth of the hostility against him, conceived of a further ambition: he resolved that the caliphate should remain for the foreseeable future in his own family. One hundred and four days after the death of Hishām and his own accession he completed a document in the form

202. Ṭabari (1966), ii, 1778.

of a letter addressed to the provincial capitals, there to be read out in public, in which he named his two sons, Ḥakam and 'Uthmān, as appointed to be his successors, one after the other, in the office of Caliph.[203]

To ensure acceptance of this arrangement, which he knew would be unpopular since both boys were under age and sons of a slave woman, Walīd deemed it advisable to declare his decision as the culmination of a religious discourse, in which he proclaimed in logical sequence the divine institution of the caliphate, the Caliph's role as mouthpiece and instrument of God's will and, as a consequence of that, the necessity of absolute obedience to his authority. We may not here enjoy the full exuberance of Walīd's eloquence expounding this syllogism, by which his nomination of the two lads was proved to be the equivalent of a decree by the Almighty; but in a condensed and shortened version of his letter we may contemplate and wonder at the extravagantly religious posture exhibited by one whom the historians universally castigated as an apostate and scoffer at religion. Here is the substance of Walīd's argument: "The glorious God of blessed name made Islam the religion of his choice and the religion of the most favoured of his creatures. Then he chose as messengers the best of the angels and of men, and sent them forth as its apostles.

Age succeeded after age while they summoned men to the path of right; until, at a time of ignorance and blindness, God's grace was consummated in Muḥammad. In him God made known the path of salvation from error, dispelled the darkness and set the seal on His revelation. In Muḥammad God gathered together His bounties to the prophets that were before him, reaffirming and enjoining all that God had revealed through them.

Thus in time there were, among his people, those who heard him and entered into the religion that God had favoured them with. They believed God's prophets of time past and accepted their exhortation; they protected and exalted the sanctuaries that had been dishonoured and despised. And of Muḥammad's people there was none that, having heard, then disbelieved or derided any of God's prophets but He made lawful their slaying and their severing from tribe and kindred.

Then God, having received up the soul of His Prophet, appointed His Caliphs to follow on the path of His mission, for the confirmation in them of Islam, the strengthening in them of its ties, the protection in them of its sanctities, for justice among its servants and for the well-being through them of its lands. So God's Caliphs followed one after the other, appointed by God to be heirs of His prophets. None opposes their right but God strikes him down; none scorns their governance, or questions their authority from God, but God gives them mastery over him and subjects him to condign punishment.

203. Ṭabari (1966), ii, 1755; 1757-64.

Thus God deals with him who has forsaken the obedience that God ordained, on which heaven and earth are sustained. And God said: 'When your lord said to the angels I am putting on earth a *khalīfa*,' they said: 'Will you put there one who will make mischief and shed blood, while we laud and sanctify you with praise?' He said: 'I know what ye know not.' So in the caliphate God preserves on earth whomsoever of His servants He does preserve; and in obedience to His appointed one there is happiness for him whom God inspires thereto. For God knows that there is neither stability nor health save in that obedience whereby He maintains His justice and averts rebellion. He who accepts it is God's friend; and he who forsakes and turns away from it, opposing God's purpose, is of those miserables whom passion has overcome, leading them to foul waters; whom God permits in this world to suffer humiliation and grievous chastisement.

Once the word is given of God's election from among His servants, it is obedience that crowns the head of this authority and command. It is by obedience that the fortunate receive from God their stations and may claim their reward; while others, by rebellion, forsaking obedience, merit and incur His anger and chastisement. So cleave to God's obedience, and be its advocate, in that lot which has befallen you.

Now, truly, God has led the nation to that best state where bloodshed is prevented, bonds of friendship hold, tongues speak as one and society stands firm and sound. That is the store of God's present favour to the nation, since He established His caliphate for the ordering and sustaining of its affairs. And that is the office and charge which God has inspired His Caliphs to administer in the solid interest of the Muslims; so that, whatever befalls, they may have in their Caliphs an assurance of shelter and refuge, a rallying point against disorder strengthening the hopes of Islam and frustrating the enticements of the Devil; whose friends are on the watch, spurred by him to the destruction of this religion and dividing of its people. So praise God your merciful lord for His beneficence in leading you to this institution of the caliphate. There He has made you a sure habitation, where you dwell in peace.

Now, ever since God appointed the Caliph to the succession, that charge has been his greatest concern and anxiety, knowing its eminent place in the affairs of the Muslims, being the means of God's generous concern for them. Through it the Caliph begs his God and Lord, in whose hand the present and the future lie, to make decisions for him and for them; for He is all-powerful. So now the Caliph has seen fit to bequeath you an order of succession, so that like your predecessors you may be at ease in your minds, peacefully and harmoniously enjoying a foreknowledge of God's ordering of your government, whereby He gives His people life, protection and well-being, repelling and frustrating every hidden transgressor who would corrupt them and destroy this religion.

So the Caliph has appointed his son Ḥakam to be his successor, and after him the Caliph's son 'Uthmān. And they are two such as God has created and fashioned for just that, perfecting in them the ideal virtues of him whom He would appoint thereto: mature judgement, true religion, manly strength and sound understanding of affairs. And in all this, for your sakes and his own, the Caliph has not spared his best efforts.

So do you now declare your allegiance, in the name of God and with His blessing, to Ḥakam the Caliph's son, and after him to his brother, in all obedience, believing that to be the good lesson taught to you by God and inculcated in you by examples in the past of general prosperity and public good, which you have enjoyed in peace and security. This is the Command which you thought slow in coming and sought to hasten; you praised God for decreeing and bringing it about for you; you saw it as your good fortune. You will preserve it and strive to fulfil your duty to God, according to the measure of God's active care for you. Furthermore, should anything happen to either one of his two heirs, the Caliph is empowered to fill his place and station by appointing whomsoever he will of his sons or of the nation, and to place him either before or after the survivor of the two, as he shall determine. So know you that, and understand it! And we pray God, who is the only God, the merciful and compassionate, who knows the visible and invisible alike, to bless the Caliph and yourselves in that which God has determined and decreed through the mouth of the Caliph; and to make its outcome full of joy, health and happiness. For that is in God's hand and in His power alone; and to Him alone can we pray. Peace and God's mercy upon you."

Walīd soon learnt the impact of his rhetoric. One of his freedmen thus describes an interview he had with the Caliph: "I came into his presence, after he had appointed his sons, and said: 'Commander of the Faithful, shall I speak as one whose counsel can be trusted or am I permitted to be silent?' He said: 'No; speak as one who can be trusted.' I said: 'The people disapprove of what you have done. They are saying: "He is proclaiming a successor who is still a boy," and I have heard things said about you which I do not like.' Said Walīd: 'Sons of uncircumcised whores. Am I to put another between me and my son? To be treated by him as I was by the Cross-eyed?' "[204]

Walīd cannot, in fact, have been surprised at his freedman's report; for he had heard the same from more important persons whom quite early he had consulted. For them it was dangerous to express an opinion. One unfortunate was Sa'īd ibn Bayhas; he pointed out to Walīd that his boys had not yet attained puberty, and advised against their nomination.[205] Instead he suggested one of the grandsons of the former Caliph Walīd ibn 'Abd

204. Iṣfahānī (1905), vi, 130.

205. Ṭabari (1966), ii, 1776.

al-Malik. Walīd, particularly disliking the families of both his uncles Walīd and Hishām, had him imprisoned; and there, in prison, Ibn Bayhas died.

Another who braved Walīd's anger was Khālid al-Qasrī.[206] His friends said to him: "The Caliph has asked you to declare for his two sons, and have you refused him?" "Of course," he said. "How can I give allegiance to one who cannot lead me in prayer, or whose witness to the faith is not acceptable?" They said: "What of Walīd, then, a scoundrel and profligate, yet you accept his witness?" Khālid replied: "About Walīd that is only vulgar talk; I know nothing of it!"

Walīd was sufficiently annoyed at Khālid's recalcitrance over the boys; he was still more vexed when Khālid, having heard that Walīd intended going on the *ḥajj*, urged him to put it off for a year. "Why so?" said Walīd. Khālid, believing in fact that Walīd would be at risk of assassination on the journey, chose to answer: "There is no obligation on me to tell you."

For a short time, it seems, while Khālid lived quietly in Damascus, Walīd, wherever he was staying, was content to treat him with contempt.[207] Then one day a letter came to Khālid. It read: "The Caliph has knowledge of the fifty million that you know of; so you will now come to him with his messenger, who has orders not to obstruct your equipment for the journey." The "fifty million" alluded to the wealth that Khālid was believed to have misappropriated during his governorate of Iraq under Hishām. Khālid showed the letter to his friends. They said: "Do not trust Walīd! You must either recruit supporters and seize the treasury in Damascus, where everyone will support you, or go into hiding." Khālid rejected their advice. He would not be the cause of a civil war, he said, and he had never hidden himself for fear of any man. He would face Walīd and trust in God.

He went. Walīd interviewed him through a messenger from his tent, while Khālid waited outside. "Where is your son Yazīd?" asked Walīd. "We do not know," said Khālid. "You do," came Walīd's reply; "you have deputed him to start a revolt." "The Caliph knows," said Khālid, "that I and my father and my grandfather—all of us are and have been a loyal family." "The Caliph tells you this," said the messenger; "you will bring him here or it will be the end of you." Raising his voice for Walīd to hear, Khālid replied: "Tell him, I know that it is what you are really after; and, by God, if I had him here in my hands I would not release him to you. Now do what you like!"

Walīd ordered one Ghaylān, chief of his guard, to take and deal with him: "And let me hear him cry!" Ghaylān took him off and gave him the chain treatment. Khālid uttered not a word. Ghaylān returned to Walīd, and said:

206. Balādhurī (1974), 46-47; Ṭabari (1966), ii, 1776-77.

207. Ṭabari (1966), ii, 1819-22.

"It's not a man, by God, I'm torturing; he says not a word nor makes a sound." "Leave him and lock him up," said Walīd.

Yūsuf ibn 'Umar arrived then from Iraq, with revenue money, and a discussion about Khālid took place. "I will buy him for fifty million," said Yūsuf. Walīd sent to Khālid: "Yūsuf will buy you for fifty million; bail yourself for that, or I sell you to him." Khālid replied: "Arabs are not for sale." He picked up a twig: "I would not give you this," he said; "so think what you will."

Walīd then sold Khālid to Yūsuf, who stripped him, wrapped him in a couple of cloaks and carried him off in an open litter toward Iraq. Somewhere along the painful journey one Zayd ibn Tamīm sent his servant Sālim with a drink of pomegranate juice for Khālid. Yūsuf heard of it and had the servant and his master severely flogged. Finally arriving at Ḥīra, Yūsuf sent simultaneously for Khālid and for the two Makhzūmī brothers, not yet executed. All three were then flogged or tortured until they died. For the gruesome details of Khālid's end the curious may turn to Ṭabarī, who quotes two accounts of barbaric torments inflicted upon him. He bore them all in total silence.

Thus Walīd repaid the man who had shown only loyalty to him; and thus he fed fuel to the hatred of his own future assassins. Khālid and the Makhzūmī brothers died in the first month of the year 126/744; Walīd had been in office for nine months.

The pursuit of personal vendettas had not put from Walīd's mind the necessity of winning affection amongst the people of Syria and Damascus. Some show of public generosity was essential to mitigate the outrage caused by acts of violence against Marwānid kindred or other well-known public figures. Accordingly, amongst the earliest acts of Walīd reported was the granting of pensions and clothing to the paralytics and blind persons of Syria; and to every man of them a servant was awarded.[208] Impoverished women, we are told, were issued with garments and aromatics; and all this in quantity exceeding any such benefactions by Hishām. Annual stipends for military service throughout the community were increased, and for the people of Syria in particular increased doubly. These last provisions gained for Walīd an immediate reputation for generosity, posthumously enhanced by his successor's reversing them.

Compensations for the Burden of Office

Walīd's political transactions did not, according to the historians, seriously

208. Ṭabari (1966), ii, 1754; Balādhurī (1974), 24.

interrupt his preferred way of life. Ṭabarī quotes Minhāl ibn ‘Abd al-Malik as declaring that on his accession to the caliphate Walīd took a dislike to any place where there were people, and was perpetually on the move, hunting, and continued so until his death, causing discontent among his retinue as well as among the people at large.[210]

Hishām's death had occurred in February, A.D.743 (6 Rabī‘ al-Ākhir, A.H.125); winter had not ended. The Ghawr would have seemed to invite; and we can guess that Walīd did not linger in Ruṣāfah or Damascus. His structural plans in the Ghawr had by no means been completed. In the palace there, parts of the roof were still without their tiles, and most of the rooms on the ground floor had not yet been paved. In the courtyard the first floor portico balustrades still lacked some of their panels, which were waiting, half carved, in a room on the site. Work in all these areas may well have been suspended when Walīd's allowance from Hishām was cut off; it was restarted on his accession to the caliphate.

In the euphoria of that time one of Walīd's first thoughts was to install above the outer portal of the music room a portrait statue of himself (**Frontispiece**). This was a carved and painted effigy in gypsum plaster, regally arrayed in surcoat and trousers in the Persian style, hand on sword, with guardian lions supporting the royal stance. We may imagine that Walīd himself was there to witness the installation; for we find him in the Ghawr soon after his accession, when he received Abū Harūn ‘Uṭarrad. In preparation for the crowning ceremony, which this truly was, a niche had been prepared in earlier years, but during the reign of Hishām had been left unoccupied; this was now filled.[211] Other statues, of girls and horsemen, were carved, painted and placed in niches within the entrance to the palace, where a lobby or waiting room, still in the hands of the decorators, was being furnished for reception of guests or delegations.

Walīd at the same time was giving thought to more domestic comforts. The arts of pre-Islamic Persia, like its costumes, were still setting standards of luxury and fashion for the aristocracy of Arabia. In Iraq Walīd had extended the responsibilities of his governor, Yūsuf ibn ‘Umar, to include also the province of Khurāsān. He now wrote to Yūsuf to prepare consignments of native luxuries for despatch to him in Syria. Yūsuf passed the word to his subordinate in the farther province, who forthwith put the people under levy

210. Ṭabari (1966), ii, 1776.

211. An interesting point of chronology is here involved, which bears on the political status of Walīd and helps to resolve a question that puzzled the excavators of al-Mafjar: who was meant to be represented by a statue designed for display on a building erected during the caliphate of Hishām by his out-of-favour nephew and heir? The solution lay in archaeological evidence for the chronology of the buildings in relation to the regnal years of the two men. See Appendix II below.

so that, we are told, there was not a slave, man or girl, nor a lively horse left in Khurāsān but he assembled them. He bought a thousand *mamlūks*, armed them and mounted them on horses. He ordered, too, the manufacture of gold and silver ewers; also statues of gazelles, ibexes and other wild animals. Furthermore, on Walīd's specific instructions the agent was required to make a selection of lutes and guitars and to look out every girl cymbal player to be found in Khurāsān. An observer of these preparations on the spot wrote a light-hearted poem, which Ṭabarī thought worth transcribing:

So rejoice, God's entrusted, here's good news and more!
The camels are loaded with treasures galore!
Mules laden with liquor, their bags full of lutes.
Pretty wantons exotic with drum, strings and flutes.
What with thrumming and trilling and boozing and love
It's good cheer for you now and in heaven above! [212]

Whatever the destiny or fabric of the gazelles and ibexes made in Khurāsān, they became models for just such creatures carved in plaster for Walīd in the Ghawr, to adorn the front of his music room, where they crouched on projecting friezes below the feet of his statue.[213] Thus, while we know today that the short span of his reign did not suffice to complete his palace in the Ghawr, Walīd at least could see resplendent on the favourite of his architectural creations, the music room, the crowning emblems and ornaments of royalty and personal fulfilment.

Marriage of the Caliph

A matter of equal or greater concern for Walīd after his accession was the consummation of his love for Salmā, the daughter of Sa'īd ibn Khālid. No certain date is remembered for the beginning of his infatuation for this girl; but the story as told suggests that it was either before or not long after the death of Yazīd ibn 'Abd al-Malik. Twenty years of thwarted passion must, then, have passed since her father, encouraged by Hishām, had rebuffed Walīd's proposal for her. Nevertheless, it was recorded by Madā'inī and others that on his accession to the caliphate the one resolve of Walīd was to marry Salmā.[214] She cannot, of course, have remained unmarried all those years; but testimonies are deficient and ambiguous concerning her marital

212. Ṭabari (1966), ii, 1765. For the original text, see Appendix III, no.80.

213. Hamilton (1959), pl.xlii, cf. **Fig.5** in this volume.

214. Balādhurī (1974), 28.

state when Walīd, as Caliph, renewed his suit. The most positive statement repeated by Balādhurī, is that her father had married her to a nephew of Walīd himself. There was a tale, perhaps never believed, that Walīd on that occasion employed an agent to prevent the consummation of that marriage. What must at least be accepted is that the nephew, who is not named, was either willing or constrained to divorce Salmā. Her father, too, was forced to agree. On one point Walīd was punctilious: he insisted on a legal divorce, and waited the necessary period before marrying her himself.

On the eve of the wedding he composed a long poem, of which a few lines are preserved:

You son of David! Hear the merry sound
    Of friendly cheer next door! Will not the bride
So long imprisoned now come forth? Day breaks!
    It's getting light! And she's not dressed! Ah, now
She comes! A new moon in a lucky night!
    No inauspicious star is seen; but five
High-breasted maidens come with her, and she's
    The noblest of the five. . .[215]

Walīd did not have long to enjoy his bride. On her way up from Madīnah to join him she had sickened; and in forty days, according to Madā'inī, or less according to others, she was dead. Walīd composed an elegy:

Salmā, you were a garden, and its fruits
    In all their kinds near ripe for harvesting.
The husbandmen with loving care kept watch,
    Nor slept, until, when spring had eased their fears,
Its fruits were scattered by the autumn winds.[216]

With less feeling, perhaps, but more elaboration, he also said:

Have you not heard, nor you, that Salmā lies
    Imprisoned in a desert grave? By your life,
Walīd, esteem, nobility and praise
    They've buried with her; and a face that far
Outshone the sun's remotest rays.
    I'd give my life for it! The sight of death
Did never bring more tears to the eyes or grief
    Or desolation to my heart.

215. Iṣfahānī (1905), vi, 112. For the original text, see Appendix III, no.81.

216. Iṣfahānī (1905), vi, 128. For the original text, see Appendix III, no.82.

Death never called for greater strength of mind
To hide your grief or show a steadfast front.[217]

Walīd's marriage was short, measured even by the brevity of his reign. He speaks of her "desert grave", and in the desert he consoled himself. Meanwhile, in the cities he was avoiding, things were going badly for him. The hunting, drinking and music-making that gave him delight were offensive to society. His cousin Bishr ibn Walīd ibn 'Abd al-Malik is quoted as summing up the state of affairs: "Walīd's unapproachability and neglect of government, his addiction to music and hunting, his persistent pursuit of pleasure and continued drinking all disgusted the people."[218] A group of notables from the family, who felt some concern, assembled to reprove him. His only answer was:

God and the holy angels hear me speak,
And all the righteous worshippers of God.
These are my heart's desire: a cup of wine,
The sound of music and a pretty cheek
To bite; a noble friend to drink with me,
A nimble serving man to fill my bowl,
A man of wit to talk; an artful minx
With round young breasts in jewelled necklaces.[219]

Hearing that they left him in despair.

Family Divisions

Walīd was too intelligent not to foresee the outcome of his attitudes; yet he remained unmoved. One well-wisher who spoke to him was Mu'āwiyah ibn 'Amr, a descendant of Abū Sufyān.[220] He visited Walīd and said: "You allow me the candour of a friend, but I still hesitate to speak. Mixing as I do with people I hear things that you do not; and I am alarmed by your assurance of safety. Shall I speak a word of advice or shall I be silent?" Walīd replied: "From you I accept anything. God knows we are aware of the hidden end to which we are moving. Did the family of Marwān but know that the brand they are lighting against me would only be thrust in their own bellies, they

217. Iṣfahānī (1905), vi, 113. For the original text, see Appendix III, no.83.

218. Iṣfahānī (1905), vi, 132.

219. Nawajī (1859), 79; Iṣfahānī (1905), vi, 108. For the original text, see Appendix III, no.83.

220. Ṭabari (1966), ii, 1785; Balādhurī (1974), 50.

would not be doing what they do. Now I'll hear what you are saying." But there the narrative breaks off.

Walīd's way of life was indeed obnoxious to the people at large, but a greater danger to his own survival was engendered by his treatment of individuals whom he had come to regard as enemies. The atrocious murder of Khālid ibn 'Abd Allāh al-Qasrī had turned the Yamanis into relentless enemies. Their desire for his blood was embittered by a satirical poem attributed to Walīd, if not composed by him, which taunted them for failing to protect Khālid.[221]

> See Khālid here, a prisoner in our hand,
> The greatest of them and their chief of old.
> And we have cast on him a cloud of shame.
> Had they been men they would have shielded him.
> Had some nobility inspired their tribes
> His deeds would not have gone for naught; and they
> Would not have left him captive and despoiled,
> In nightly converse with our heavy chains.[222]

Amongst the Yamanis, then, and in the families of Hishām and Walīd ibn 'Abd al-Malik, and amongst the Qa'qa' family, of whom four had lost their lives under Walīd's orders, a brooding hatred spread. It was the Yamanis, according to Ṭabarī, who took the crucial step: they called on Yazīd ibn al-Walīd, Walīd's cousin, and offered him their allegiance.[223]

Yazīd consulted one 'Amr ibn Yazīd al-Ḥakamī. 'Amr warned him that the support of the Yamanis was not enough. He should consult his brother 'Abbās, the leader of the Marwān family. "If he accepts you," said 'Amr, "everyone else will; but if he refuses, people will obey him rather than you." Yazīd, accordingly, went to see 'Abbās. Damascus at the time was plague-ridden, and both were encamped in the steppe—'Abbās at Qasṭal and Yazīd a few miles away. In Ṭabarī's pages this visit of Yazīd's precedes the rebuke administered to him by 'Abbās in consequence of Marwān's letter from Armenia. But no correlation of time or place is suggested between the two interviews; and we cannot even be sure that one single occasion has not been duplicated in the record. However that may be, at Qasṭal, we read, Yazīd told his brother what was happening, asked his advice and spoke abusively of Walīd. 'Abbās said: "Gently, Yazīd! Breaking an oath before God is the break-up of religion and of this life on earth!"

Yazīd returned home. He got to work in secret, and began secretly to receive promises of allegiance. A movement spread from his friends among

221. Ṭabari (1966), ii, 1781.

222. For the original text, see Appendix III, no.85.

223. Ṭabari (1966), ii, 1784.

other leaders of society. Then, accompanied by a freedman of the family named Qaṭan, he made another call on ʻAbbās. He told him more this time of the followers urging him to be proclaimed. Again ʻAbbās forbade him to proceed: "If you go on," he said, "I swear by God I will tie you up and carry you to the Caliph!" So Yazīd again retired. ʻAbbās sent for Qaṭan: "Look, Qaṭan," he said, "is Yazīd really in earnest?" Qaṭan replied: "Honestly I do not think so. But he feels deeply about Walīd's treatment of our families and his notorious contempt for religion." ʻAbbās said: "He is the black sheep of the family of Marwān, and were it not for Walīd's rash prejudice, I would have bound Yazīd fast and handed him over. So you warn him off; he listens to you." When Qaṭan told Yazīd what ʻAbbās had said, Yazīd said: "I am not drawing back!"

ʻAbbās came under pressure again, from another brother, Bishr ibn al-Walīd.[224] Bishr's son tells of the interview, hinting at the division that had begun to plague the Umayyads: "My father called on my uncle ʻAbbās ibn al-Walīd, and I was with him; and he talked to him about unseating Walīd and proclaiming Yazīd. ʻAbbās said: 'No!' But my father argued with him. I was delighted, and said to myself: 'I see my father dares to speak to my uncle and speak again!' And I saw that what my father said was right: and so, too, was what my uncle said."

It was then that ʻAbbās pronounced the ominous words: "O Banū Marwān! I verily perceive that God has permitted your destruction." And he recited those despairing verses that I have quoted on page 15 above.

Revolt and Flight

Yazīd, with his mind now made up, set out for Damascus. Those who have recorded the sequel, in particular Balādhurī, Ṭabarī and Iṣfahānī, have described his movements in curious detail, giving their very triviality a certain quality of drama.[225] Yazīd travelled in disguise with seven companions. They had four days' journey before them, and rode on asses. It was late in the evening of the third day that they reached Jarūd, one day out from Damascus. There they thought to buy some food; but the householder they approached insisted that they were his guests. While he killed some hens, and prepared to serve them with honey and other condiments, Yazīd lay down and slept. His friends covered him up. He was described by the host as tall and stout. When their supper was ready, the host told Yazīd's companions to wake him up; but they said that he had a fever and would not eat.

224. Iṣfahānī (1905), vi, 132; Ṭabari (1966), ii, 1787-88.

225. Ṭabari (1966), ii, 1788; Iṣfahānī (1905), vi, 133; Balādhurī (1974), 51.

Staying no longer than necessary, they rode on in time to reach Damascus by the next night. There, the historians record, the majority of people were prepared in secret to give allegiance to Yazīd; so also, they add, were most of the people of Mizzah, a suburb of Damascus. The headman of Mizzah, however, named Mu'āwiyah ibn Maṣād al-Kalbī, had not yet declared himself. Yazīd decided to visit him with a small party that same night. Mu'āwiyah's house was a mile or so from the city, and they went on foot. On the way they were caught in a violent rain storm. A servant answered their knock and welcomed them in. "It is Yazīd ibn al-Walīd," they said. "God's peace on you," said the servant. "My feet are muddy," said Yazīd, "and I do not like to spoil your carpet." Mu'āwiyah had appeared and said: "The man you want my help against is worse than a spoilt carpet." And he promised his allegiance.

Yazīd returned to Damascus by night, riding beside a canal on a black ass. He lodged for a time incognito in the house of one Thābit ibn Sulaymān al-Khushānī. Soon, confident of his support amongst the inhabitants, he resolved to reveal himself. The governor of Damascus at that time, 'Abd al-Malik ibn Muḥammad ibn al-Ḥajjāj, had left the city to escape the plague, leaving his son in charge. This man, told that Yazīd was leading a revolt, refused to believe it. The Chief of Police, Abū'l-'Aj al-Kuthayr ibn 'Abd Allāh al-Sulamī, was an ineffective character. So things were favourable. It was the month of Jumāda al-Ukhrā in the year A.H.126 (the spring of A.D.744); on the evening of Friday, Yazīd sent messages to his friends to meet him by the mosque. They assembled quietly at an ablution place near Bāb al-Farādīs. At the dusk call to prayer they joined the crowd, entered the mosque and mixed with the congregation. When the prayers were ended and the time came for doors to be locked for the night, the guardians began to order the people out. Yazīd's party lingered behind, or went out by one door and came in by another, until they alone remained in the mosque and were able to overpower the guardians. Thus the Great Mosque became the first centre of power for the rebels.

Here the historians all record what they must have judged to be a critical event in the progress of affairs: one of the notables in the city, Yazīd ibn 'Anbasah al-Saksakī, approached Yazīd, saluted him and, taking him by the hand, said: "Rise, Commander of the Faithful, rejoice in God's help and aid!" Yazīd rose and said: "O God! If that be your pleasure, give me your aid and guide me thereto! But if not, let death be my discharge!"

Yazīd set out the next day with twelve companions to walk through the city, visiting the several markets and gathering supporters as they went—forty in the donkey market, and in the grain market something like two hundred.

Returning to the mosque they numbered more than two hundred and sixty. A party of them then went to the castle. Knocking at the gate they called out: "Emissaries of the Caliph Walīd!" The gate was opened and they passed in. There they found Abū'l-'Aj intoxicated. They took him prisoner and all the staff of the Treasury and the Master of Posts. By the middle of next day the whole of the city was in their hands, and most of the population had declared for Yazīd; those who hesitated were arrested.

Yazīd then sent 'Abd al-Raḥmān ibn Maṣād of Mizzah with two hundred horsemen to arrest 'Abd al-Malik, the absent Governor. He had a castle at Qaṭan, where he could defend himself. But being promised immunity he came out and gave himself up. The rebel party entered the castle and were lucky to find two saddle-bags containing sixty thousand *dīnārs*, which they carried back to Mizzah. There one of the party suggested to 'Abd al-Raḥmān that he should appropriate the *dīnārs*: "You will never get anything like that from Yazīd," said he. "Treachery!" said 'Abd al-Raḥmān virtuously. "No, by God! Never shall Arabs say that I was the first traitor in this affair!" He handed the money to Yazīd.

With this windfall and whatever he had found in the Treasury, Yazīd was able to promote his cause. He stationed a cousin, 'Abd al-'Azīz ibn al-Ḥajjāj ibn 'Abd al-Malik, at Bāb al-Jābiyah to proclaim: "Anyone due an allowance, come and collect it! For the rest, a gratuity of a thousand *dirhams*!"

In the mosque the rebels had found a great quantity of arms; their next step was to recruit men to carry them. Yazīd appointed a crier: "Who volunteers to fight Walīd the Libertine? A thousand *dirhams*!" Something less than a thousand came forward. He advanced the bidding: "Who comes to fight the Libertine? Fifteen hundred *dirhams*!" That day fifteen hundred volunteered. Finally he advanced to two thousand, and got precisely a proportionate response. Thus predictably in the city money played its due part in the progress of affairs.

But from outlying regions, too, as far afield as Jarash, there was a gathering of contingents. To check on these Yazīd gave orders that the gates were to be kept on the chain and all arrivals required to give a password. Amongst these was a party of fifteen hundred from Mizzah, who arrived at Bāb al-Jābiyah and found the gate closed. There, outside, was a messenger from Walīd, angrily demanding to know what was afoot: "I must certainly," said he, "let the Commander of the Faithful know." He was quickly killed. Hardly more fortunate was another dependant of Walīd, who took to his horse and hurried off to let him know what was going on. He rode without a break to Walīd's residence in the south, where on arrival the horse died of its exertions. Its rider, bearing unpleasant news, was rewarded with prison and a hundred lashes.

Meanwhile in Damascus Yazīd was organizing his followers as an army grouped in sections under separate commanders with his cousin, 'Abd al-'Azīz ibn al-Ḥajjāj ibn 'Abd al-Malik, in command of them all. Walīd, when the news of these events reached him, was at his far southern property named by Ṭabarī as Aghdaf, in the territory of 'Ammān.[226] His friends there knew his position was precarious and began to consider the options open to him. Said one: "Commander of the Faithful, march and install yourself in Ḥimṣ, which is well fortified. There you may send troops to kill or capture Yazīd." Another said: "It is not fitting for the Caliph to leave his women and soldiers without a worthy fight; God is his strength and will give him victory." The first said: "What is there to fear for the women? It is only 'Abd al-'Azīz who comes against him, and he is their cousin." Another, Sa'īd ibn al-Walīd al-Kalbī, named Abrash, then said: "Tadmur is strong and I have people there who will defend you." Walīd doubted they could reach it; and, beside, the Banū 'Āmir were there, who belonged to the rebels. He added: "And its name is what it is!" (*tadmur*: "thou perishest!") "Well then," said Abrash, "there is Bakhrā', with the castle of Nu'mān ibn Bashīr." "The name stinks," said Walīd, (*al-bakhrā'*: "she that stinks") "and I fear the plague." They said: "What they have in store for you is worse than the plague." At this critical moment Ṭabarī puts into the mouth of Walīd philosophical and defiant verses:

If with the evil there's no good,
 In time of fear you'll find
No counsellor nor friend in need.
 While they were working at their little plot
I bared my head to them
 And scorned to cover it.[227]

Walīd finally settled for Bakhrā', the scene of former pleasures, where the old Persian fort was still defensible in a settlement some twenty miles south of Tadmur. From Aghdaf he had over two hundred and thirty miles to ride, a twelve-day journey at the least, before reaching Bakhrā'. They set off eastwards along the desert road, which would lead ultimately to Samawa on the lower Euphrates. Turning off that northwards, at sundry points on the road they were met by small groups of supporters on horseback, the most important of them a party of five hundred horsemen from Ḥimṣ, who reached Walīd shortly before Bakhrā' itself. Here the horses were an immediate embarrassment, for no sooner had they arrived than the men complained they they had no feed for them. "Tell them," said Walīd, "that the Caliph has bought corn from the village." "We cannot give our beasts green corn," said the men; "they go sick on it." And they demanded money. Just so was it when Walīd offered a prize of five hundred *dirhams* for an enemy

226. Ṭabari (1966), ii, 1795-96.

227. For the original text, see Appendix III, no.86.

head.[228] When some heads came in, Walīd said: "Write down their names!" "Commander of the Faithful," said they, "this is no time for business on credit!" but for such money as he possessed Walīd had a different need: the faint hope of buying off his enemies.

Meanwhile 'Abd al-'Azīz, aware of Walīd's movements, had sent a contingent to intercept his passage. They did not catch Walīd himself, but met and seized his baggage train. Following hard on his heels, the rebels encamped, to the number of eight hundred men, not long after Walīd's arrival, quite close to the walled settlement of Bakhrā'. At this point a bizarre episode is related: Walīd ordered his dais to be brought out and set up in the midst of his little army.[229] He mounted upon it and addressed the troops: "So they attack me, do they! Me! Who will pounce on a lion and strangle serpents!" Words that the sequel was not to vindicate.

A messenger had lately come from 'Abbās ibn al-Walīd ibn 'Abd al-Malik that he was coming to join Walīd, in loyalty, with such members of his household and family as he could muster. Walīd waited in expectation of their arrival. Hearing of this, 'Abd al-'Azīz sent one of his subordinate commanders, Manṣūr ibn Jamhūr, with a body of horses to intercept and capture the party. The road 'Abbās must traverse from Qasṭal, where he lived, to Bakhrā' passed through a range of high ground and could be predicted. You will meet them, said 'Abd al-'Azīz, at al-Shi'b, the Pass. And so it was. At al-Shi'b 'Abbās, with thirty of his sons and retainers, was caught and forced by the threats and superior numbers of the enemy to divert to the encampment of 'Abd al-'Azīz. On arrival before 'Abd al-'Azīz, 'Abbās found himself with his sons separated from his other companions. 'Abd al-'Azīz ordered him to make acknowledgement of his brother Yazīd. 'Abbās in his predicament gave way. The rebels set up a flag and announced: "This is the flag of 'Abbās ibn al-Walīd; he has sworn allegiance to Yazīd ibn al-Walīd, Commander of the Faithful! Who follows 'Abbās ibn al-Walīd is safe." "Treachery most foul," said 'Abbās, "the devil's own treachery! We are in God's hands. Verily the House of Marwān is dead!"

Willing or unwilling, the appearance of 'Abbās in the rebel camp had the intended effect of drawing waverers over to Yazīd.[230] 'Abbās was to suffer for it later. When news of Walīd's death and the circumstances of it reached his friends in Ḥimṣ, they reacted in anger. "We could keep the people under control," they said, "until 'Abbās came along; then they followed him over to 'Abd al-'Azīz." So the people of Ḥimṣ, loyal to Walīd, rose up, looted and destroyed the home of 'Abbās, plundered his women and seized and

228. Ṭabari (1966), ii, 1809; Iṣfahānī (1905), vi, 134.
229. Ṭabari (1966), ii, 1797.
230. Ṭabari (1966), ii, 1826.

imprisoned his sons. He himself they sought; but 'Abbās had perforce taken refuge with the usurper.

That was in the future. Around Bakhrā', in the meantime, Walīd and 'Abd al-'Azīz confronted each other. There was sporadic fighting, too confused for historians to give it a clear account. There were losses on both sides and allegiance was in a flux.[231] The rebels held aloft on a spear a call to Walīd's men: "We summon you to God's book and the law of his Prophet!" Walīd, on his way to Bakhrā', had been joined by one Walīd ibn Khālid with a party of the Banū 'Āmir. When battle was joined the Banū 'Āmir, on Walīd's left, found their own kinsmen opposite, on the rebel side. They would not fight, and all (except, apparently, their leader) deserted. Walīd sent Walīd ibn Khālid to 'Abd al-'Azīz, with an offer of fifty thousand *dīnārs* and the governorship of Ḥimṣ for life, if he would but depart and desist. 'Abd al-'Azīz refused. Walīd repeated the message. It had no effect. The envoy, Walīd ibn Khālid, set off on his return journey, but shortly turned his horse and approached 'Abd al-'Azīz once more. "Will you settle with me," he said, "for five thousand *dīnārs*, and the same for Abrash (the Kalbī, his uncle) if I join you with my people, as their leader, and share in your enterprise?" "Yes," said 'Abd al-'Azīz, "but on condition, here and now, you attack Walīd's people." He did so.

Another traitor, in Ṭabarī's narrative, was Mu'āwiyah ibn Abī Sufyān, successor to a famous name, who had stood on the right of Walīd's troops. He offered his services for an even higher price, twenty thousand *dīnārs* and the governorship of Jordan, with partnership in the revolt. 'Abd al-'Azīz replied as before: "Yes, but you must instantly attack Walīd's people." Which he did.

With these betrayals and defections the battle was lost for Walīd.[232] The enemy at close quarters began to pelt him with stones, shouting: "Kill God's enemy! Stone the Sodomite!" Walīd managed to escape into the castle and lock the door. The rebels surrounded him.

From within the gate Walīd then called out: "Is there not amongst you a nobleman of standing with whom I can talk?" There came a reply: "Speak to me!" "Who are you?" said Walīd. "I am Yazīd ibn 'Anbasah al-Saksakī," he answered. "Why, brother of the Saksakīs," said Walīd: "did I not increase your bounties, and remove burdens from you? Did I not endow your poor, and minister to your cripples?" Yazīd replied: "On our own account we have nothing against you. We condemn you for doing what God has forbidden: for drinking wine, for debauching the mothers of your father's children, for your sodomizing and for your belittling of God's rule." "Enough, brother Saksakī!" said Walīd. "On my life you have gone too far and spoken overmuch. What God permitted has sufficed for me without the things you speak of! And now,

231. Ṭabari (1966), ii, 1804-05.

232. Iṣfahānī (1905), vi, 134-35.

God knows, there will be no closing the rifts you are making, nor repairing your disorders; and there will be no unity in your counsels!" And he went back inside the castle.

Death of Walīd

The last hours and death of Walīd are variously described, and the event in its true details will never be known. What reads like a fictitious interlude, worthy of some Italian opera, is introduced, with dramatic effect but little historical probability, by Iṣfahānī.[233] On hearing the cry: "stone the Sodomite," he relates, "Walīd entered the castle, locked the door and recited:

> Leave me Sulaymah, wine, a girl to sing, a cup:
> That's wealth enough for me!
> Though life be on a bare sand hill, with Salmā in my arms
> I would not have it changed.
> Take your possessions! God has made them not so sure
> As that which binds my life.
> Unharness me before my eyes can blink, nor grudge
> Me that I starve to death.
> Do I ask in wealth perpetual to dwell with you?
> How often wealth will come to nought!
> How many a house, its people loaded up,
> By noon is void
> And its abodes a wilderness!"

Iṣfahānī records this outburst (which Walīd then bade 'Umar al-Wādī to sing) before the conversation with the Saksakī. But did it really happen? Sulaymah (little Salmā), alas, had died before all these events; and it is hard to believe that, with Salmā dead, Walīd at this fateful moment could have relived the passionate sentiments of that receding time when hopeful love and rupture with Hishām had first inspired those verses.

That 'Umar al-Wādī had accompanied Walīd and was present at Bakhrā' there need be no doubt. With him, too was another of the singers, Mālik ibn Abī Samḥ. In a later figment of his imagination 'Umar claimed to have been singing up to the moment when he saw Walīd's head come off and his body bathed in blood. What really happened was less heroic. The story is told by Ṭabarī and Balādhurī.[234] When Walīd's friends deserted him and he was

233. Iṣfahānī (1905), vi, 134; Ibn 'Abd Rabbihī (1876), ii, 345.

234. Ṭabari (1966), ii, 1810; Balādhurī (1974), 64. Ṭabari in this passage changes 'Umar's name to 'Amr.

besieged, Mālik said to 'Umar: "Let us be off!" 'Umar said: "Why, this is not the end; we are not fighters, so we shall be all right." "You poor fool," said Mālik, "if they catch us, you and I will be the first to be killed. His head will be stuck up between our two and they'll say to the people: look who was with him! And you and I will be the worst of his offences!" So they made off. Iṣfahānī brings this story into his portrait of Mālik. "He was the stupidest of men," says his companion there, "and that was the first time I ever heard him talk sense!"

Walīd was now practically alone. The singers were able to escape; but the rebels had surrounded the castle. There is a hint that Walīd offered to come out and parley; but 'Abd al-'Azīz scorned the offer. Then a tall young man on horseback managed to scale the wall of the castle and get inside. Others followed him, amongst them Yazīd ibn 'Anbasah, who in other accounts is credited with being the first. Walīd, returning from his conversation with Yazīd, conceived of himself as the central character in a drama. He remembered the murder of 'Uthmān, the third Caliph, and resolved to play out the same role.[235] He took up a copy of the Qur'ān, and sat down and began to read. He said: "It is a day as the day of 'Uthmān!"

Thus Yazīd found him, seated with his sword in its sheath beside him. "Draw your sword," said Yazīd. "If I had wished for the sword," said Walīd, "things between us would have been different from this!"

Yazīd grasped his wrist, thinking to make him his prisoner and use that to negotiate some bargain with Yazīd ibn al-Walīd. But ten others had by then entered the castle, and one of them, 'Abd al-Salām al-Lakhmī, struck Walīd on the head; another, Sirrī ibn Ziyād, then wounded him in the face; then one after the other all struck him to death with their swords. A mêlée developed with five of the attackers seeking to drag Walīd's corpse out into the open. Then a strange thing happened: a woman in the house cried out, and the plunderers dropped him. What the woman had said is not recorded. The body stayed where it was until the bravest of them, one Abū 'Alāqah, decapitated the late Commander of the Faithful.

Yazīd ibn al-Walīd had set a price on the head of Walīd, a hundred thousand *dirhams*. Since there was only one head, a bizarre scramble ensued amongst participants in the murder, each intent to secure some prize or plunder from the corpse. There were ten who claimed the credit for themselves. The first necessity was to repair the damaged face; someone produced a length of gut and stitched that up. The person who carried the mended head to Yazīd was Rawḥ ibn Muqbil; but he was outrun. For 'Amr ibn Marwạn al-Kalbī had severed Walīd's left hand and with that relic reached Damascus first on a Friday evening; the head only arrived early the

235. Iṣfahānī (1905), vi, 135.

next day. Presenting it, Rawḥ saluted Yazīd with the words: "Rejoice, Commander of the Faithful! The transgressor is slain! His affair is finished and he has his reward!"

Yazīd was at his morning meal. He and those with him rose and prostrated themselves in prayer. Yazīd ibn 'Anbasah al-Saksakī had also reached the scene. He re-enacted his gesture in Damascus at the beginning of the revolt, grasping Yazīd by the hand and saying: "Rise, Commander of the Faithful! Rejoice in God's aid!" Yazīd withdrew his hand and said: "O God! If this is your pleasure, direct me aright!" He then said to the Saksakī: "Did Walīd speak to you?" he replied: "Yes; he spoke to me through the door." The Saksakī then recounted in detail their conversation ending in Walīd's prediction of irreparable schism amongst the Umayyads.

Yazīd ordered the head of Walīd to be exhibited.[236] He was reproved by a dependant of the family, Yazīd ibn Farwah, who protested: "It is only the heads of strangers that are exhibited; this was your cousin and a Caliph. I fear that if you display it people will become sorry for him and his family will be outraged." "Display it I shall," said Yazīd, and stuck it on a spear. Then to Ibn Farwah: "Take it and be off with you," he said. "Go round the city and carry it into his father's house." So the man obeyed. There was an outcry—whether of horror or satisfaction or both we know not—in the city and in the household. The man carried the head back to Yazīd. "Take it to your own house," said he. After a month Yazīd ordered him to hand the head over to Walīd's brother Sulaymān. Ibn Farwah accordingly washed the head, put it in a basket and carried it to Sulaymān. This brother was one of those who had tried to influence Walīd. He took one look at the head and said: "Take it away! He was a wine-drinker, without shame or conscience. He tried to seduce me!" Ibn Farwah left the house. Encountering a freedwoman of Walīd's household, he told her what Sulaymān had said. "He is a filthy liar," said she; "if Walīd had wanted to do it, he could not have stopped him."

Sanctimonious Sermon by an Assassin

Having thus disposed of his kinsman, the lawful Caliph, Yazīd resolved on a public statement. Walīd's murder was not universally welcomed; and it was expedient for the assassin to speak with candour of his enemy's vices and, without concealment, of his own virtues. Accordingly he thus addressed the people:"I come before you," he said, after praising God and blessing the Prophet, "not to boast or exult, nor in eager desire for this world's goods. I seek not kingship and know not self-praise. Except for my Lord's mercy I would be tyrant to myself.

236. Ṭabari (1966), ii, 1807.

No! It was in anger for God's cause that I came forward: for His prophet and His religion. I came exhorting to God's book and to the law of His Prophet (God's blessing on him), at a time when the pointers to truth were demolished, the light of the God-fearing extinguished and the rebel tyrant made manifest, for whom nothing was sacred; who embarked on every heresy; who believed not in the book nor in the day of reckoning. True, he was reckoned my cousin and my equal in lineage. Seeing that, I sought God's will concerning him, praying God not to leave me to my own discretion. I summoned to that task those in my command who answered my call. And therein I strove until God, by His power and strength, not mine, gave to His servants and lands rest from that man.

O People! You have my word that I will not place stone on stone nor brick on brick. I will dig no canal; I will pile up no wealth, nor bestow it on wife or child. I will not transfer property from one place to another except I make good the loss to that place and to its poor, to their advantage; and, if any excess remain, I will assign that to their near neighbour who may be in need of it. I will not post you for long spells on your frontiers, to the sore trial of yourselves and your families. Nor will I shut my door against you, for the strong amongst you to devour the weak. I will not lay on those in your protection burdens that will drive them forth from their lands and curtail their progeny.

With me your stipends year by year are safe, and your subsistence month by month. Thus for Muslims, far and near alike, their livelihood abounds. If, then, I fulfil my word to you it is for you to hear and obey, and to give loyal support. But if I do not fulfil it you may reject me, except only you seek my repentance and, if I repent, you accept it. And if you have knowledge of any man of known rectitude who will of himself give you what I give you, and if you wish to proclaim him, then I myself will be the first to do that and give him my obedience.

People! Obedience to the creature allows not rebellion against the creator; nor can keeping faith lie in the breaking of it. Obedience is to God alone; so submit with God's obedience to such a one as obeys. But if he himself rebel against God and call to rebellion, then is he deserving of rebellion against himself and of death. So say I, and beg God's forgiveness for me and for you."[237]

So preached Yazīd. He had assumed and was allowed the character of a devout Muslim. His promise to eschew the building extravagance of his predecessors may have impressed his hearers; but his assurances concerning their stipends were a deception, for he shortly cancelled the increases that Walīd had granted and earned for himself the sobriquet of "Curtailer" or

237. Ṭabari (1966), ii, 1834-35.

"Defrauder"—"Yazīd al-Nāqiṣ"—which clung to him thereafter. To press home the immediate impact of his eloquence, Yazīd called on his audience forthwith to renew their pledge of loyalty. This the people of Damascus were ready to do; but others elsewhere would not necessarily be so amenable. To the volatile people of Iraq, where he sent as governor one of his active supporters in the revolt, Manṣūr ibn Jamhūr, Yazīd thought it desirable to address a letter expatiating on the crimes and godlessness of Walīd. Ṭabarī has recorded the gist of his diatribe.[238] After recalling that Islam was the religion chosen by God to embody His commands and prohibitions, and how its administration and maintenance had been satisfactorily sustained through the succession of Caliphs, Yazīd continued: "So it was until the death of Hishām. Then the command passed to God's enemy, Walīd, the violator of sanctities such as Muslims and pagans alike hold untouchable and unapproachable. Therein his acts ranged far and wide, unto notoriety, becoming a sore affliction, with bloodshed, unlawful confiscations and abominations such as God will not long tolerate. Then it was that I went to him, reprobating his behaviour and reckless rebellion against God and seeking to recall him by reasoning to contrition. It was my hope that God would bring to completion that which I had in mind: the re-edification of religion and the acceptance among His people of God's good pleasure."

Here Yazīd, as quoted by Ṭabarī, omits to mention how Walīd received his reproof. We may probably fill the gap by inserting the little poem quoted from a similar, perhaps the same, incident given on page 149 above. Yazīd's letter continues: "Then at last I found a troop of men whose hearts burned with anger to see the acts of God's enemy. (For God's enemy saw no ordinance of Islam but he sought to change it and to act contrary to God's revelation. That was notorious and undisputed; God gave no cover to his nakedness.) So I told them of my fears for the corruption of religion and society, which I must avenge, rousing them to the defence and repair of their religion. For a while they hesitated, fearing to perpetuate for themselves that which they opposed, until I called upon them to change it. Then they responded swiftly.

So God sent me an army of such as He knew and had made trial of, good men of religion. And I set over them 'Abd al-'Azīz ibn al-Ḥajjāj ibn 'Abd al-Malik, who found God's enemy beside a place called Bakhrā'. They called on him to parley, for the Muslims themselves to consult and agree on whom they would invest. But God's enemy responded not, being set only to rush headlong forward in his error, knowing not God. But of God's power and wisdom he soon learnt, and the fierce pain of His chastisement. So God killed him for his evil acts and rebellion. And among his companions the inner circle of evil men numbered not ten. The rest of those who were with him,

238. Ṭabari (1966), ii, 1843-45.

being summoned to the right course, took it. So God quenched his fire and gave God's servants rest. Thus perish he and all who follow him!"

So much for the virtuous Yazīd the Curtailer. Within six months he was dead, having achieved nothing but the further disintegration of Umayyad fortunes. Not much remains to be told in the lamentable story of Walīd ibn Yazīd. Not always in his own or in later generations was his memory reprobated. Of his contemporaries one steadfast supporter was Marwān ibn Muḥammad, who had endeavoured, though unsuccessfully, to stop the revolt while that was still possible. Marwān was still on the Armenian frontier when news reached him of Walīd's assassination and Yazīd's promotion. He did not take it well. One of the details conveyed to him concerned the acclamations received by Yazīd after he had addressed the people of Damascus.[239] A certain Qays ibn Hanī' al-'Abasī had responded with the zeal of a sycophant to Yazīd's harangue. "Commander of the Faithful," said this man, "hold to your course in the fear of God! Of all your house not one has stood so high as you! They may say: ''Umar ibn 'Abd al-'Azīz!' But I say that you achieved it by righteous means, 'Umar by evil." "God curse him," said Marwān when he heard this. "He degrades 'Umar and he degrades us all!" And so incensed was he that having himself very shortly succeeded to the Caliphate he caused Qays to be slain while at prayer in the mosque at Damascus.

Later Memories

More than thirty years after Walīd's death it happened one night in the presence of the 'Abbāsid Caliph al-Mahdī that conversation turned on Walīd ibn Yazīd.[240] The Caliph remarked: "I reckon he was godless." But one Ibn 'Ulāthah the Faqīh stood up and said: "Commander of the Faithful, God is too great to entrust the succession as Prophet and Governor of the nation to one who does not believe in God. And I have been told about Walīd ibn Yazīd, by one who witnessed him at his sport and in his drinking, how correct he was in his ablutions and prayer. As the time of prayer approached, he would throw off the clothes he was wearing, perfumed and dyed as they were; then he would wash himself with the utmost care and would be handed clean white clothes such as pertain to the office of Caliph. In them he would pray to perfection. His reading was faultless; his silence and his stillness exemplary; and his prostrating and seating himself alike impeccable. When he had finished he would resume the dress he had worn before and then return to his relaxation and his drinking. Is this the behaviour of an unbeliever?" "You are right, God bless you, Ibn 'Ulāthah," said al-Mahdī.

239. Ṭabari (1966), ii, 1835-36.

240. Iṣfahānī (1905), vi, 136.

A few years later one of the sons of Ghamr ibn Yazīd, Walīd's brother, came into the presence of Hārūn al-Rashīd. The Caliph asked him where he was from. "I am of Quraysh," replied the young man. "What family?" said Rashīd. Then, when the other hesitated: "You are quite safe," he assured him, "though you be a Marwānī." "I am a son of Ghamr ibn Yazīd," said the young man. "God have mercy on your uncle," said Rashīd, "and curse Yazīd the Curtailer and your uncle's murderers—deliberately they killed a Caliph!"

The poet Marwān ibn Sulaymān, commonly called Ibn Abī Ḥafṣah after his great-grandfather Abū Ḥafṣah, freedman of the Umayyad Marwān I, relates how he once attended on the Caliph Hārūn al-Rashīd and was asked by him if he ever met Walīd ibn Yazīd: "'Yes,' said I. 'Tell me about him,' said Rashīd. I hesitated in embarrassment. He said: 'Speak out! The Caliph will not object to anything you say.' I said: 'Commander of the Faithful, he was the best-looking, the strongest and the cleverest man of his time, and the best poet.' Rashīd said: 'Do you remember any of his poems?' I said: 'Yes. I visited him once with my uncles. He had a rod in his hand and began to poke it into my hair, which was long and thick. He called me "my lad" and told me about my ancestress, Sukkār, who was the mother of sons to Marwān ibn al-Ḥakam, and was given by him as wife to Abū Ḥafṣah from whom I am descended. Walīd was Caliph at the time, and spoke of Hishām and how he had tried to prevent his succession. Then I heard him sing his verses which began: "He should have lived, Hishām, to see his brimming bushels filled"...'" Ibn Abī Ḥafṣah sang the lines to Rashīd, who sent for paper and ink, and had them copied out.[241]

Thus the 'Abbāsid Caliph helped to generate one of two strands composing the posthumous history of Walīd ibn Yazīd. For although on that disastrous day in April A.D.744 Walīd's life was ignominiously extinguished, that was not quite the end of him. Two groups among his posterity preserved his memory: the censorious (amongst them most of the chroniclers) reprobating his morals, and the literati and poets admiring his accomplishments. Enough has been told here of the atrocities and follies that destroyed him; the story may be ended less disagreeably by lingering briefly amongst some pleasanter memories.

Iṣfahānī's informant remarks that beside the verses quoted to Rashīd by Marwān many other of Walīd's poems were current and popular in those years, including a well-known encomium on wine.[242] This piece, he relates, had so powerful an effect on one singer, Abū Ghassān Muḥammad ibn Yaḥyā, that the artist could hardly refrain from dancing as he sang:

241. Iṣfahānī (1905), vi, 106.

242. Iṣfahānī (1905), vi, 106-07.

Let whispering cares be cloven by delight,
    And let the vineyard's daughter cheer your days.
Embrace the easeful opulence of life,
    And shun the trails that lead you to regret.
With wine that mellowing years have beautified,
    Time's aged mistress, more desirable
To dally with upon her bridal day
    Than virgin daughter of nobility.
Clear as the day, in essence delicate,
    The very sight of her is wonderful.
Unmixed she is a stream of sparks; dilute
    She's liquid gold, a firebrand in the glass,
A blaze of lights before the eager eye.
    And have with you Umayya's sprightly sons,
The heirs of honour and esteem; amongst
    Mankind none equals them, and of them none
Can equal me or my paternal line.

In a shorter poem preserved by Mas'ūdī Walīd has more to say of his golden mistress:

A golden wine like saffron in the cup,
    That merchants carried up from Ascalon.
The smallest mote is clear; an ample jug
    Shields it from finger's touch. And as it's poured
The bubbles gleam as lightning in the south.[243]

In a more lyrical and ebullient mood, which the translator may slightly inflate, he celebrated a bibulous all-night session with his friend Abū Kāmil, who became the favoured recipient of a princely headpiece.

A wine-skin!
    A both-ways bulging, full-to-bursting
        Proper camel of a wine-skin!
I ran with it!
    To my friend and fellow-drinker, to
        Abū Kāmil did I run with it!
We drank it!
    On the roof-top of the convent, by
        The sea we spent the night with it!

243. Mas'ūdī (1830), ii, 186. For the original text of the poetry on this page, see Appendix III, nos.87-89.

The slanderer!
His reception we rejected it,
Rejected the reception of a foul-mouthed ignoramus! [244]

There were other nights that Walīd prized rather for their intimacy and quiet. An unnamed woman had promised him a night in her house. Leaving her he said:

She rose to me with kisses, and her arms
She put about my neck.
Plump curves fleshed out her bones, her mouth was musk.
Come in! I pledge myself
There's none to see us, and my soul to yours
Is pledged no ill shall fall!
So passed our night. Each held the other close.
We loved too much for sleep;
Till, when the threads of night and dawn appeared,
I said: "It's time to part."
She sobbed in grief; and then I left unseen.
None was aware of us.
May God reward her for that noble night![245]

Walīd once saw a Christian girl and imagined himself in love:

Your heart is sick, Walīd! That lissom girl
It was, this morning, going out to church.
Love at first sight! And then, before my eyes,
She kissed a piece of wood, a wooden cross!
Poor soul of mine, to see that cross adored;
It could be me! God, put me in its place!
And I'll be fuel for the flames of hell![246]

But more often it was Salmā who inspired his raptures. He saw her in dreams and in imagination:

The wounded heart could not forget its pain,
Nor eye could stem the flow of flooding tears.
Till Salmā met you in the quiet of night,
The horses bowing low beside us there.

244. Iṣfahānī (1905), vi, 140. For the original text of the poetry on this page, see Appendix III, nos.89-92.

245. Iṣfahānī (1905), vi, 120.

246. Gabrieli (1934), xxxii.

So all that night I lay with her in joy;
  Until the clarion herald crowed: It's dawn![247]

The changing moods and fortunes of a lover he accepted with philosophy:

I ask not God to change her ways; she sleeps,
  Albeit her eyes keep mine awake.
Missing her, nothing's longer than my night;
  Finding her, nothing's shorter.[248]

One of his dreams seemed sad and fraught with foreboding:

I slept, and in my sleep Salmā appeared,
  Disquieted. "Come near," I said, "Don't go!
That I may question you on love." She turned.
  "My friend, my comrade, rise! Light me a lamp
Here in this desert, where none graze, where thorn
  And wormwood only grow!"[249]

Another seems to picture Salmā braving and surviving the long and hazardous journey from Madīnah for her marriage in Syria:

To me by night, while my companions slept,
  There came a dappled fawn, white as the moon,
Or like the sun's first rays that soar and touch
  The mountain tops. Perils she met for me!
What desert, murderous lands she crossed! But then
  With us, in bridal bowers, Salmā found home.[250]

Not all Walīd's thoughts on Salmā were sentimental; they came to him also in convivial moments;

A drink for me, you Sālim's son,
  The morning star's alight and shining clear!
A drink for me of nectar pure
  That's fresh distilled from little Salmā's tongue!

247. Gabrieli (1934), xxvi. For the original text of the poetry on this page, see Appendix III, nos.92-96.

248. Gabrieli (1934), iv.

249. Iṣfahānī (1905), vi, 118.

250. Iṣfahānī (1905), vi, 118.

And for my fellow-drinker here
A cup of incapacitating wine![251]

There may have been in Walīd's mind occasionally some conflict between his devotion for Salmā and his addiction to other enjoyments. Something of the sort is hinted at in an introspective poem apparently composed after his receipt of a sobering communication from Salmā herself:

Ah me! If Salmā saw me now
My troubles surely would be hers;
My substance all on pleasures spent,
On bright-eyed singing girls my love!
For it was only Salmā's word
That coming filled my heart with grief.
Careless I'd lived till then, but now
Heart's ache for Salmā lays me waste.
And yet for Salmā I'm rebuked,
And sage advisers tell me: "No!"[252]

Still in comparatively serious mood he declared himself to Salmā direct:

I see myself a full-grown man who played
The lad. Were love to leave me I would fast
And pray. If you so willed, I would endure;
Or if you willed it not, then would I not.
But no, by God! Leviathan will not
Endure life in the desert waterless!
No, little Salmā! I've no patience more.
If you but let me, I will come and kiss
Two thousand thousand kisses on your mouth,
And swear my life away to give you life!
With all my heart and strength through all the world
Salmā's my love, an antelope I love
For her dark eyes and spotless neck and throat.[253]

Again he declared his devotion with impassioned and fantasizing hyperbole:

251. Iṣfahānī (1905), vi, 115. For the original text of the poetry on this page, see Appendix III, nos. 96-98.

252. Iṣfahānī (1905), vi, 116.

253. Iṣfahānī (1905), vi, 113. In lines 3 and 4 I read *idha shi'ti*, "if you so willed." The reading of Gabrieli and Abyarī is *idha shi'tu* "if I wished," which seems to make less sense.

God let me see you as I see you now,
Salmā, in life and at the Judgement Day.
Have you no recompense for him you've long
Enslaved, who'd answer every claim you made?
Who, if you died (but do not die!) would die
Himself; or, doomed by Fate to live, would live
In tears. Who, if his every hope were met
In this wide world, would turn to none but you.
Salmā! Requite a lover sick with care;
Who, if he tripped, would call no name but yours.
Who, if you told him: Die!—and he could die—
Obedient would taste of death for you.[254]

Apart from the attempt on his life, Walīd had some pleasant adventures while hunting. One day he came across a group of women of the Minjāb clan of Banū Kalb. He stopped by them to ask for some water, and they entertained him. A girl amongst them caught his eye and inspired a short poem:

I passed by women of Minjāb,
Bright flashing eyes. They bade me sup.
Amongst them was a tender sylph,
A pretty flirt, with slender waist
And sharp eye teeth. Where'er she stayed,
She graced their houses in the sown,
She graced her desert-dwellers' tents.[255]

On another day Walīd's dogs caught a gazelle, or antelope. When it was brought to him he said: "Let it go! Its throat and eyes are the nearest I ever saw to Salmā's." Then he recited:

We caught and would have killed an antelope
That ran auspicious from the right.
But then it gently turned its eyes and looked—
The very image of your look!
We let it go. And know: but for our love
For you, it surely would have died.
Now, little antelope, you're free and safe.
So off you go,
Happy among the other antelopes.[256]

254. Iṣfahānī (1905), vi, 116. For the original text of the poetry on this page, see Appendix III, nos.99-101.

255. Iṣfahānī (1905), vi, 120.

256. Iṣfahānī (1905), vi, 121.

Lahw and levity were perpetual factors in Walīd's life, and these reminiscences may end with a light fancy, which Abū'l-Faraj describes as one of the least substantial of his poems:

> They told me on a Friday Salmā had
>   Gone out to prayers.
> Just then, upon a branch a pretty bird
>   Sat preening.
> I said: "Who here knows Salmā?" "Ha!" said he;
>   Then up he flew.
> I said: "Come hither, birdie!" "Ha!" said he;
>   Then down he came.
> I said: "Have you seen, Salmā?" "Ha!" said he;
>   Then turned his tail,
> And struck a secret wound within my heart.
>   Then off he flew.[257]

257. Iṣfahānī (1905), vi, 115. For the original text, see Appendix III, no. 102

Appendix I: Some Other Buildings of Walīd

Hishām censuring Walīd's architectural extravagance wrote of his "places" in the plural. The establishment in the Ghawr was one of them, authenticated for us by approximately datable inscriptions (A.D.724-43) and by a "signature", but as yet unrecognized among places named in published sources. Identification of Walīd's other places is a matter of conjecture. He certainly stayed at Bakhrā', identifiable with the ruined site of Bakhrā' near Tadmur and was assassinated there;[258] but whether he spent money reconstructing the pre-Islamic buildings at Bakhrā' we cannot say. It has been thought likely that another of Walīd's places was the vast ruin known as Qaṣr al-Ṭubah or Ṭubat al-Ghadaf in the Wādī'l-Ghadaf. One reason for that conjecture has been the statement of Ṭabarī and Abū'l-Faraj that to avoid harassment by Hishām Walīd settled "at a watering place (*'alā mā'in*) called al-Aghdaf", which in common speech is interchangeable with Ghadaf, the present name of the area. But there is a difficulty; for at Ṭubah there is no water and none, according to Musil,[259] nearer than Ghadīr al-Dhib, fifteen miles away. To identify Walīd's place of self-imposed exile with Qaṣr al-Ṭubah would therefore require us to ignore the words *'alā mā'in*.

That brings into consideration another possible allusion to Qaṣr al-Ṭuba, the famous account by Severus ibn al-Muqaffa', cited by Lammens, of Walīd's disastrous attempt to build a "city" in the desert fifteen miles from water, and of the sufferings of his heterogeneous work force.[260] Lammens wished to link that with Mshattā; but the fatal distance from water is much better suited to Ṭubah.

Ibn al-Muqaffa' explicitly states that Walīd began his venture after the death of Hishām; we need not therefore connect it with the "watering place", for there is no reason to assume that the "desert city" was to be sited just where Walīd had been staying during the last years of Hishām's life.

If Qaṣr al-Ṭubah was indeed one of Walīd's buildings (though not one of those Hishām had lived to object to), it is remarkable that nothing in its architecture suggests a close connection with his buildings in the Ghawr. Certainly its perimeter was furnished with round towers and its construction combined bricks with stone: brick on stone courses for walls and brick for vaults. But at al-Mafjar bricks were used only for vaults, not at all for walls; and brick vaults at the two sites were constructed by entirely different methods, implying different work forces. Stone sculpture survives at Ṭuba, but only on doorways, and is not matched by any of the sculpture, in stone or plaster, at al-Mafjar. At Ṭubah there was no stone vaulting, while in the

258. Musil (1928), 234.
259. Musil (1928), 285.
260. Lammens (1930), 348.

Ghawr masons capable of the most sophisticated ashlar stone vaulting were present, as we have seen in the cross-vault spanning the palace entrance porch.

If both sites belonged to the same man, the differences between them need some explanation. It could be either difference in time or difference in geography. Walīd was a rich man for most of Hishām's caliphate of twenty years. His resources for building must have fallen short when Hishām cut off his allowance. But I believe that happened only a few years before Hishām's death. At any time, then, for say fifteen years during Hishām's lifetime, and again for the fourteen months of his own caliphate, building for Walīd could have taken place. In theory, then, some such lapse of time could have separated the buildings in Wādī'l-Ghadaf (at the end of Walīd's life) from the buildings in the Ghawr. But since the palace in the Ghawr was left, like Qaṣr al-Ṭuba, unfinished at Walīd's death, it does not seem that so great an interval can have separated them as to explain the differences in their construction. We must conclude that it was their geographical separation which brought those differences about.

In the Ghawr Walīd was operating close to the centre of the ancient Phoenician building tradition based on abundance of limestone in all qualities and timber equally available. Bricklaying in the Ghawr was a cheap and easy innovation, but masons there used bricks for vaulting as they would use stone, with beds at right angles to the thrust of a vault and with timber centring during construction. In Wādī'l-Ghadaf, eighty miles away, whether for lack of suitable timber or following the practice of foreign workmen, bricks for vaulting were laid on edge in rings sloping toward an end wall, by a Mesopotamian device for dispensing with timber framing. The appearance of this technique, exotic in Syria and Palestine, may recall Ibn Muqaffa''s statement that Walīd conscripted workers from all quarters.

The structural features that distinguish Qaṣr al-Ṭubah from al-Mafjar link it closely with Mshattā, another building commonly ascribed to Walīd ibn Yazīd. Creswell, in characteristic style, counts the points of resemblance between the two buildings and finds them to number fourteen, including the unfinished state of both.[261] The palace in the Ghawr was also left unfinished, but much nearer to completion. We know from graffiti that it was begun during the caliphate of Hishām, while the bath and music room had been both completed and used for some years. On archaeological evidence (Appendix II below) I believe that work on the palace had been interrupted toward the end of Hishām's reign and then resumed on Walīd's accession. The main building may therefore have preceded by some years the construction of Mshattā as well as that of Ṭubah.

261. Creswell (1969), 623.

If Qaṣr al-Ṭubah came too late to vex Hishām, there is more reason to conjecture that Mshattā was one of those buildings that he could have known and disapproved of. And Mshattā, though distinguished from al-Mafjar by the same major structural differences, is not altogether devoid of parallels in ornament. For example, beside the presence in both buildings of sculptured nudes or semi-nudes one can compare the six-lobed rosettes built into the spandrels of the triple arch before the basilical hall at Mshattā to the twelve lobed medallions on the facade of the gate tower at al-Mafjar.[262] Then, I have noticed that the pilaster capitals at the front of the basilical hall are almost identical in composition and detail with the big pier capitals of Walīd's pool pavilion in the Ghawr.[263] Again, the double vine scroll carved on the arch of the triple apse at Mshattā is very similar to linked vine ornaments on certain balustrade posts at al-Mafjar.[264]

On a more general view one may see in the supremely lavish façade sculpture of Mshattā, unprotected and exposed to the desert, on the face of a building retaining the conventional outline of a defended castle, a defiant paradox analogous on a more extravagant scale to the arcaded façade of the palace in the Ghawr, and eloquent perhaps of the same eccentric personality.

Appendix II: The Chronology of Walīd's Statue

The sequence of bath and music room built first, to be followed later by palace, mosque and pool pavilion, is deduced from the presence of ash in the bath furnaces and lime incrustation in pipes, proving the bath to have been finished and used for some years; while roof tiles stacked and balustrade panels lying half carved in a workroom showed that the palace was still unfinished. The siting of the mosque and pavilion implies that the palace was there before them.

The passage of time is further suggested by stylistic differences detectable between figure sculptures in the two buildings. The distinction most easily observed lies in their rendering of the human or animal eye. **Fig.29** illustrates this with just two examples out of many. The head on the right is from the *bahw* of the music room, that on the left from the entrance hall of the palace. It can be seen that the eyelids of the head on the left project abruptly from the cheeks and brow ridges, while those on the right are rendered with smooth, natural contours. Exactly the same difference distinguishes the other human and animal statuary in the palace from that in the porch and *bahw* of the

262. Creswell (1969), 585, fig.639; cf. Hamilton (1959), pl.ci.

263. Schulz & Strzygowski (1904), 254, fig.35; cf. Hamilton (1959), 125, fig.65.

264. Creswell (1969), pl.116, c; cf. Hamilton (1959), 274, fig.229.

Figure 29. Plaster heads from the palace and bath, showing different techniques.

music room. We can be sure that the sculptors working in the palace were operating at a later date than those in the music room.

A surprise, therefore, confronts us on the façade of the music room porch, where the most important statue of all, standing majestically on heraldic lions above the entrance portal, declares itself through its eyes to belong unequivocally to the palace group (**Fig.30**). It follows that while the interior of the porch was completed and furnished with the statues of girls and athletes, the royal figure destined for the façade was postponed and its niche left empty. When it came to be filled it was the new group of sculptors, working in the palace, who made the figure.

All this can readily be linked with events in the political field. During Hishām's lifetime, Walīd, having before his final rupture with the Caliph completed construction and equipment of his bath and music room, diplomatically refrained from flaunting his own image on the front of the building. Hishām's he would not have wanted. Work in the meantime continued on the other buildings until, at some moment toward the end of Hishām's life, Walīd's stipend was cancelled. All building work on the site

Figure 30. Statue of Walīd.

will then surely have been stopped. So will it have been at any other of Walīd's "places", including Mshattā, if that was one of them and if that, unlike Ṭuba, had been started before Hishām's death.

Walīd could continue to frequent his bath, with such of his friends as he had not been compelled to dismiss. But to finish the buildings he must wait for Hishām to die. I believe, from the presentiment of death in Hishām's letter, that the time was not long. But fresh workmen were engaged to complete the internal decoration of the palace entrance and, on the front of the music room, to model the effigy of their master and his attendant lions and other beasts.

Postscript

Throughout this book I have taken the attribution of our buildings in the Ghawr to Walīd ibn Yazīd as sufficiently authenticated by archaeological and documentary evidence previously described. Now I have been kindly allowed to read the first draft of a yet unpublished note by Mr Robert Schick quoting a Syriac chronicler of the 13th century, who records that Sulaymān ibn 'Abd al-Malik (Caliph 96-99/715-17) built constructions on a stream near Jericho where were "arches, gardens and mills", all of which perished in the great earthquake. While accepting a date for the palace in the reign of Hishām, Mr Schick's suggestion is that the bath at al-Mafjar might be one of Sulaymān's constructions as described by the chronicler.

Mr Schick rightly observes that if his suggestion "holds up", my interpretation of the bath, the stone chain and the mosaic pictogram "may have to be re-examined". So also will Iṣfahānī's mention of Walīd's wine bath, scented pool and music room, so curiously foreshadowed by features present at al-Mafjar. Interpreters of the ruins may be reluctant to discount this coincidence of literary and archaeological evidence. Further, if they note that the bath had a private entrance linked by a covered passage and stairs to domestic quarters in the palace,[265] they will probably infer that whoever owned the bath looked forward, while building it, to one day living in the palace. But Sulaymān died some seven years before Hishām became Caliph, and if it was he who built the bath it is difficult to explain the link between the two buildings if, as we know, the palace was only begun under Hishām.

265. Hamilton (1959), 3, pl.cix.

Appendix III: Arabic Text of Quoted Poems

Extract **1**. is to be found on page 7.

إِنِّى أُعِيذُكُمُ بِٱللهِ مِنْ فِتَنٍ   مِثْلِ ٱلجِبَالِ تَسَامَى ثُمَّ تَنْدَفِعُ
إِنَّ ٱلبَرِيَّةَ قَدْ مَلَّتْ سِيَاسَتَكُمُ   فَٱسْتَمْسِكُوا بِعَمُودِ ٱلدِّينِ وَٱرْتَدِعُوا
لَا تُلْحِمُنَّ ذِئَابَ ٱلنَّاسِ أَنْفُسَكُمْ   إِنَّ ٱلذِّئَابَ إِذَا مَا أُلْحِمَتْ رَتَعُوا
لَا تَبْقُرُنَّ بِأَيْدِيكُمْ بُطُونَكُمُ   فَثَمَّ لَا حَسْرَةٌ تُغْنِى وَلَا جَزَعُ

2. Ṭabarī (1966), ii, 1788.

وَلَقَدْ قَضَيْتُ وَإِنْ تَجَلَّلَ لِمَّتِى   شَيْبٌ عَلَى رَغْمِ ٱلْعِدَى لَذَّاتِى
مِنْ كَاعِبَاتٍ كَٱلدُّمَى وَنَوَاصِفَ   وَمَرَاكِبَ لِلصَّيْدِ وَٱلنَّشَوَاتِ
فِى فِتْيَةٍ تَأْبَى ٱلهَوَانَ وُجُوهُهُمْ   شُمِّ ٱلأُنُوفِ جَحَاجِحَ سَادَاتِ
إِنْ يَطْلُبُوا بِتِرَاتِهِم يُعْطَوا بِهَا   أَوْ يُطْلَبُوا لَا يُدْرَكُوا بِتِرَاتِ

3. Iṣfahānī (1905), vi, 103–04.

لَا عَيْشَ إِلَّا بِمَالِكِ بْنِ أَبِى ٱلـ   سَّمْحِ فَلَا تَلْحُنِى وَلَا تَلُمْ
أَبْيَضُ كَٱلبَدْرِ أَوْ كَمَا يَلْمَعُ ٱلـ   بَارِقُ فِى حَالِكٍ مِنَ ٱلظُّلَمْ

4. Iṣfahānī (1905), iv, 170–71.

أَحْوَلُ كَٱلقِرْدِ أَوْ كَمَا يَرْقُبُ ٱلـ   سَّارِقُ فِى حَالِكٍ مِنَ ٱلظُّلَمْ

5. Walid's parody.

حَيَّ ٱلحُمُولَ بِجَانِبِ ٱلعُزْلِ   إِذْ لَا يُلَائِمُ شَكْلُهَا شَكْلِى
ٱللهُ أَنْجَحَ مَا طَلَبْتَ بِهِ   وَٱلبِرُّ خَيْرُ حَقِيبَةِ ٱلرَّحْلِ
إِنِّى بِحَبْلِكَ وَاصِلٌ حَبْلِى   وَبِرِيشِ نَبْلِكَ رَائِشٌ نَبْلِى
وَشَمَائِلِى مَا قَدْ عَلِمْتَ وَمَا   نَبَحَتْ كِلَابُكَ طَارِقاً مِثْلِى

6. Iṣfahānī (1905), iii, 94.

أَيَذْهَبُ عُمْرِى هٰكَذَا لَمْ أَنَلْ بِهَا   مَجَالِسَ تَشْفِى قَرْحَ قَلْبِى
وَقَالُوا تَدَاوَى إِنَّ فِى ٱلطِّبِّ رَاحَةً   فَعَلَّلْتُ نَفْسِى بِٱلدَّوَاءِ فَلَمْ يَجِدِ

7. Iṣfahānī (1905), iii, 96.

القَصْرُ فَٱلنَّخْلُ فَٱلجَمَّاءُ بَيْنَهُمَا   أَشْهَى إِلَى ٱلنَّفْسِ مِنْ أَبْوَابِ جَيْرُون

8. Iṣfahānī (1905), i, 21.

لَهْفِي عَلَى فِتْيَةٍ ذَلَّ الزَّمَانُ لَهُم   فَمَا أَصَابَهُمُ إِلَّا بِمَا شَاءُوا
مَا زَالَ يَعْدُو عَلَيْهِم رَيْبُ دَهْرِهِم   حَتَّى تَفَانُوا وَرَيْبُ الدَّهْرِ عَدَّاءُ
أَبْكَى فِرَاقُهُمُ عَيْنِي وَأَرَّقَها   إِنَّ التَّفَرُّقَ لِلأَحْبَابِ بِكَآءُ

9. Iṣfahānī (1905), i, 25.

يَا رَبْعُ مَا لَكَ لا تُجِيبُ مُتَيَّماً   قَدْ عَاجَ نَحْوَكَ زَائِراً وَمُسَلِّماً
جَادَتْكَ كُلُّ سَحَابَةٍ هَطَّالَةٍ   حَتَّى تُرَى عَنْ زَهْرَةٍ مُتَبَسِّماً
لَوْ كُنْتَ تَدْرِي مَن دَعَاكَ أَجَبْتَهُ   وَبَكَيْتَ مِنْ حَرْقٍ عَلَيهِ إِذاً دَماً

10. Iṣfahānī (1905), i, 25.

عَجِبَتْ لَمَّا رَأَتْنِي   أَنْدُبُ ٱلرَّبْعَ ٱلمَحِيلَا
وَاقِفاً فِي ٱلدَّارِ أَبْكِي   لَا أَرَى إِلَّا ٱلطُّلُولَا
كَيْفَ تَبْكِي لِأَناسٍ   لَا يَمَلُّونَ ٱلذَّمِيلَا
كُلَّمَا قُلْتُ ٱطْمَأَنَّتْ   دَارُهُمْ قَالُوا ٱلرَّحِيلَا

11. Iṣfahānī (1905), i, 25–26.

إِنَّنِي فَكَّرْتُ فِي عُمَرٍ   حِينَ قَالَ ٱلقَوْلَ فَٱخْتَلَجا
إِنَّهُ لِلمُسْتَنِيرِ بِهِ   قَمَرٌ قَدْ طَمَسَ ٱلسُّرُجَا
وَيُغَنِّي الشِّعْرَ يَنْظِمُهُ   سَيِّدُ ٱلقَوْمِ الَّذِي فَلَجَا
أَكْمَلَ ٱلوَادِيُّ صَنْعَتَهُ   فِي لُبَابِ ٱلشِّعْرِ فَٱنْدَمَجَا

12. Iṣfahānī (1905), vi, 137.

أَلَا يُسْلِيكَ عَنْ سَلْمَى   قَتِيرُ ٱلشَّيْبِ وَٱلْحِلْمُ
وَأَنَّ ٱلشَّكَّ مُلْتَبِسٌ   فَلَا وَصْلٌ وَلَا صَرْمُ
فَلَا وَٱللهِ رَبِّ ٱلنَّا   سِ مَا لَكِ عِنْدَنَا ظُلْمُ
وَكَيْفَ بِظُلْمِ جَارِيَةٍ   وَمِنْهَا ٱللِّينُ وَٱلرُّحْمُ

13. Iṣfahānī (1905), vi, 139.

مَا أَحْسَنَ ٱلجِيدَ مِنْ مُلَيِكَةَ وَٱلْـ ... لَّبَاتِ إِذْ زَانَهَا تَرَائِبُهَا
يَا لَيْتَنِى لَيْلَةً إِذَا هَجَعَ ٱلـ ... نّاسُ وَنَامَ ٱلكِلَابُ صَاحِبُها
فِى لَيْلَةٍ لَا يُرَى بِهَا أَحَدٌ ... يَسْعَى عَلَيْنَا إِلَّا كَوَاكِبُهَا

14. Iṣfahānī (1905), xiii, 148.

لَقَد فَتَّنَت رَيَّا وَسَلَّامَةُ ٱلقَسَّا ... فَلَمْ تَتْرُكَا لِلْقَسِّ عَقْلاً وَلَا نَفْسَا
فَتَاتَانِ أَمَّا مِنْهُمَا فَشَبِيهَةُ ٱلـ ... هِلَالِ وأُخْرَى مِنْهُمَا تُشْبِهُ ٱلشَّمْسَا
تَكُنَّانِ أَبْشَاراً رِقَاقاً وَأَوْجُهاً ... عِتَاقاً وَأَطْرَافاً مُخَضَّبَةً مُلْسَا

15. Iṣfahānī (1905), viii, 7.

فَارَقُونِى وَقَدْ عَلِمْتُ يَقِيناً ... مَا لِمَنْ ذَاقَ مِيتَةً مِنْ إِيَابِ
إِنَّ أَهْلَ الحِصَابِ قَدْ تَرَكُونِى ... مُولَعاً مُوزَعاً بأَهْلِ الحِصَابِ
أَهْلُ بَيْتٍ تَتَابَعُوا لِلمَنَايَا ... مَا عَلَى ٱلدَّهْرِ بَعْدَهُمْ مِنْ عِتَابِ
سَكَنُوا الجِزْعَ جِزْعَ بَيْتِ أَبِى مُو- ... سَى إِلَى ٱلنَّخْلِ مِن صُفِىِّ السِبَابِ
كَمْ بِذَاكَ ٱلحُجُونِ مِنْ حَىِّ صِدْقٍ ... وَكُهُولَ أَعِفَّةَ وَشَبَابَ

16. Iṣfahānī (1905), viii, 10.

لِى لَيْلَتَانِ فلَيْلَةٌ مَسْعُولَةٌ ... أَلْقَى ٱلحَبِيبَ بِهَا بِنَجْمِ الأَسْعُدِ
وَمُرِيحَةٌ هَمِّى عَلَىَّ كَأَنَّنِى ... حَتَّى ٱلصُّبَاحِ مُعَلَّقٌ بِٱلفَرْقَدِ

17. Iṣfahānī (1905), iv, 53.

مَا مِن مُصِيبَةِ نكْبَةٍ أُمْنَى بِهَا ... إِلَّا تُعَظِّمُنِى وَتَرْفَعُ شَأْنِى
إِنِّى إِذَا خَفِىَ ٱللِّئَامُ رَأَيْتَنِى ... كَٱلشَّمْسِ لَا تَخْفَى بِكُلِّ مَكَانِ

18. Iṣfahānī (1905), iv, 44.

كَرِيمُ قُرَيْشٍ حِينَ يُنْسَبُ وَٱلَّذِى ... أَقَرَّتْ لَهُ بِٱلمُلْكِ كَهْلاً وَأَمْرَدَا
وَلَيْسَ وَإِنْ أَعْطَاكَ فِى ٱليَوْمِ مَانِعاً ... إِذَا عُدْتَ إِضْعَافَ إِعْطَائِهِ غَدَا
أَهَانَ تِلَادَ ٱلمَالِ فِى ٱلحَمْدِ أَنَّهُ ... إِمَامُ هُدىً يَجْرِى عَلَى مَا تَعَوَّدَا
تَشَرَّفَ مَجْداً مِنْ أَبِيهِ وَجَدِّهِ ... وَقَدْ أُورِثَا بُنْيَانَ مَجْدٍ تَشَيَّدَا

19. Iṣfahānī (1905), iv, 49–50.

أَلَا لَا تَلُمْهُ ٱلْيَوْمَ أَنْ يَتَبَلَّدَا   فَقَدْ غُلِبَ ٱلْمَحْزُونُ أَنْ يَتَجَلَّدَا
بَكَيْتُ ٱلصِّبا جَهْدِى فَمَنْ شَاءَ لَامَنى   وَمَن شَاءَ آسَى فى ٱلْبُكاءِ وَأَسْعَدَا
وَإِنّى وَإِن فُنِّدتُ فى الطَّلْبِ الغِنَى   لَأَعْلِمُ أَنّى لَسْتُ فى ٱلْحُبِّ أَوْحَدَا
إِذَا أَنْتَ لَمْ تَعْشِقْ وَلَمْ تَدْرِ مَا ٱلْهَوَى   فَكُنْ حَجَراً مِنْ يَابِسِ ٱلصَّخْرِ جَلْمَدَا
فَمَا ٱلعَيْشُ إِلّا مَا تَلَذُّ وَتَشْتَهِى   وَإِنْ لَامَ فِيهِ ذُو ٱلشَّنَانِ وَفَنَّدَا

20. Iṣfahānī (1905), xiii, 151.

كَفَى حَزَناً لِلهَائِمِ ٱلصَّبِّ أَنْ يَرَى   مَنَازِلَ مَن يَهْوَى مُعَطَّلَةً قُفْرَى

21. Iṣfahānī (1905), xiii, 158.

إِذَا ٱسْتَبَقَ ٱلنّاسُ ٱلعُلَا سَبَقَتْهُمْ   يَمِينُكَ عَفْواً ثُمَّ صَلَّتْ شِمَالُهَا

22. Iṣfahānī (1905), i, 131.

أَعَتَبْتَ أَمْ عَتَبَتْ عَلَيْكَ صَدُوفُ   وَعِتَابُ مِثْلِكَ مِثْلَهَا تشرِيفُ
لَا تَقْعُدَنَّ تَلُومُ نَفْسَكَ دَائِباً   فِيهَا وَأَنْتَ تَحُبُّهَا مَشْغُوفُ
إِنَّ الصَّرِيْمَةَ لَا يَقُومُ بِثَقْلِهَا   إِلَّا ٱلقَوِىُّ بِهَا وَأَنتَ ضَعِيْفُ
الحُبُّ أَمْلَكُ بِٱلفَتى مِنْ نفْسِهِ   وَٱلذُّلُّ فِيهِ مَسْلَكٌ مَأْلُوفُ

23. Iṣfahānī (1905), xv, 177; vi, 119.

أَيُّهَا ٱلشَّامِتُ ٱلمُعَيِّرُ بِٱلدَّهْـ   ـرِ أَأَنْتَ ٱلمُبَرَّأُ ٱلمَوْفُورُ
أَمْ لَدَيكَ العَهْدُ الوَثِيقُ مِنَ ٱلأَ   يامِ بَلْ أَنتَ جَاهِلٌ مَغْرُورُ
مَنْ رَأَيتَ ٱلمَنُونَ خَلَّدْنَ أم مَنْ   ذَا عَلَيْهِ مِنْ أَن يُضَامَ خَفِيرُ
أَيْنَ كِسْرَى كِسْرَى ٱلمُلُوكِ أَنُوشِرْ   وَانُ أَمْ أَينَ قَبْلَهُ سَابُورُ
وَبَنُو ٱلأَصْفَرُ الكِرَامُ مُلُوكُ ٱلرُّ   ومِ لَمْ يَبْقِ مِنْهُمُ مَذْكُورُ
وَأَخُو ٱلحَضْرِ إِذْ بَنَاهُ وَإِذْ دِجْـ   ـلَةُ تُجْبَى إِلَيْهِ وَٱلخَابُورُ
شَادَهُ مَرْمَراً وَجَلَّلَهُ كِلْـ   ـساً فَلِلطَّيْرِ فى ذُرَاه وُكُورُ
لَمْ يَهَبْهُ رَيْبُ ٱلمَنُونِ فَبَادَ ٱلْـ   ـمُلْكُ عَنْهُ فَبَابُهُ مَهْجُورُ
وَتَذَكَّرْ رَبَّ ٱلخَوَرْنَقِ إِذْ أَشْـ   ـرَفَ يَوْماً وَلِلهُدَى تَفكيرُ
سَرَّهُ مَالُهُ وَكَثْرَةُ مَا يَمْـ   ـلِكُ وَٱلبَحْرُ مُعرِضاً وَٱلسَّدِيرُ
فَٱرْعَوَى قَلْبُهُ فَقَالَ وَمَا غِبْـ   ـطَةُ حَيٍّ إِلَى ٱلمَمَاتِ يَصِيرُ
ثَمَّ بَعْدَ ٱلفَلَاحِ وَٱلمُلْكِ وَٱلإِمَّـ   ـةِ وَارَتْهُمُ هُنَاكَ ٱلقُبُورُ
ثُمَّ صَارُوا كَأَنَّهُمْ وَرَقٌ جَفَّ   فَأَلْوَتْ بِهِ ٱلصَّبَا وَٱلدَّبُورُ

24. Iṣfahānī (1905), ii, 34.

أَلَا سُقِيَ ٱلخَوَرْنَقُ مِنْ مَحَلٍّ   ظَرِيفِ ٱلرَّوْضَ مَعْشُوقٍ أَنِيقِ
أَقَمْتُ بِدَيْرِ حَنَّتِهِ زَمَاناً   بِسُكْرٍ فِي ٱلصَّبُوحِ وفِي ٱلغُبُوقِ
وَمِنَّا لَابِسٌ إِكْلِيلَ زَهْرٍ   وَمُخْتَضِبٌ ٱلسَّوَالِفَ بِٱلخَلُوقِ
كَأَنَّ رِيَاضَهُ حُسْناً وَنَوْراً   سَحَائِبُ ذُهِّبَتْ بِسَنَا ٱلبُرُوقِ
كَأَنَّ تَقَاطُرَ ٱلأَشْجَارِ فِيهِ   إِذَا غَسَقَ ٱلظَّلَامُ قِطَارُ نُوقِ
وَمَاذَا شِئْتَ مِنْ دُرِّ ٱلأَقَاحِي   هُنَاكَ وَمِنْ يَوَاقِيتِ ٱلشَّقِيقِ

25. ʿUmarī (1924), i, 313.

فَدَيْتُ مَن مَرَّ بِنَا مُسْرِعاً   يَسْعَى إِلَى ٱلدَّيْرِ بِأَسْفَارِهِ
خَدَمْتُ رَبَّ الدَّيرِ مِنْ أَجْلِهِ   حَتَّى كَأَنِّى بَعْضُ أَحْبَارِهِ
حَذَّرَنِى ٱلنَّارَ وَلَمْ يَدْرِ مَا   فِى ٱلقَلْبِ وَٱلأَحْشَاءِ مِنْ نَارِهِ
حَيَّرَنِى تَفْتِيرُ أَجْفَانِهِ   وَحَلَّ عَقْدِى عَقْدُ زُنَّارِهِ

26. ʿUmarī (1924), i, 321.

وَبِٱلحِيرَةِ لِى يَومٌ   وَيَوْمُ بِٱلأُكَيْرَاحِ
إِذَا عَزَّ بِنَا ٱلمَاءُ   مَزَجْنا ٱلرَّاحَ بِالرَّاحِ

27. ʿUmarī (1924), i, 321.

يَا لُبَيْنَى أَوْقِدِى ٱلنَّارَا   إِنَّ مَن تَهْوَيْن قَدْ جَارَ
رُبَّ نَارٍ بِتُّ أَرْمُقُهَا   تَقْضَمُ ٱلهِنْدِيَّ وٱلغَارَا
عِنْدَهَا ظَبْىٌ يُؤَجِّجُها   عَاقِدٌ فِى ٱلخَصْرِ زُنَّارَا

28. ʿUmarī (1924), i, 350.

حَبَّذَا لَيلَتِى بِدَيْرِ بَوَانَّا   حَيْثُ نُسْقَى شَرَابَنَا وَنُغَنَّى
كَيْفَ مَا دَارَتِ ٱلزُّجَاجَةُ دُرْنَا   يَحْسِبُ ٱلجَاهِلُونَ أَنَّا جُنِنَّا
وَمَرَرْنَا بِنِسْوَةٍ عَطِرَاتٍ   وَغِنَاءٍ وَقَهْوَةٍ فَنَزَلْنَا
وَجَعَلْنَا خَلِيفَةَ ٱللهِ فُطْرُو   سَ مُجُوناً وَٱلمُسْتَشَارَا يُحَنَّا
فَأَخَذْنَا قُرْبَانَهُم ثُمَّ كَفَّرْ   نَا لِصُلْبَانِ دَيْرِهِم فَكَفَرْنَا
وَٱشْتَهَرْنا لِلنَّاسِ حَيثُ يَقُو   لُونَ إِذَا خُبِّرُوا بِمَا قَد فَعَلْنا

29. Yāqūt (1866-73), ii, 649.

يَا أَيّها ٱلسَّائِلُ عَن دِينِنَا   نَحْنُ عَلَى دِينِ أَبِى شَاكِرِ

نَشْرُبُهَا صِرْفاً وَمَمْزُوجَةً   بِالسُّخْنِ أَحْيَاناً وَبِالْفَاتِرِ

30. Ṭabarī (1966), ii, 1742.

إِنَّ كَأْسَ ٱلْعَجُوزِ كَأْسُ رَوَاءٍ   لَيْسَ كَأْسُ كَكَأْسِ أُمِّ حَكِيمِ

إِنَّهَا تَشْرَبُ ٱلرَّسَاطُونَ صِرْفاً   فِى إِنَاءٍ مِنَ ٱلزُّجَاجِ عَظِيمِ

لَوْ بِهِ يَشْرَبُ ٱلْبَعِيرُ أَوِ ٱلْفِي   لُ لَظَلَّا فِى سُكْرَةٍ وَغُمُومِ

وَلَدَتْهُ سُكْرَى فَلَمْ تُحْسِنِ ٱلطَّلْ   قَ فَوَافَى لِذَاكَ غَيْرَ حَكِيمِ

31. Iṣfahānī (1905), xv, 48.

عَلِّلَانِى بِعَاتِقَاتِ ٱلْكُرُومِ   وَٱسْقِيَانِى بِكَأْسِ أُمِّ حَكِيمِ

إِنَّهَا تَشْرَبُ ٱلْمَدَامَةَ صِرْفاً   فِى إِنَاءٍ مِنَ ٱلزُّجَاجِ عَظِيمِ

جَنِّبُونِى أَذَاةَ كُلِّ لَئِيمٍ   إِنَّهُ مَا عَلِمْتُ شَرُّ نَدِيمِ

ثُمَّ إِنْ كَانَ فِى ٱلنَّدَامَى كَرِيمٌ   فَأَذِيقُوهُ بَعْضَ مَسِّ ٱلنَّعِيمِ

لَيْتَ حَظِّى مِنَ ٱلنِّسَاءِ سُلَيْمَى   إِنَّ سَلْمَى جُنَيْنَتِى وَنَعِيمِى

فَدَعُونِى مِنَ ٱلْمَلَامَةِ فِيهَا   إِنَّ مَنْ لَامَنِى لَغَيْرُ رَحِيمِ

32. Iṣfahānī (1905), xv, 48.

عَرَفْتُ دِيَارَ ٱلْحَيِّ خَالِيَةً قَفْراً   كَأَنَّ بِهَا لَمَّا تَوَهَّمْتُهَا سَطْراً

وَقَفْتُ بِهَا كَيْمَا تَرُدُّ جَوَابَهَا   فَمَا بَيَّنَتْ لِىَ ٱلدَّارُ عَنْ أَهْلِهَا خَبْراً

33. Iṣfahānī (1905), iii, 113.

أَنَا ٱبْنُ أَبِى ٱلْعَاصِى وَعُثْمَانُ وَالِدِى   وَمَرْوَانُ جَدِّى ذُو ٱلْفِعَالِ وَعَامِرِ

أَنَا ٱبْنُ عَظِيمِ ٱلْقَرْيَتَيْنِ وَعَزِّهَا   ثَقِيفُ وَفِهْرِ وَٱلْعُصَاةِ ٱلْأَكَابِرِ

نَبِىُّ ٱلْهُدَى خَالِى وَمَنْ يَكُ خَالُهُ   نَبِىُّ ٱلْهُدَى يَقْهَرْ بِهِ مَنْ يُفَاخِرِ

34. Iṣfahānī (1905), vi, 100.

أَنَا ٱلْوَلِيدُ أَبُو ٱلْعَبَّاسِ قَدْ عَلِمَتْ   عُلْيَا مَعَدِّ مَدَى كَرِّى وَإِقْدَامِى

إِنِّى لَفِى ذُرْوَةِ ٱلْعُلْيَا إِذَا ٱنْتَسَبُوا   مُقَابَلٌ بَيْنَ أَخْوَالِى وَأَعْمَامِى

بَنَى لِى ٱلْمَجْدَ بَانٍ لَمْ يَكُنْ وَكَلَّا   عَلَى مَنَارٍ مُضِيَاتٍ وَأَعْلَامِ

حَلَلْتُ مِنْ جَوْهَرِ ٱلْأَعْيَاصِ قَدْ عَلِمُوا   فِى بَاذِخٍ مُشْمَخِرِّ ٱلْعِزِّ قَمْقَامِ

صَعْبِ ٱلْمَرَامِ يُسَامِى ٱلنَّجْمَ مَطْلَعُهُ   يَسْمُو إِلَى فَرْعِ طَوْدٍ شَامِخٍ سَامِى

35. Iṣfahānī (1905), vi, 103.

أَتَانا بَرِيدَانِ مِنْ وَاسِطٍ   يَخُبَّانِ بِٱلْكُتُبِ ٱلْمُعْجَمَه
أَقُولُ وَمَا ٱلْبُعْدُ إِلَّا ٱلرَّدَى   أَمَسْلَمَ لا تَبْعُدَنْ مَسْلَمَه
فَقَدْ كُنْتَ نُوراً لَنَا فِى ٱلْبِلَادِ   تُضِىءُ فَقَدْ أَصْبَحَتْ مُظْلِمَه
كَتَمْنا لِنَعْيِكَ نَخْشَى ٱلْيَقِينَ   فَجَلَّى ٱلْيَقِينُ عَنِ الجَمْجَمَه
وَكَمْ مِنْ يَتِيمٍ تَلَافَيْتَهُ   بِأَرْضِ ٱلْعَدُوِّ وَكَمْ أَيِّمَه
وَكُنْتَ إِذَا ٱلْحَرْبُ دَرَّتْ دَماً   نَصَبْتَ لَهَا رَأْيَةً مُعْلَمَه

36. Iṣfahānī (1905), vi, 101.

أَهَيْنَمَةُ حَدِيثُ القَوْمِ أَمْ هُمْ   سُكُوتٌ بَعْدَ مَا مَتَعَ ٱلنَّهَارُ
عَزِيْزٌ كَانَ بَيْنَهُمُ نَبِيّاً   فَقَوْلُ ٱلْقَوْمِ وَحْىٌ لَا يَحَارُ
كَأَنَّا بَعْدَ مَسْلَمَةَ ٱلْمُرَجَّى   شُرُوبٌ طَوَّحَتْ بِهِمُ عُقَارُ
أَوُ ٱلْآفٌ هِجَانٌ فِى قُيُودٍ   تَلَفَّتَ كُلَّمَا حَنَّتْ ظُؤَارُ
فَلَيْتَكَ لَمْ تَمُتْ وَفَدَاكَ قَوْمٌ   تُرِيحُ غَبِيَّهُم عَنْهَا ٱلدِّيارُ
سَقِيمُ ٱلصَّدْرِ أَوْ شَكِسٌ نَكِيدٌ   وَآخَرُ لَا يَزُورُ وَلَا يُزَارُ

37. Iṣfahānī (1905), vi, 101.

أَلَمْ تَرَ لِلنّجْمِ إِذْ سَبَّعَا   يُبَادِرُ فِى بُرْجِهِ ٱلْمَرْجِعَا
تَحَيَّرَ عَنْ قَصْدِ مَجْرَاتِهِ   إِلَى ٱلْغَوْرِ وَٱلْتَمَسَ ٱلْمَطْلَعَا
فَقُلْتُ وَأَعْجَبَنِى شَأْنُهُ   وَقَدْ لَاحَ إِذْ لَاحَ لِى مُطْمِعَا
لَعَلَّ ٱلْوَلِيْدَ دَنَا مُلْكُهُ   فَأَمْسَى إِلَيْهِ قَدِ ٱسْتُجْمَعَا
وَكُنَّا نُؤَمِّلُ فِى مُلْكِهِ   كَتَأْمِيلِ ذِى ٱلْجُدْبِ أَن يُمْرِعَا
عَقَدْنَا لَهُ مُحْكَمَاتِ ٱلْأُمُو   رِ طَوْعاً فَكَانَ لَهَا مَوْضِعَا

38. Iṣfahānī (1905), vi, 102.

أَنَا ٱلنَّذِيْرُ لِمُسْدِى نِعْمَةٍ أَبَداً   إِلَى ٱلْمَقَارِيفِ مَا لَمْ يَخْبُرِ ٱلدَّخَلَا
إِنْ أَنْتَ أَكْرَمْتَهُمْ أَلْفَيْتَهُمْ بُطُراً   وَإِنْ أَهَنْتَهُمُ أَلْفَيْتَهُمْ ذُلُلَا
أَتَشْمَخُونَ وَمِنّا رَأْسُ نِعْمَتِكُمْ   سَتَعْلَمُونَ إِذَا كَانَتْ لَنَا دُوَلَا
أُنْظُرْ فَإِن كُنْتَ لَمْ تَقْدِرْ عَلَى مَثَلٍ   لَهُ سِوَى ٱلْكَلْبِ فَٱضْرِبْهُ لَهُ مَثَلَا
بَيْنَا يُسَمِّنُهُ لِلصَّيْدِ صَاحِبُهُ   حَتَّى إِذَا مَا نَوَى مِنْ بَعْدِ مَا هُزِلَا
عَدَا عَلَيْهِ فَلَمْ تَضْرُرْهُ عَدْوَتُهُ   وَلَوْ أَطَاقَ لَهُ أَكْلاً لَقَدْ أَكَلَا

39. Iṣfahānī (1905), vi, 102.

أَلَيْسَ عَظِيماً أَنْ أَرَى كُلَّ وَارِدٍ   حِيَاضَكَ يَوْماً صَادِراً بِٱلنَّوَافِلِ
فَأَرْجِعَ مَحْمُودَ ٱلرَّجَاءِ مُصَرَّداً   بِتَخْلِيَةٍ عَنْ وِرْدِ تِلْكَ ٱلْمَنَاهِلِ
فَأَصْبَحْتُ مِمَّا كُنْتُ آمُلُ مِنْكُمُ   وَلَيْسَ بِلَاقٍ مَا رَجَا كُلُّ آمِلِ
كَمُقْتَبِضٍ يَوْماً عَلَى عَرْضِ هَبْوَةٍ   يَشُدُّ عَلَيْهَا كَفَّهُ بِٱلْأَنَامِلِ

40. Iṣfahānī (1905), vi, 104.

رَأَيْتُكَ تَبْنِى جَاهِداً فِى قَطِيعَتِى   فَلَوْ كُنْتَ ذَا إِرْبٍ لَهَدَّمْتَ مَا تَبْنِى
تُثِيرُ عَلَى ٱلبَاقِينَ مَجْنَى ضَغِينَةٍ   فَوَيْلٌ لَهُمْ إِنْ مِتَّ مِنْ شَرِّ مَا تَجْنِى
كَأَنِّى بِهِمْ وَٱللَّيْتَ أَفْضَلُ قَوْلِهِم   أَلَا لَيْتَنَا وَٱللَّيْتَ إِذْ ذَاكَ لَا يُغْنِى
كَفَرْتَ يَداً مِنْ مُنْعِمٍ لَوْ شَكَرْتَهَا   جَزَاكَ بِهَا ٱلرَّحْمَانُ ذُو ٱلفَضْلِ وَٱلمِنِّ

41. Iṣfahānī (1905), vi, 101; Ṭabarī (1966), ii, 1749–50.

فَبِيْنِى وَإِنِّى لَا أُبَالِى وَأَيْقِنِى   أَصَعَّدَ بَاقِى حُبِّكُمْ أَمْ تَصَوَّبَا
أَلَمْ تَعْلَمِى أَنِّى غَرُوفٌ عَنِ ٱلْهَوَى   إِذَا صَاحِبِى مِنْ غَيْرِ شَىْءٍ تَغَضَّبَا

42. Iṣfahānī (1905), iii, 113–14.

إِنَّنِى أَبْصَرْتُ شَيْخاً   حَسَنَ الوَجْهِ مَلِيحْ
وَلِبَاسِى ثَوْبُ شَيْخ   مِنْ عِبَاءٍ وَمُسُوحْ
وَأَبِيعُ ٱلزَّيْتَ بَيْعاً   خَاسِراً غَيْرَ رَبِيحْ

43. Iṣfahānī (1905), vi, 111; Balādhurī (1974), xvii,
(variant for line 2): لَابِساً   أَثوابَ   سُوءٍ

فَمَا مِسْكٌ يُعَلُّ بِزَنْجَبِيلٍ   وَلَا عَسَلٌ بِأَلْبَانِ ٱللِّقَاحِ
بِأَشْهَى مِنْ مُجَاجَةِ رِيقِ سَلْمَى   وَلَا مَا فِى ٱلزِّقَاقِ مِنَ ٱلقَرَاحِ
وَلَا وَٱللهِ لَا أَنْسَى حَيَاتِى   وِثَاقَ ٱلبَابِ دُونِى وَٱطِّرَاحِى

44. Iṣfahānī (1905), vi, 111.

أَبَا عُثْمَانَ هَلْ لَكَ فِى صَنِيعٍ   تُصِيبُ ٱلرُّشْدَ فِى صِلَتِى هُدِيتَا
فَأَشْكُرُ مِنْكَ مَا تُسْدِى وَتُحْيِى   أَبَا عُثْمَانَ مَيِّتَةً وَمَيْتَا

45. Iṣfahānī (1905), vi, 112.

عَتَبَتْ سَلْمَى عَلَيْنَا سَفَاهاً   أَنْ سَبَبْتُ ٱليَوْمَ فِيهَا أَبَاهَا
كَانَ حَقُّ ٱلعَتْبِ يا قَوْمُ مِنّى   لَيْسَ مِنْهَا كَانَ قَلْبِى فِدَاهَا
فَلَئِنْ كُنْتُ أَرَدتُّ بِقَلْبِى   لِأَبِى سَلْمَى خِلَافَ هَوَاهَا
فَثَكِلْتُ ٱليَوْمَ سَلْمَى فَسَلْمَى   مَلَأَتْ أَرْضِى مَعاً وَسَمَاهَا
غَيْرَ أَنّى لَأَظُنُّ عَدُوًّا   قَدْ أَتَاهَا كَاشِحاً وَأَذَاهَا
فَلَهَا ٱلعُتْبَى لَدَيْنَا وَقَلَّتْ   أَبَداً حَتَّى أَنالَ رِضَاهَا

46. Iṣfahānī (1905), vi, 114.

أَسَعْدَةُ هَلْ إِلَيكِ لَنَا سَبِيلٌ   وَهَلْ حَتَّى ٱلقِيَامَةِ مِنْ تَلَاقِ
بَلَى وَلَعَلَّ دَهْراً أَنْ يُؤَاتِى   بِمَوْتٍ مِنْ حَلِيلِكِ أَوْ طَلَاقِ
فَأُصْبِحَ شَامِتاً وَتَقِرَّ عَينِى   وَيُجْمَعَ شَمْلُنَا بَعْدَ ٱفْتِرَاقِ

47. Iṣfahānī (1905), vi, 110.

أَتَبْكِى عَلَى لُبْنَى وَأَنْتَ تَرَكْتَهَا   فَقَدْ ذَهَبَتْ لُبْنَى فَمَا أَنْتَ صَانِعُ

48. Iṣfahānī (1905), vi, 111.

لَعَلَّ ٱللّٰهَ يَجْمَعُنى بِسَلْمى   أَلَيْسَ ٱللّٰهُ يَفْعَلُ مَا يَشَاءُ
فَيُخْرِجُهَا فَيَطْرَحُهَا بِأَرْضٍ   وَيُرْقِدُهَا وَقَدْ سَقَطَ ٱلرِّدَاءُ
وَيَأْتِى بِى وَيَطْرُحُنى عَلَيهَا   فَيُوقِظُنى وَقَد قُضِىَ ٱلقَضَاءُ
وَيُرْسِلُ دَيْمَةً مِنْ بَعْدِ هَذَا   فَتَغْسِلُنَا وَلَيْسَ بِنَا غَنَاءُ

49. Ibn ʿAbd Rabbihī (1876), ii, 342.

بَكَّرَ ٱلعَاذِلُونَ فِى وَضَحِ ٱلصُّبْـ　　حِ يَقُولُونَ لِى أَلَا تَسْتَفِيقُ
وَيَلُومُونَ فِيكِ يَا ٱبْنَةَ عَبْدِ ٱللّٰـ　　هِ وَٱلقَلْبُ عِنْدَكُمْ مَوْهُوقُ
لَسْتُ أَدْرِى إِذَا كَثَرُوا ٱلعَذْلَ عِنْدِى　　أَعَدُوٌّ يَلُومُنِى أَوْ صَدِيقُ
زَانَهَا حُسْنُهَا وَفَرْعٌ عَمِيمٌ　　وَأَثِيثٌ صَلْتُ ٱلجَبِينِ أَنِيقُ
وَثَنَايَا مُفَلَّجَاتٌ عِذَابٌ　　لَا قِصَارٌ تُرَى وَلَا هُنَّ رُوقُ
فَدَعُوا بِٱلصُّبُوحِ يَوْماً فَجَاءَتْ　　قَيْنَةٌ فِى يَمِينِهَا إِبْرِيقُ
قَدَّمَتْهُ عَلَى عُقَارٍ كَعَيْنِ ٱلدِّ　　يكِ صَفَّى سُلَافَهَا ٱلرَّاوُوقُ
مَرَّةً قَبْلُ مَزْجِهَا فَإِذَا مَا　　مُزِجَتْ لَذَّ طَعْمَهَا مَنْ يَذُوقُ
وَطَفَتْ فَوْقَهَا فَقَاقِيعُ كَٱلدُّرِّ　　صِغَارِ يُثِيرُهَا ٱلتَّصْفِيقُ
ثُمَّ كَانَ ٱلمِزَاجُ مَاءَ سَمَاءٍ　　غَيْرَ مَا آجِنٍ وَلَا مَطْرُوقُ

50. Iṣfahānī (1905), v, 158.
(p.165 variant on line 7): قَدَّمَتْهُ عَلَى سُلَافٍ كَرِيحِ ٱلمِسْكِ

شَمَّاءُ وَاضِحَةُ ٱلعَوَارِضِ طَفْلَةٌ　　كَٱلبَدْرِ مِنْ خَلَلِ ٱلسَّحَابِ ٱلمُنْجَلِى
وَكَأَنَّمَا رِيحُ ٱلقَرَنْفُلِ نَشْرُهَا　　أَوْ حَنْوَةٌ خُلِطَتْ خُزَامَى حَوْمَلِ
وَكَأَنَّ فَاهَا بَعْدَ مَا طَرَقَ ٱلكَرَى　　كَأْسٌ تُصُفِّقَ بِٱلرَّحِيقِ ٱلسَّلْسَلِ
لَوْ أَنَّهَا عَرَضَتْ لِأَشْمَطَ رَاهِبٍ　　فِى رَأْسِ مُشْرِفَةِ ٱلذُّرَا مُتَبَتِّلِ
جَأْرِ سَاعَاتِ ٱلنِّيَامِ لِرَبِّهِ　　حَتَّى تَخَدَّدَ لَحْمُهُ مُتَبَهِّلِ
لَصَبَا لِبَهْجَتِهَا وحُسْنِ حَدِيثِهَا　　وَلَهَمَّ مِنْ نَامُوسِهِ بِتَنَزُّلِ

51. Iṣfahānī (1905), xix, 92.

عَهِدَتْنِى نَاشِئًا ذَا غِرَّةٍ　　رَجِلَ ٱلجُمَّةِ ذَا بَطْنٍ أَقَبّْ
أَتْبَعُ ٱلوِلْدَانَ أُرْخِى مِئْزَرِى　　إِبْنُ عَشْرٍ ذَا قَرِيطٍ مِنْ ذَهَبْ
وَهِىَ إِذْ ذَاكَ عَلَيْهَا مِئْزَرٌ　　وَلَهَا بَيْتُ جَوَارٍ مِنْ لُعَبْ

52. Iṣfahānī (1905), ii, 64.

جَرَتْ سُنُحاً فَقُلْتُ لَهَا أَجِيزِى　　نَوًى مَشْمُولَةً فَمَتَى ٱللِّقَاءُ
بِنَفْسِى مِنْ تَذَكُّرِهِ سَقَامٌ　　أُعَانِيهِ وَمَطْلَبُهُ عَنَاءُ

53. Iṣfahānī (1905), ii, 62.

أَلَا لِلّٰهِ دَرُّكَ مِنْ فَتَى قَوْمٍ إِذَا رَهِبُوا
وَقَالُوا مَنْ فَتًى لِلْحَرْ بِ يَرْقُبُنا وَيَرْتَقِبُ
فَكُنْتَ فَتَاهُمُ فِيهَا إِذَا تُدْعَى لَهَا تَثِبُ
ذَكَرْتُ أَخِي فَعَاوَدَنِى رُدَاعُ ٱلسُّقْمِ وَٱلوَصَفُ
كَمَا يَعْتَادُ ذَاتَ ٱلبَوِّ بَعْدَ سُلُوِّهَا ٱلطَّرَبُ
عَلَى عَبْدِ بْنِ زُهْرَةِ بِـ تُّ طُولَ ٱللَّيْلِ أَنْتَحِبُ

54. Iṣfahānī (1905), ii, 61.

قُلْ لِلمَنَازِلِ بِٱلظَّهْرَانِ قَدْ حَانَا أَن تَنْطَقِى فَتُبَيِّنِى ٱلقَوْلَ تَبْيَانَا
قَالَتْ وَمَن أَنتَ قُلْ لِى قُلْتُ ذُو شَغَفٍ هِجْتِ لَهُ مِنْ دَوَاعِى ٱلحُبِّ أَحْزَانَا

55. Iṣfahānī (1905), ii, 70.

أَبَعْدَكَ مَعْقِلاً أَرْجُو وَحِصْناً قَدْ أَعْيَتْنِى ٱلمَعَاقِلُ وَٱلحُصُونُ

56. Iṣfahānī (1905), ii, 70.

سَقَى بَلَداً أَمْسَتْ سُلَيْمَى تَحُلُّهُ مِنَ ٱلمُزْنِ مَا يُرْوَى بِهِ وَيُسِيمُ
وَإِنْ لَمْ أَكُنْ مِنْ قَاطِنِيهِ فَإِنَّهُ يَحُلُّ بِهِ شَخْصٌ عَلَيَّ كَرِيمُ
أَلَا حَبَّذَا مَنْ لَيْسَ يَعْدِلُ قُرْبُهُ لَدَيَّ وَإِنْ شَطَّ ٱلمَزَارُ نَعِيمُ
وَمَنْ لَامَنِى فِيهِ حَمِيمٌ وَصَاحِبٌ فَرُدَّ بِغَيْظٍ صَاحِبٌ وَحَمِيمُ

57. Iṣfahānī (1905), ii, 73.

إِذَا ٱلصَّبُّ ٱلغَرِيبُ رَأَى خُشُوعِى وَأَنْفَاسِى تَزَيَّنَ بِالخُشُوعِ
وَلِى عَيْنٌ أَضَرَّ بِهَا ٱلتِفَاتِى إِلَى الأَجْزَاعِ مُطْلَقَةَ ٱلدُّمُوعِ
إِلَى ٱلخَلَوَاتِ يَأْنَسُ فِيْكِ قَلْبِى كَمَا أَنِسَ ٱلغَرِيبُ إِلَى ٱلجَمِيعِ

58. Iṣfahānī (1905), ii, 73.

إِنِّى رَأَيْتُ صَبِيحَةَ ٱلنَّحْرِ حُوْراً نَفَيْنَ عَزِيمَاةَ ٱلصَّبْرِ
مِثْلَ ٱلكَوَاكِبِ فِى مَطَالِعِهَا بَعْدَ ٱلعَشَاءِ أَطَفْنَ بِالبَدْرِ
وَخَرَجْتُ أَبْغِى ٱلأُجْرَ مُحْتَسِباً فَرَجَعْتُ مَوْفُوراً مِنَ ٱلوِزْرِ

59. Mas'ūdī (1830), ii, 187; Iṣfahānī (1905), ii, 70.

عَلِّلَانِى وَٱسْقِيَانِى مِنَ شَرَابٍ إِصْبَجَانِى
مِنْ شَرَابِ ٱلشَّيخِ كِسْرَى أَوْ شَرَابِ ٱلقَيْرَوَانِى
إِنَّ فِى ٱلكَأْسِ لَمِسْكًا أَوْ بِكَفَّىْ مَنْ سَقَانِى
أَوْ لَقَدْ غُودِرَ فِيهَا حِينَ صُبَّتْ فِى ٱلدِّنَانِ
كَلِّلَانِى تَوِّجَانِى وَبِشِعْرِى غَنِّيَانِى
أَطْلِقَانِى بِوَثَاقِى وَٱشْدُدَانِى بِعِنَانِى
إِنَّمَا ٱلكَأْسُ رَبِيعٌ يُتَعَاطَى بِٱلبَنَانِ
وَحُمَيَّا ٱلكَأْسِ دَبَّتْ بَيْنَ رِجْلِى وَلِسَانِى

60. Iṣfahānī (1905), viii, 84.

أَنْتَ ٱبْنُ مُسْلَنْطِحِ ٱلبِطَاحِ وَلَمْ تُطْرِقْ عَلَيْكَ ٱلحُنِىُّ وَٱلوُلُجُ
طُوبَى لِفَرْعَيْكَ مِنْ هُنَا وَهُنَا طُوبَى لِأَعْرَاقِكَ ٱلَّتِى تَشِجُ
لَوْ قُلْتَ لِلسَّيْلِ دَعْ طَرِيقَكَ وَالـ مَوْجُ عَلَيْهِ كَٱلهِضْبِ يَعْتَلِجُ
لَسَاحَ وَٱرْتَدَّ أَوْ لَكَانَ لَهُ فِى سَائِرِ ٱلأَرْضِ عَنْكَ مُنْعَرَجُ

61. Iṣfahānī (1905), iv, 80.

وَقَدْ قَالَتْ لِأَتْرَابٍ لَهَا زَهْرٌ تَلَاقِينَا
تَعَالَيْنَ فَقَدْ طَابَ لَنَا ٱلعَيْشُ تَعَالَيْنَا

62. Iṣfahānī (1905), ii, 75.

سَقَيْتُ أَبَا كَامِلٍ مِنَ ٱلأَصْفَرِ ٱلبَابِلِى
وَسَقَيْتُهَا مَعْبَداً وَكُلَّ فَتًى بَازِلِ
لِىَ ٱلمَحْضُ مِنْ وُدِّهِمْ وَيَغْمُرُهُمْ نَائِلِى
فَمَا لَامَنِى فِيهِمُ سِوَى حَاسِدٍ جَاهِلِ

63. Iṣfahānī (1905), vi, 140.

أَدِرِ ٱلكَأْسَ يَمِيناً لَا تُدِرْهَا لِيَسَارِ
إِسْقِ هٰذَا ثُمَّ هٰذَا صَاحِبَ ٱلعُودِ ٱلنُّضَارِ
مِنْ كُمَيْتٍ عَتَّقُوهَا مُنْذُ دَهْرٍ فِي جِرَارِ
خَتَّمُوهَا بِٱلْأَفَاوِيـ ـهِ وَكَافُورٍ وَقَارِ
فَلَقَدْ أَيْقَنْتُ أَنِّي غَيْرُ مَبْعُوثٍ لِنَارِ
سَأَرُوضُ ٱلنَّاسَ حَتَّى يَرْكَبُوا أَيْرَ ٱلحِمَارِ
وَذَرُوا مَنْ يَطْلُبُ ٱلْجَنَّةَ يَسْعَى لِتَبَارِ

64. Iṣfahānī (1905), vi, 119–20.

إِكْلِيلُهَا أَلْوَانٌ وَوَجْهُهَا فَتَّانُ
وَخَالُهَا فَرِيدٌ لَيْسَ لَهَا جِيْرَانُ
إِذَا مَشَتْ تَثَنَّتْ كَأَنَّهَا ثُعْبَانُ
قَدْ جَدَلَتْ فَجَاءَتْ كَأَنَّهَا عِنَانُ

65. Iṣfahānī (1905), xii, 77.

أَبُو يَحْيَى أَخُو ٱلغَزْلِ ٱلْمُغَنِّي بَصِيرٌ بِٱلثِّقَالِ وَبِٱلخِفَافِ
عَلَى ٱلعِيْدَانِ يُحْسِنُ مَا يُغَنِّي وَيُحْسِنُ مَا يَقُولُ عَلَى ٱلدِّفَافِ

66. Iṣfahānī (1905), vi, 62.

أَتُوْعِدُ كُلَّ جَبَّارٍ عَنِيْدٍ فَهَا أَنَا ذَاكَ جَبَّارٌ عَنِيدُ
إِذَا لَاقَيْتَ رَبَّكَ يَوْمَ حَشْرٍ فَقُلْ لِلّٰهِ مَزَّقَنِي ٱلوَلِيدُ

67. Iṣfahānī (1905), vi, 121.

اِسْقِنِي يَا يَزِيدَ بِٱلقَرْقَارَةِ قَدْ طَرِبْنَا وَحَنَّتِ ٱلزَّمَّارَه
اِسْقِنِي اِسْقِنِي فَإِنَّ ذُنُوبِي قَدْ أَحَاطَتْ فَمَا لَهَا كَفَّارَه

68. Mas'ūdī (1830), ii, 186.

لَوْ رَدَّ ذُو شَفَقٍ حِمَامَ مَنِيَّةٍ لَرَدَدْتُ عَنْ عَبْدِ ٱلعَزِيزِ حِمَامَا
صَلَّى عَلَيكَ ٱللّٰهُ مِنْ مُسْتَوْدَعٍ جَاوَرْتَ بُوماً فِي ٱلقُبُوْرِ وَهَامَا

69. Iṣfahānī (1905), v, 135.

أَلَمْ تَرَ أَنِّى بَيْنَ مَا أَنَا آمِنٌ   يَخُبُّ بِيَ ٱلسِّنْدِىُّ قَفْراً فَيَافِيَا
تَطَلَّعْتُ مِنْ غَوْرٍ فَأَبْصَرْتُ فَارِساً   فَأَوْجَسْتُ مِنْهُ خِيفَةً أَنْ يَرَانِيَا
وَلَمَّا بَدَا لِى أَنَّمَا هُوَ فَارِسٌ   وَقَفْتُ لَهُ حَتَّى أَتَى فَرَمَانِيَا
رَمَانِى ثَلَاثاً ثُمَّ إِنِّى طَعَنْتُهُ   فَرَوَّيْتُ مِنْهُ صَعْدَتِى وَسِنَانِيَا

70. Iṣfahānī (1905), vi, 128.

نَحْنُ سَبَقْنَا خَيْلَ ٱللُّوَمَه   وَصَرَّفَ ٱللّٰهُ إِلَيْنَا ٱلْمَكْرُمَه
كَذَاكَ كُنَّا فِى ٱلدُّهُورِ ٱلْمُقْدَمَه   أَهْلُ ٱلْعُلَا وَٱلرُّتَبِ ٱلْمُعْظَمَه

71. Mas‘ūdī (1830), ii, 188.

قُلْ لِوَالِى ٱلْعَهْدِ إِنْ لَاقَيْتُهُ   وَوَلِىُّ ٱلْعَهْدِ أَوْلَى بِٱلرَّشَدْ
إِنَّهُ وَٱللّٰهِ لَوْ لَا أَنْتَ لَمْ   يَنْجُ مِنِّى سَالِماً عَبْدُ ٱلصَّمَدْ
إِنَّهُ قَدْ رَامَ مِنِّى خُطَّةً   لَمْ يَرُمْهَا قَبْلَهُ مِنِّى أَحَدْ
فَهْوَ مِمَّا رَامَ مِنِّى كَٱلَّذِى   يَقْنِصُ ٱلدُّرَّاجَ مِنْ خِيسِ ٱلْأَسَدْ

72. Iṣfahānī (1905), iv, 120.

أَتَانِى سِنَانٌ بِٱلْوَدَاعِ لِمُؤْمِنٍ   فَقُلْتُ لَهُ إِنِّى إِلَى ٱللّٰهِ رَاجِعُ
أَلَا أَيُّهَا ٱلْحَاثِى عَلَيْهِ تُرَابَهُ   هَبِلْتَ وَشُلَّتْ مِنْ يَدَيْكَ ٱلْأَصَابِعُ
يَقُولُونَ لَا تَجْزَعْ وَأَظْهِرْ جَلَادَةً   فَكَيْفَ بِمَا يَحْنِى عَلَيْهِ ٱلْأَضَالِعُ

73. Iṣfahānī (1905), vi, 130.

عَيْنَىَّ لِلْحَدَثِ ٱلْجَلِيلِ   جُودَا بِأَرْبَعَةٍ هُمُولِ
جُودَا بِدَمْعِى إِنَّهُ   يَشْفِى ٱلْفُؤَادَ مِنَ ٱلْغَلِيلِ
لِلّٰهِ قَبْرٌ ضُمِّنَتْ   فِيهِ عِظَامُ ٱبْنِ ٱلطَّوِيلِ
مَا ذَا تَضَمَّنَ إِذْ ثَوَى   فِيهِ مِنَ ٱللُّبِّ ٱلْأَصِيلِ
قَدْ كُنْتُ آوِى مِنْ هَوَا   كَ إِلَى ذَرَى كَهْفٍ ظَلِيلِ
أَصْبَحْتُ بَعْدَكَ وَاحِداً   فَرْداً بِمَدْرَجَةِ ٱلسُّيُولِ

74. Iṣfahānī (1905), vi, 129.

قَدْ لَعَمْرِى بِتُّ لَيلى   كَأَخِى ٱلدَّاءِ ٱلوَجِيعِ
وَنجِىُّ ٱلهَمِّ مِنّى   بَاتَ أَدْنَى مِن ضَجِيعِى
كُلَّمَا أَبْصَرْتُ رَبْعاً   خَالِياً فَاضَتْ دُمُوعِى
قَدْ خَلَا مِنْ سَيِّدٍ كَا   نَ لَنَا غَيْرَ مُضِيعِ
لَا تَلُمْنَا إِنْ خَشَعْنا   أَوْ هَمَمْنَا بِخُشُوعِ

75. Iṣfahānī (1905), i, 18.

طَابَ يَوْمِى وَلَذَّ شُرْبُ ٱلسُّلَافَه   إِذْ أَتَانَا نَعِىُّ مَنْ بِٱلرُّصَافه
وَأَتَانَا ٱلبَرِيدُ يَنْعَى هِشَاماً   وَأَتَانَا بِخَاتِمٍ لِلْخِلَافَه
فَٱصْطَبَحْنَا بِخَمْرِ عَانَةَ صِرْفاً   وَلَهَوْنَا بِقَيْنَةٍ عَزَّافَه

76. Iṣfahānī (1905), vi, 105.

لَيْتَ هِشَاماً عَاشَ حَتَّى يَرَى   مِكْيَالَهُ ٱلأَوْفَرَ قَدْ طُبِّعَا
كِلْنَاهُ بِٱلصَّاعِ ٱلَّذِى كَالَهُ   وَمَا ظَلَمْنَاهُ بِهِ إِصْبَعَا
وَمَا أَتَيْنَا ذَاكَ عَنْ بِدْعَةٍ   أَحَلَّهُ ٱلفُرْقَانُ لِى أَجْمَعَا

77. Iṣfahānī (1905), vi, 106.

إِنِّى سَمِعْتُ بِلَيْلٍ   نَحْوَ ٱلرُّصَافَةِ رَنَّه
أَقْبَلْتُ أَسْحَبُ ذَيلى   أَقُولُ مَا شَأْنُهُنَّهُ
إِذَا بَنَاتُ هِشَامٍ   يَنْدُبْنَ وَالِدَهُنَّه
يَنْدُبْنَ قَرْماً جَلِيلاً   قَدْ كَانَ يَعْضُدُهُنَّه
يَقُلْنَ وَيْلى وَعَوْلِى   وَٱلوَيلُ حَلَّ بِهِنَّه
أَنَا ٱلمُخَنَّثُ حَقّاً   إِنْ لَمْ أُنَيِّكْهُنَّه

78. Iṣfahānī (1905), vi, 106.

قَدْ رَاحَ نَحْوَ ٱلعِرَاقِ مَشْخَلَبَه   قُصَارُهُ ٱلسِّجْنُ بَعْدَهُ ٱلخَشَبَه
يَرْكَبُهَا صَاغِراً بِلَا قَتَبٍ   وَلَا خِطَامٍ وَحَوْلَهُ جَلَبَه
فَقُلْ لِدَعْجَاءَ إِنْ مَرَرْتَ بِهَا   لَنْ يُعْجِزَ ٱللهَ هَارِبٌ طَلَبَه
قَدْ جَعَلَ ٱللهُ بَعْدَ غَلْبَتِكُمْ   لَنَا عَلَيْكُمْ يَا دُلْدُلُ ٱلغَلَبَه
لَسْتَ إِلَى هَاشِمٍ وَلَا أَسَدٍ   وَلَا إِلَى نَوْفَلٍ وَلَا ٱلحَجَبَه
لَكِنَّمَا أَشْجَعُ أَبُوكَ سَلِ ٱلـ   كَلْبِى لَا مَا يُزَوِّقُ الكَذَبَه

79. Iṣfahānī (1905), i, 160.

فَأَبشِرْ يَا أَمِينَ ٱللّـٰ ـهِ أَبْشِرْ بِتَبَاشِيرْ
بِإِبْلٍ يُحْمَلُ ٱلمَالُ عَلَيْهَا كَٱلأَنَابِيرْ
بِغَالٌ تَحْمَلُ ٱلخَمْرَ حَقَائِبُهَا طَنَابِيرْ
وَدَلُّ ٱلبَرْبَرِيَّاتِ بِصَوْتِ ٱلبَمِّ وَٱلزِّيرْ
وَقَرْعُ ٱلدُفِّ أَحْيَاناً وَنَفْخٌ بِٱلمَزَامِيرْ
فَهَذَا لَكَ فِى ٱلدُّنْيَا وَفِى ٱلجَنَّةِ تَحْبِيرْ

80. Ṭabarī (1966), ii, 1765.

خَفَّ مِنْ دَارِ جِيرَتِى يَا ٱبْنَ دَاوُودَ أُنْسُهَا
أَوَلَا تَخْرُجُ ٱلعَرُو سُ فَقَدْ طَالَ حَبْسُهَا
قدْ دَنَا ٱلصُّبْحُ أَوْ بَدَا وَهْىَ لَمْ تَقْضِ لُبْسَهَا
بَرَزَتْ كَٱلْهِلَالِ فِى لَيْلَةٍ غَابَ نَحْسُهَا
بَيْنَ خَمْسٍ كَوَاعِبَ أَكْرَمُ ٱلخَمْسِ جِنْسُهَا

81. Iṣfahānī (1905), vi, 112.

يَا سَلْمَ كُنْتِ كَجَنَّةٍ قَدْ أُطْعِمَتْ أَفْنَانُهَا دَانٍ جَنَاهَا مُوْضِعُ
أَرْبَابُهَا شَفَقاً عَلَيْهَا نَوْمُهُمْ تَحْلِيلُ مَوْضِعِهَا وَلَمَّا يَهْجَعُوا
حَتَّى إِذَا فَسَخَ ٱلرَّبِيعُ ظُنُونَهُمْ نَشَرَ ٱلخَرِيفُ ثِمَارَهَا فَتَصَدَّعُوا

82. Iṣfahānī (1905), vi, 128.

أَلَمَّا تَعْلَمَا سَلْمَى أَقَامَتْ مُضَمَّنَةً مِنَ ٱلصَّحْرَاءِ لَحْدَا
لَعَمْرُكَ يَا وَلِيدُ لَقَدْ أَجَنُّوا بِهَا حَسَباً وَمَكْرَمَةً وَمَجْدَا
وَوَجْهاً كَانَ يُقْصِرُ عَنْ مَدَاهُ شُعَاعُ ٱلشَّمْسِ أَهْلٌ أَن يُفَدَّى
فَلَمْ أَرَ مَيّتاً أَبْكَى لِعَيْنٍ وَأَكْثَرَ جَازِعاً وَأَجَلَّ فَقْدَا
وَأَجْدَرَ أَن تَكُونَ لَدَيْهِ مِلْكاً يُرِيكَ جَلَادَةً وَيُسِرُّ وَجْدَا

83. Iṣfahānī (1905), vi, 113.

أُشْهِدُ ٱللهَ وَٱلمَلَائِكَةَ ٱلأَبْـ رَارَ وَٱلعَابِدِينَ أَهْلَ ٱلصَّلَاحِ
أَنَّنِى أَشْتَهِى ٱلسَّمَاعَ وَشُرْبَ ٱلـ كَأْسِ وَٱلعَضَّ لِلْخُدُودِ ٱلمِلَاحِ
وَٱلنَّدِيمَ ٱلكَرِيمَ وَٱلخَادِمَ ٱلفَا رِهَ يَسْعَى عَلَىَّ بِٱلأَقْدَاحِ
وَظَرِيفَ الحَدِيثَ وَالكَاعِبَ ٱلطُّفْـ لَةَ تَحْتَالُ فِى سُمُوطِ ٱلوِشَاحِ

84. Iṣfahānī (1905), vi, 108; Nawajī (1859), 79.

وَهَذَا خَالِدٌ فِينَا أَسِيراً   أَلَا مَنَعُوهُ إِن كَانُوا رِجَالَا
عَظِيمُهُمُ وسَيِّدُهُمْ قَدِيماً   جَعَلْنَا ٱلمُخْزِيَاتِ لَهُ ظِلَالَا
فلَوْ كَانَتْ قَبَائِلَ ذَاتَ عِزٍّ   لَمَا ذَهَبَتْ صَنَائِعُهُ ضَلَالَا
وَلَا تَرَكُوهُ مَسْلُوباً أَسِيراً   يُسَامِرُ مِنْ سَلَاسِلِنَا ٱلثِّقَالا

85. Ṭabarī (1966), ii, 1781.

إِذَا لَمْ يَكُنْ خَيْرٌ مَعَ ٱلشَّرِّ لَمْ تَجِدْ   نَصِيحاً وَلَا ذَا حَاجَةٍ حِيْنَ تَفْزَعُ
إِذَا مَا هُمُ هَمُّوا بِإِحْدَى هَنَاتِهِم   حَسَرْتُ لَهُم رَأْسِى فَلَا أَتَقَنَّعُ

86. Ṭabarī (1966), ii, 1796.

إِصْدَعْ نَجِيَّ ٱلهُمُومِ بِٱلطَّرَبِ   وَٱنْعَمْ عَلَى ٱلدَّهْرِ بِٱبْنَةِ ٱلعِنَبِ
وَٱسْتَقْبِلِ ٱلعَيْشَ فِى غَضَارَتِهِ   لَا تَقْفُ مِنْهُ آثَارَ مُعْتَقَبِ
مِنْ قَهْوَةٍ زَانَهَا تَقَادُمُهَا   فَهْىَ عَجُوزٌ تَعْلُو عَلَى ٱلحِقَبِ
أَشْهَى إِلَى ٱلشُّرْبِ يَوْمَ جَلْوَتِهَا   مِنَ ٱلفَتَاةِ ٱلكَرِيمَةِ ٱلنَّسَبِ
فَقَدْ تَجَلَّتْ وَرَقَّ جَوْهَرُهَا   حَتَّى تَبَدَّتْ فِى مَنْظَرٍ عَجَبِ
فَهْىَ بِغَيْرِ ٱلمَزَاجِ مِنْ شَرَرٍ   وَهْىَ لَدَى ٱلمَزْجِ سَائِلُ ٱلذَّهَبِ
كَأَنَّهَا فِى زُجَاجِهَا قَبَسٌ   تَذْكُو ضِيَاءً فِى عَيْنِ مُرْتَقِبِ
فِى فِتْيَةٍ مِنْ بَنِى أُمَيَّةَ أَهْـ   ـلِ ٱلمَجْدِ وَٱلمَأْثُرَتِ وَٱلحَسَبِ
مَا فِى ٱلوَرَى مِثْلُهُمْ وَلَا بِهِم   مِثْلِى وَلَا مُنْتَمٍ بِمِثْلِ أَبِى

87. Iṣfahānī (1905), vi, 106.

وَصَفْرَاءَ فِى ٱلكَأْسِ كَٱلزَّعْفَرَانِ   سَبَاهَا لَنَا ٱلتَّجْرُ مِنْ عَسْقَلَانِ
تُرِيكَ ٱلقَذَاةَ وَعَرْضُ ٱلإِنَا   ءِ سِتْرٌ لَهَا دُونَ لَمْسِ ٱلبَنَانِ
لَهَا حَبَبٌ كُلَّمَا صُفِّقَتْ   تَرَاهَا كَلَمْعَةِ بَرْقٍ يَمَانِ

88. Mas'ūdī (1830), ii, 186.

وَزِقٍّ وَافِرِ ٱلجَنْبَيْـ   ـنِ مِثْلِ ٱلجَمَلِ البَازِلْ
بِهِ رُحْتُ إِلَى صَحْبِى   وَنَدْمَانِى أَبِى كَامِلْ
شَرِبْنَاهُ وَقَدْ بِتْنَا   بِأَعْلَى ٱلدَّيْرِ بِٱلسَّاحِلْ
وَلَمْ نَقْبَلْ مِنَ ٱلوَاشِى   قُبُولَ ٱلجَاهِلِ ٱلخَاطِلْ

89. Iṣfahānī (1905), vi, 140.

قَامَتْ إِلَيَّ بِتَقْبِيلٍ تَعَانِقُنِى   رَيَّا ٱلعِظَامِ كَأَنَّ ٱلمِسْكَ فِى فِيهَا
أُدْخُلْ فَدَيْتُكَ لَا يَشْعُرْ بِنَا أَحَدٌ   نَفْسِى لِنَفْسِكَ مِنْ دَاءٍ تُفَدِّيهَا
بِتْنَا كَذٰلِكَ لَا نَوْمٌ عَلَى سُرُرٍ   مِنْ شِدَّةِ ٱلوَجْدِ تُدْنِينِى وَأُدْنِيهَا
حَتَّى إِذَا مَا بَدَا ٱلخَيْطَانِ قُلْتُ لَهَا   حَانَ ٱلفِرَاقُ فَكَادَ ٱلحُزْنُ يُشْجِيهَا
ثُمَّ ٱنْصَرَفْتُ وَلَمْ يَشْعُرْ بِنَا أَحَدٌ   وَٱللّٰهُ عَنِّى بِحُسْنِ ٱلفِعْلِ يَجْزِيهَا

90. Iṣfahānī (1905), vi, 120.

أَضْحَى فُؤَادُكَ يَا وَلِيدُ عَمِيدَا   بَرَزَتْ لَنَا نَحْوَ ٱلكَنِيسَةِ غِيدَا
لا زِلْتُ أُومِقُهَا بِعَيْنَىْ وَامِقٍ   حَتَى بَصُرْتُ بِهَا تُقَبِّلُ عُودَا
عُودَ ٱلصَّلِيبِ فَوَيْحَ نَفْسِى مَنْ رَأَى   مِنْكُم صَلِيباً مِثْلَهُ مَعْبُوداً
فَسَأَلْتُ رَبِّى أَن أَكُونَ مَكَانَهُ   وَأَكُونَ فِى لَهَبِ ٱلجَحِيمِ وَقُودَا

91. Gabrieli (1934), xxxii.

تَذَكَّرَ شَجْوَهُ ٱلقَلْبُ ٱلقَرِيحُ   فَدَمْعُ ٱلعَيْنِ مُنْهَلٌّ سَفُوحُ
أَلَا طَرَقَتْكَ بِٱللِّقَاءِ سَلْمَى   هُدُوءًا وَٱلمَطِىُّ بنا جَنُوحُ
فَبِتُّ بِهَا قَرِيرَ ٱلعَيْنِ حَتَّى   تَكَلَّمَ نَاطِقُ ٱلصُّبْحِ ٱلفَصِيحُ

92. Gabrieli (1934), xxvi.

لَا أَسْأَلُ ٱللهَ تَغْيِيراً لِمَا صَنَعَتْ   نَامَتْ وَإِنْ أَسْهَرَتْ عَيْنَىَّ عَيْنَاهَا
فَٱللَّيْلُ أَطْوَلُ شَىْءٍ حِينَ أَفْقِدُهَا   وَٱللَّيْلُ أَقْصَرُ شَىْءٍ حِينَ أَلْقَاهَا

93. Gabrieli (1934), iv, (Ibrāhīm b. ʿAlī al-Ḥuṣrī, iii, 46.)

طَافَ مِنْ سَلْمَى خَيَالٌ   بَعْدَمَا نِمْتُ وَهَاجَا
قُلْتُ عُجْ نَحْوِى أُسَائِلْـ   ـكَ عَنِ ٱلحُبِّ فَعَاجَا
يَا خَلِيلِى يَا نَدِيمِى   قُمْ فَأَنْفِثْ لِى سِرَاجَا
بِفَلَاةٍ لَيْسَ تُرْعَى   أَنْبَتَتْ شِيحاً وَحَاجَا

94. Iṣfahānī (1905), vi, 118.

طَرَقَتْنِى وَصِحَابِى هُجُوعٌ   ظَبْيَةٌ أَدْمَاءُ مِثْلَ ٱلْهِلَالِ
مِثْلَ قَرْنِ ٱلشَّمْسِ لَمَّا تَبَدَّتْ   وَٱسْتَقَلَّتْ فِى رُؤُوسِ ٱلْجِبَالِ
تَقْطَعُ ٱلأَهْوَالَ نَحْوِى وَكَانَتْ   عِنْدَنَا سَلْمَى أَلُوفَ ٱلْحِجَالِ
كَمْ أَجَازَتْ نَحْوَنَا مِنْ بِلَادٍ   وَحْشَةٍ قَتَّالَةٍ لِلرِّجَالِ

95. Iṣfahānī (1905), vi, 118.

إِسْقِنِى يَا ٱبْنَ سَالِمٍ قَدْ أَنَارَا   كَوْكَبُ ٱلصُّبْحِ وَٱنْجَلَى وَٱسْتَنَارَا
إِسْقِنِى مِنْ سُلَافِ رِيقِ سُلَيْمَى   وَٱسْقِ هٰذَا ٱلنَّدِيمَ كَأْساً عُقَارَا

96. Iṣfahānī (1905), vi, 115.

وَيْحَ سَلْمَى لَوْ تَرَانِى   لَعَنَاهَا مَا عَنَانِى
مُتْلِقاً فِى ٱللَّهْوِ مَالِى   عَاشِقاً حُورَ ٱلْقِيَانِ
إِنَّمَا أَحْزَنَ قَلْبِى   قَوْلُ سَلْمَى إِذْ أَتَانِى
وَلَقَدْ كُنْتُ زَمَاناً   خَالِيَ ٱلذَّرْعِ لِشَانِى
شَاقَ قَلْبِى وَعَنَانِى   حُبُّ سَلْمَى وَبَرَانِى
وَلَكَمْ لَامَ نَصِيحٌ   فِى سُلَيْمَى وَنَهَانِى

97. Iṣfahānī (1905), vi, 116.

أَرَانِى قَدْ تَصَابَيْتُ   وَقَدْ كُنْتُ تَنَاهَيْتُ
وَ لَوْ يَتْرُكُنِى ٱلْحُبُّ   لَقَدْ صُمْتُ وَصَلَّيْتُ
إِذَا شِئْتِ تَصَبَّرْتُ   وَلَا أَصْبِرُ إِنْ شِئْتِ
وَلَا وَٱللهِ لَا يَصْبِـ   ـرُ فِى ٱلدَّيْمُومَةِ ٱلْحُوتُ
سُلَيْمَى لَيْسَ لِى صَبْرٌ   وَإِنْ رَخَّصْتِ لِى جِيتُ
فَقَبَّلْتُكِ أَلْفَيْنِ   وَفَدَّيْتُ وَحَيَّيْتُ
أَلَا أَحْبِبْ بِزَوْرٍ زَا   رَ مِنْ سَلْمَى بِبَيْرُوتُ
غَزَالٍ أَدْعَجِ ٱلْعَيْنَيْنْ   نَقِيِّ ٱلْجِيدِ وَٱللِّيتُ

98. Iṣfahānī (1905), vi, 113.

أَرَانِى ٱللهُ يَا سَلْمَى حَيَاتِى   وَفِى يَوْمِ ٱلحِسَابِ كَمَا أَرَاكِ
أَلَا تَجْزِينَ مَنْ تَيَّمْتِ عَصْراً   وَمَنْ لَوْ تَطْلُبِينَ لَقَدْ قَضَاكِ
وَمَنْ لَوْ مِتِّ مَاتَ وَلَا تَمُوتِى   وَلَوْ أُنْسِىءُ لَهُ أَجَلٌ بَكَاكِ
وَمَنْ حَقًّا لَوُ ٱعْطِىَ مَا تَمَنَّى   مِنَ ٱلدُّنْيَا ٱلعَرِيضَةِ مَا عَدَاكِ
وَمَنْ لَوْ قُلْتِ مُتْ فَأَطَاقَ مَوْتاً   إِذاً ذَاقَ ٱلمَمَاتَ وَمَا عَصَاكِ
أَثِيبِى عَاشِقاً كَلِفاً مُعَنىًّ   إِذَا خَدِرَتْ لَهُ رِجْلٌ دَعَاكِ

99. Iṣfahānī (1905), vi, 116.

لَقَدْ مَرَرْتُ بِنِسْوَةٍ أَعْشَيْنَنِى   حُورِ ٱلمَدَامِعِ مِنْ بَنِى ٱلمِنْجَابِ
فِيهِنَّ خَرْعَبَةٌ مَلِيحٌ دَلُّهَا   غَرْثَى ٱلوِشَاحِ دَقِيقَةُ ٱلأَنْيَابِ
زَيْنُ ٱلحَوَاضِرِ مَا ثَوَتْ فِى حَضْرِهَا   وَتَزِينُ بَادِيَهَا مِنَ ٱلأَعْرَابِ

100. Iṣfahānī (1905), vi, 120.

وَلَقَدْ صِدْنَا غَزَالاً سَانِحاً   قَدْ أَرَدْنَا ذَبْحَهُ لَمَّا سَنَحْ
فَإِذَا شَبْهُكِ مَا نُنْكِرُهُ   حِينَ أَزْجَى طَرْفَهُ ثُمَّ لَمَحْ
فَتَرَكْنَاهُ وَلَوْ لَا حُبُّكُمْ   فَٱعْلَمِى ذَاكَ لَقَدْ كَانَ ٱنْذَبِحْ
أَنْتَ يَا ظَبْىُ طَلِيقٌ آمِنٌ   فَٱغْدُ فِى ٱلغِزْلَانِ مَسْرُوراً وَرُحْ

101. Iṣfahānī (1905), vi, 121.

خَبَّرُونِى أَنَّ سَلْمَى   خَرَجَتْ يَوْمَ ٱلمُصَلَّى
فَإِذَا طَيْرٌ مَلِيحٌ   فَوْقَ غُصْنٍ يَتَفَلَّى
قُلْتُ مَنْ يَعْرِفُ سَلْمَى   قَالَ هَا ثُمَّ تَعَلَّى
قُلْتُ يَا طَيْرُ ٱدْنُ مِنِّى   قَالَ هَا ثُمَّ تَدَلَّى
قُلْتُ هَلْ أَبْصَرْتَ سَلْمَى   قَالَ هَا ثُمَّ تَوَلَّى
فَنَكَى فِى ٱلقَلْبِ كَلْماً   بَاطِناً ثُمَّ تَعَلَّى

102. Iṣfahānī (1905), vi, 115.

Bibliography

Avi-Yonah (1938)	Avi-Yonah, "Mosaic Pavements in Palestine", *Q.D.A.P.*, 2, 1938.
al-Balādhurī (1974)	Aḥmad ibn Yaḥyā al-Balādhurī, *Ansāb al-Ashrāf*, parts edited and transcribed by Dieter Derenk, *Leben und Dichtung des Omaiyadenkalifen al-Walīd ibn Yazīd*, (Freiburg im Bresgau, 1974), page references to the end section of that book.
Creswell (1969)	Creswell, K.A.C., *Early Muslim Architecture*, Oxford, 1969.
Ettinghausen (1972)	Ettinghausen, R., *From Byzantium to Sasanian Iran and the Islamic World*, Leiden, 1972, pp.28-34.
Gabrieli (1934)	Gabrieli, Francesco , "al-Walīd ibn Yazīd. Il califfo e il poeta", *Rivista degli Studi Orientali*, 15, fasc. i, 1934, pp.1-64.
Grabar (1973)	Grabar, Oleg, *The Formation of Islamic Art*, Yale, 1973.
Hamilton (1946)	Hamilton, Robert, "Khirbat al Mafjar. Stone Sculpture", *Quarterly of the Department of Antiquities in Palestine*, 12, 1946, pp.12-13.
Hamilton (1959)	Hamilton, Robert, *Khirbat al Mafjar, an Arabian Mansion in the Jordan Valley*, Oxford, Clarendon Press, 1959.
Hamilton (1969)	Hamilton, Robert, "Who built Khirbat al Mafjar?", *Levant*, 1, 1969, pp.61-67.
Hamilton (1978)	Hamilton, Robert, "Khirbat al-Mafjar: The Bath Hall reconsidered", *Levant*, 10, 1978, pp.126-38.
Ibn 'Abd Rabbihī (1876)	Aḥmad ibn Muḥammad ibn 'Abd Rabbihī, *al-'Iqd al-Farīd*, Bulaq, 1876.
al-Iṣfahānī (1905)	Abū'l-Faraj al-Iṣfahānī, *Kitāb al-Aghānī*, Cairo, 1905, 21 vols. (Checked at points against the edition by Ibrāhīm al-Abyarī, Dār al-Sha'b, Cairo, 1969).
Lammens (1930)	Lammens, H., *Études sur le siècle des Omayyades*, Beyrouth, 1930.
al-Mas'ūdī (1830)	Abū'l-Ḥasan 'Alī ibn al-Ḥusayn al-Mas'ūdī, *Murūj al-Dhahab wa Ma'ādin al-Jawhar fī'l-Ta'rīkh*, Cairo, 1246/1830, 2 vols.
Migne (1857 *et seq.*)	Migne, J.P., *Patrologia Graeca*, cxxi, 1857 *et seq.*, pp.885-86.
al-Muqaffa' (1910)	Severus ibn al-Muqaffa', *Patrologia Orientalis*, v, 1910, pp.139-40.
Musil (1928)	Musil, Alois, *Palmyrena. A Topographical Itinerary*, New York, 1928.
al-Nawajī (1859)	Muḥammad al-Nawajī, *Ḥalbat al-Kumayt*, Bulaq, 1859.
Schulz & Strzygowski (1904)	Schulz, B. and Strzygowski, J., "Mschatta": *Jahrbuch der königlichen preussischen Kunstsammlungen*, xxv, 1904.
al-Ṭabarī (1966)	Abū Ja'far Muḥammad ibn Jarīr al-Ṭabarī, *Ta'rīkh al-Rusul wa'l-Mulūk*, Cairo, Dār al-Ma'ārif, 1966, vol.7, using de Goeje's pagination.
Thompson (1976)	Thompson, D., *Stucco from Chal Tarkhan—Eshqabad near Rayy*, Warminster, 1976.
al-'Umarī (1924)	Ibn Faḍl Allāh al-'Umarī, *Masālik al-Abṣār fī Mamālik al-Amṣār*, Cairo, Dār al-Kutub, 1924, vol.i.
Yāqūt (1866-73)	Yāqūt ibn 'Abd Allāh al-Rūmī, *Mu'jam al-Buldān*, ed. F. Wüstenfeld, Leipzig, 1866-73.